African Union Law

This book explores the emergence of African Union (AU) law as a legal order and its implications for existing order in the region. As an authoritative text on the development of AU law, the book covers such pertinent issues as legislative powers, competences, direct effect in AU law, subsidiarity, interventionism, and enforcement of laws.

Olufemi Amao argues that there is a gradual movement from intergovernmentalism to supranationalism in the African Union legal order, and explores how this trajectory gradually and incrementally de-emphasises the discourse on nation state sovereignty; a concept that has caused many problems in the African context. Drawing upon EU law as a comparison, the book also examines how the development of supranationalism affects crucial issues such as human rights, democratic reforms, territorial matters, tribal and religious disputes, and economic relations.

As a comprehensive examination of the development of law within a union, this book will be of great interest and use to students, scholars and practitioners in international law, international relations, and African studies.

Olufemi Amao is currently Senior Lecturer at the Sussex Law School, University of Sussex. He was previously a lecturer at Brunel Law School, the director for Undergraduate Studies, Brunel University, London, and a lecturer at University College Cork, Ireland. He is the author of *Corporate Social Responsibility, Human Rights and the Law: Multinational Corporations in Developing Countries* (Routledge, 2011).

African Union Law

The Emergence of a Sui Generis Legal Order

Olufemi Amao

Routledge
Taylor & Francis Group
LONDON AND NEW YORK

First published 2019
by Routledge

2 Park Square, Milton Park, Abingdon, Oxfordshire OX14 4RN
52 Vanderbilt Avenue, New York, NY 10017

Routledge is an imprint of the Taylor & Francis Group, an informa business

First issued in paperback 2020

British Library Cataloguing-in-Publication Data
A catalogue record for this book is available from the British Library

Library of Congress Cataloging-in-Publication Data
Names: Amao, Olufemi, author.
Title: African Union law : the emergence of a sui generis legal order / Olufemi Amao.
Description: Abingdon, Oxon [UK] ; New York, NY : Routledge, 2018. Identifiers: LCCN 2018003028| ISBN 9781138914940 (hbk) | ISBN 9781315690551 (ebk)
Subjects: LCSH: African Union. | Law—Africa—Economic aspects. | Human rights—Africa. | African cooperation. | Africa—Politics and government. | Subsidiarity.
Classification: LCC KQE721 .A43 2018 | DDC 341.24/9—dc23
LC record available at https://lccn.loc.gov/2018003028

ISBN: 978-1-138-91494-0 (hbk)
ISBN: 978-0-367-90028-1 (pbk)

Typeset in ITC Galliard Std
by Swales & Willis Ltd, Exeter, Devon, UK

Contents

This book is dedicated to the great builders of modern Africa (in no particular order):

> Nelson Mandela, Kwame Nkrumah, Patrice Lumumba, Julius Nyerere, Hailie Selassie, Leopold Sedar Senghor, Muhamad Anwal-EL Sadat, Herbert Macaulay, Obafemi Awolowo, Abubakar Tafawa Balewa, Nnamdi Azikwe, Aminu Kano and all others too numerous to mention who contributed to the emergence of modern Africa, the African Union and its legal order.

And to my beloved late brother, Olusegun Amao.

The best of us, now in the company of the greatest, in the presence of the Most High.

Foreword

African Union Law: The Emergence of a Sui Generis Legal Order is a scholarly, carefully argued and beautifully written analysis of the emerging legal order that is the African Union (AU). In this book Amao makes a significant contribution to African legal scholarship, and to the emerging body of research on African Union law. Arguing that a new continental legal order is emerging in Africa, Amao analyses the historical, contextual and normative underpinnings of the Union legal order and its 'peculiar characteristics'. Those peculiar characteristics include a distinct colonial history, a plurality of legal systems and constitutional traditions, and contested visions of socio-economic integration in the African Union.

The book clearly situates the Constitutive Acts of the African Union as a marker of progress towards a Pan-African ideal of political and economic unity. The African Union is presented by Amao as a norm-generating institution, in contrast to its predecessor, the Organisation of African Unity (OAU). As Amao notes, this potential for norm entrepreneurship is beginning to bear fruit in an expanding body of African human rights law and the engagement of a plurality of legal sources to further the political objective of a closer Union.

The question of legal sources is central to this book and Amao takes an open and expansive view of the role that diverse sources, including European Union law, can play. The emerging continental legal order is characterised as both diverse and as dynamic. Plurality and openness to a diverse family of legal systems are not viewed by Amao with the usual legal caution. The fragmentation of legal sources and of the underpinning norms of the Union order is not a matter for concern, but rather a rich resource for the emerging legal order.

Amao presents a skilful, masterly critique of the denial of African laws and legal systems in western jurisprudence and in the canons of international law. The rules of conduct that regulated individuals, groups and tribal collectives, he argues, provided the foundations for concepts of restorative and reconciliatory justice as well as for collective responsibility – concepts that continue today to influence the development of African legal systems and the Union order itself. Drawing on the work of Elias and others, Amao notes the place of African customary law in the Statute of the OAU, and the subsequent move to the more 'radical integrationist' law and politics of the African Union. It is a move that he largely welcomes.

Law and the unique legal order of the African Union are positioned as central to the integrationist project, and Amao presents the evolving legal order as both '*sui generis*' and not dissimilar, in aspiration and legal form, to the supranational order of European Union law. Citing Edozie, he argues that the AU may justifiably be described as an emerging suprastate organisation. While the OAU was limited, he argues, by its adherence to the principle of non-intervention, the AU legal order is premised on a distinct set of norms, including a norm of 'non-indifference', a human rights norm, and the norms of responsibility to protect and democratic constitutionalism. While Amao notes the human rights norm as being the most expansive of the emerging AU norms, he views economic integration and the work of the Organisation for the Harmonisation of Business Law in Africa (OHADA) as critical to the achievement of the Pan African ideal of ever closer union.

A significant contribution of Amao's book is its engagement with economic integration, as well as with the politics and practice of human rights. Unlike most legal scholars, Amao does not shy away from engaging both with the complexities of transnational economic integration and with the local challenges to human rights, including gender equality norms. Drawing on his own scholarly standing in international business law and human rights law, Amao provides a compelling analysis of African Union law's contributions in both fields. Taking on the regulation of same-sex sexual conduct and relationships, Amao challenges the appeals to African specificity to justify criminalisation of same-sex relationships. The othering of sexual minorities and of diverse forms of sexual orientation is due in large part, he argues, to the legacies of colonialism and to the introduction of Christianity and Islam into the African continent and its legal orders. African human rights law, and the African Union itself, has the opportunity both to harmonise domestic laws on equality and non-discrimination, and to ensure compliance with expanding international norms on recognition and rights. The task, he admits, however, is a daunting one, complicated by the legacies of colonialism, and appeals to distinct religious traditions and the politics of national sovereignty claims. Though Amao looks to developments in the Inter-American human rights system on relationship recognition in particular, he reluctantly acknowledges the more limited recognition of the rights claims of sexual minorities in African human rights law to date.

At a time when free movement of persons is being challenged and restricted elsewhere, including in the neighbouring European Union, Amao rightly identifies the moves towards greater freedom of movement in the African Union as a critical step in economic and political integration. It is a move that is driven less by humanitarian concerns and more by the concern to facilitate the expansion of trade and the attendant need for an expanding labour market and mobility of workers. The role played by the Organisation for the Harmonisation of African Business Laws in West and Central Africa is acknowledged as a model and a potential driver for the continental efforts at harmonisation of legal norms, identified as key to facilitating greater ease in commercial transactions, and consequently greater predictability and certainty in the Union's legal order.

Amao's book makes a significant contribution not only to our understanding of the African Union and its unique legal order, but also to the evolution of supranational legal orders and projects of integration. At a time when such projects are under threat elsewhere, most notably in the European Union, Amao's careful analysis of the normative and legal architectural requirements of greater unity is not only timely, it is also critical to our understanding of law's potentially transformative role in facilitating greater cooperation between diverse nation states.

Siobhán Mullally,
Galway,
11 March 2018

Acknowledgements

I thank my wife Anne-Marie and our twins Brian Olusegun and Máire Agnes for giving me the time to work on this book and for their encouragement and unwavering support. I also wish to express my gratitude to my mentor at the Sussex Law School, Professor Lindsay Stirton, for his support. I thank the members of the African Union Law Research Network (http://africanunionlaw.org) for the insights they provided at the workshops of the network. I also thank the leadership of the Sussex Law School for providing the enabling environment to do this research. I thank Dr Charles Olubokun and Chosen Udorji for providing research assistance for parts of this book. In addition, I thank the staff at Cashel Library, Co. Tipperary, Republic of Ireland, for allowing me the use of their facilities during my holidays to work on this book. Finally, I am grateful to Professor Siobhán Mullally for writing the foreword to this book.

This work was supported by funding from the Arts and Humanities Research Council, UK.

Femi Amao
Cashel, Republic of Ireland,
January 2018

1 Introduction

The core argument that this book seeks to provide evidence for is that, either wittingly or unwittingly through the activities of the Organisation of African Unity (OAU) and particularly its successor, the African Union (AU), a new continental legal order is evolving in Africa. While it is acknowledged that the emerging legal order is a work in progress, this book shows how the legal order has developed in its own peculiar and unique way. The book considers the AU and its institutions as norm 'entrepreneurs' or generators, standard setters and lawmakers at the continental level. It also considers the Constitutive Act of the AU as a continental-level social contract and a constitutional instrument. This is contrasted with the Organisation of African Unity, which was not designed or conceived as a norm- or law-generating institution. Nonetheless, the OAU played a noteworthy role in the development of the AU legal order.

A key driver behind the emergence of the AU legal order is the need to find collective solutions to problems and challenges peculiar to the African continent. As shown in Chapter 2, the OAU was created with the aim of collectively responding to some of the major challenges facing the continent post-independence. These include eradication of all forms of colonialism, defending the sovereignty and territorial integrity of Member States and developmental challenges. This limited and somewhat restrictive role shaped the contribution that the OAU could make to the emergent AU legal order. Indeed, the OAU fell short of the Pan-African idea of a united Africa that was influential in the lead up to the independence of Member States. The emergence of the AU appears to have revived that idea and it is helping to drive forward the emergent AU legal order. As discussed in Chapter 2, it is notable that the African Union legal order is developing with its own peculiar characteristics that are different from any existing legal order. These peculiar characteristics are reflected in the core instruments underpinning the continental legal order.

In Chapter 3, an attempt is made to identify and categorise the various sources of AU law. This task is challenging because the norms and standards have developed in a wide variety of ways, over several decades, and range from non-binding soft law to binding norms. Chapter 3 also addresses the question of the legal personality of the AU. This question was dealt with and laid to rest by the African Court on Human and Peoples' Rights (African Court) in *Femi Falana* v. *African Union*.[1] It is noteworthy that some of the AU (and OAU) instruments made references to 'Laws of the Union' or 'African Law' without defining what it is or identifying its sources. By adopting and adapting Maluwa's categorisation of AU/OAU treaties, the chapter provides a useful categorisation of AU/OAU legal instruments.[2]

This book is designed to be less focused on the political and the institutional issues but instead focuses more on aspects of the development of the AU and its predecessor and their institutions that have normative and legal standard-setting implications. The Constitutive Act of the AU is a fundamental source because of its constitutional status and its extensive scope. It is also observed that continental level judicial and quasi- judicial jurisprudence have emerged as an important source of AU law. The Pan-African Parliament, which was inaugurated in 2004, is expected to play a significant role as a source of law in the future. It is also noted in Chapter 3, that some borrowed principles from the EU legal order are playing a notable role in the AU legal order. These include the principles of subsidiarity, proportionality and direct effect.

Chapter 4 addresses the issue of membership of the AU. The recent accession of the newly created Republic of South Sudan and the return of Morocco to the African Union membership show why the issue is important. It is notable that under the OAU regime the conditionalities for membership were regarded as being very lax. The AU regime introduced a level of control over the admission to membership but, compared with the European Union (EU) regime, the conditions introduced are still very weak. Robust membership conditionalities have the potential of enabling the AU to shape Member States' behaviour and ensure that prospective Member States have the capacity to meet their membership obligations. In addition, there is also the question of whether States that are not based in the African continent but with close connection to Africa could join the membership of the AU. Indeed, Haiti, a Caribbean State with its population consisting mostly of people of African descent, attempted unsuccessfully to join the AU in 2012. The ability of the AU to impose sanctions on Member States for failure to comply with AU policies and decisions under Article 23 and 30 of the Constitutive Act is a major development in relation to the enforcement process within the AU legal order and forms part of the discussion in the chapter. The chapter also covers the implication of membership for Member States' citizens and the bid to harmonise citizenship rules at the continental level.

Since independence from colonial rule, Member States of the OAU/AU have recognised the importance of economic integration in the quest for development. Despite this recognition, progress has been slow in this sphere when compared with the human rights sphere. As discussed in Chapter 5, the adoption of the Treaty Establishing the African Economic Community (also known as the Abuja Treaty or the AEC Treaty) in 1991 has significant implications for

1 *Femi Falana* v. *African Union*, Application 001/2011.

2 See Chapter 3.

standard setting and norm creation in the economic sphere. It is notable that the design and structure of the AEC have supranational features and have been co-opted into the AU framework. The utilisation of regional economic communities (RECs) as building blocks to achieve the objective of the AEC has led to key developments at the regional levels in areas such as trade and tariff, currency unification and freedom of movement. It is also contended that the relative success of the Organisation for the Harmonisation of Business Law in Africa (OHADA) shows the potential for supranational norms in the economic sphere in the continent. Notably, the compatibility of the OHADA legal order with AU legal instruments was considered in *Kevin Mgwanga Gunme* et al. v. *Cameroon*, ACHPR.[3] This decision is discussed in Chapter 5.

Chapter 6 focuses on the theme of peace, security and the rule of law in the AU legal order. The challenges posed by conflicts, insecurity and lack of respect for rule of law have led to a keen focus on these issues, which has resulted in the development of new norms and standards. The OAU played a role in this sphere but, because of its adherence to its norm of non-interference, its role was limited. The development of new norms, especially under the AU, has led to significant and potentially radical changes. These new norms, which have expanded the AU's ability to impact Member States, include the non-indifference norm, the norm of unconstitutional change of government, the human rights norm, and the responsibilities to protect and of democratic constitutionalism.

Perhaps the most developed norm to date is the human rights norm. At the heart of the human rights system at the continental level is the African Charter on Human and Peoples' Rights. As discussed in Chapters 7 and 8, the application of the provisions of the Charter by the African Court on Human and Peoples' Rights and the African Commission have shaped the emergence of a credible jurisprudence on human rights in the continent. The jurisprudence is also significant because of the peculiar and distinctive features of the African human rights system. The evolving use of provisional or interim measures and the expanding powers of the continental court system also has significant implications for the future. In addition, the African human rights jurisprudence is having notable impact in Member States' courts and also on individual rights in Member States.

One of the key challenges facing the AU legal order is reconciling its emerging norms and standards with prevailing conception of custom and morality across the continent. In Chapter 9, the controversial issue of sexual orientation is used as a case study to explore this tension and the ways in which the AU institutions are grappling with it. Chapter 10 focuses on the mechanism for enforcement of AU law, which, it is acknowledged, is a major challenge to the AU legal order. The chapter focuses mainly on the available judicial and quasi-judicial enforcement mechanisms at the continental level. It is envisaged that with the introduction of the African Court system there is a possibility that the enforcement process could become more robust in the future.

3 *Kevin Mgwanga Gunme* et al. v. *Cameroon*, ACHPR, Communication No. 266/03 (2009).

2 The development of the concepts of African law and African Union law

Africa: an introduction

There is no consensus as to the origin of the name 'Africa' and to how it came to refer to the modern continent of Africa. It has been suggested that the word may have originated from a Greek word with the meaning 'without cold' or the reference in Latin to a 'land of Afri'.[1] It has further been suggested that it may have been the Romans or the Carthaginians who first called the continent by that name.[2] In pre-colonial times the region that comprises modern-day Africa was made up of disparate tribal kingdoms and communities with the main commonality being the geographical contiguity of these entities. Pre-colonial communities identified themselves by their tribe or community. This will have a significant bearing on the development of laws and legal systems. The use of the word 'Africa' was popularised by European contact with the region and their need to give an identity to a region that was previously known as the 'dark continent'.[3]

Africa is the second largest continent on the planet. It is the second most populous continent after Asia. There are 55 sovereign countries in Africa including Sahrawi Arab Democratic Republic (Western Sahara), a Member State of the African Union (AU) whose statehood is disputed by Morocco. The continent has an estimated population of 1,032,532,974, accounting for over 14% of the world's population. The continent is bordered by the Mediterranean Sea to the north, the Suez Canal and the Red Sea along the Sinai Peninsula to the northeast, the Indian Ocean to the east and southeast, and the Atlantic Ocean to the west. In 2015 Africa accounted for 5.1% of global gross domestic product (GDP)[4] and had a GDP growth rate of 5% between 2000 and 2010, slowing down to

1 P. Finkelman (ed.) *Encyclopaedia of African American History: 1896 to the Present: From the Age of Segregation to the Twenty-First Century*, Vol. 1 (OUP, 2009) 17.

2 W. D. Wright, *Critical Reflections on Black History* (Praeger Publishers, an imprint of Greenwood Publishing Group, Inc., 2002) 7.

3 J. I. Levitt (ed.), *Africa: Mapping New Boundaries in International Law* (Hart Publishing, 2010) 2, 4; W. Menski, *Comparative Law in a Global Context: The Legal Systems of Asia and Africa* (Cambridge University Press, 2006) 380.

4 Office for National Statistics, available at: www.ons.gov.uk/economy/nationalaccounts/balanceofpayments/articles/theukstradeandinvestmentrelationshipwithafrica/2016, accessed 5 December 2017.

3.3% between 2010 and 2015.[5] The continent's global share of Foreign Direct Investment (FDI) grew from 3.2% in 2007 to 5.6% in 2012 but has since fallen back in recent times to 3.4%.[6] The continent is undoubtedly a significant part of the global architecture.

An unwritten 'Magna Carta': African customary law and its role in the development of African Union law

It is trite to say that, on contact with the African continent, the Europeans failed to understand the concept or workings of law in African societies. Indeed, the Scottish explorer Mungo Park (1771–1806) presented what he called 'the standard law of Africa' in one paragraph in his classic autobiography, where he stated as an afterthought,

> In case it should escape my memory, I take this opportunity of observing that the standard law of Africa runs thus: If an ass should break a single stem of corn, the proprietor of the corn has a right to seize the ass; and if the owner of the ass will not satisfy him for the damage he thinks he has sustained, he can *retain* his ass. He cannot *sell* or *work* him but he can *kill* him: and as the Bambarrans esteem ass-flesh as a great luxury, this part of the law is often put in force.[7]

This anecdotal approach to the perception of laws in African societies persisted in decades afterward as the contact of the African continent with the wider world increased. Law in Africa was generally perceived as primitive customs that needed to be replaced. That is why legal tradition in Africa has previously and controversially been described as 'folk law'.[8]

Menski has observed that there existed 'a barely hidden undercurrent of denial of African laws and their potential contributions to jurisprudence'.[9] This attitude, in his view, is borne out of 'a serious deficiency of plurality-consciousness in understanding non-western laws, mainly implicating positivist presuppositions' and denying 'the existence of law in social contexts'.[10] Menski went on to observe that Africans were widely assumed to lack the capacity for sophisticated rational thought and modern administrative arrangements but this assumption 'ignored

5 World Economic Forum, '3 reasons things are looking up for African economies', available at: www.weforum.org/agenda/2016/05/what-s-the-future-of-economic-growth-in-africa, accessed 5 December 2017.

6 UNCTAD, *World Investment Report* 2017, available at: http://unctad.org/en/Publications Library/wir2017_en.pdf, accessed 5 December 2017.

7 M. Park, *Travels in the Interior of Africa* (Wordsworth Classics of World Literature, 2002) 363.

8 H. P. Glenn, *Legal Traditions of the World: Sustainable Diversity in Law*, 5th ed. (Oxford University Press) 62.

9 *Supra*, Menski, 380.

10 Ibid.

massive evidence of mainly oral African laws and brushed it aside as "culture"'.[11] Reflecting on this point, Kuwali posited that,

> The Europeans transplanted their Western laws to African soil. In so doing, the colonialists did not take any interest in analysing the received European law's interaction and impact on the indigenous laws and customs which it co-existed within the colonial territories. The colonialist concluded that native laws were pagan customs which ought to be destroyed and substituted with higher colonial laws.[12]

A preliminary (albeit naïve) question to begin with is whether 'law' was a recognised concept in Africa before the contact with the West. In so far as one does not hold a very narrow view of 'law' to mean the presence of a parliament, court, policing system, a prison service, a written code and the like, one can confidently answer that question in the affirmative. Law was indeed part of the African society, though in a different form and not as a written code.[13] According to Allott, a prominent proponent of the idea of African law, it is possible to have a purely oral legislated law that essentially is customary law.[14] A common characteristic of African legal systems is therefore that they are customary in nature and unwritten. Unlike ancient European customary law whose historical jurisprudence is dominated by speculative thoughts, evidence of African customary law is much fuller and less speculative.[15] Furthermore, unlike the European ancient tradition, African customary law is not the domain of the 'aristocracy' or a 'judicial oligarchy' or a privileged minority but rather a collective/community endeavour.[16] Furthermore, it was a localised institution, which was available at all levels in the community and administered by a wide variety of entities and individuals including chiefs, village headman, elders and family heads.[17]

One may also see African law or legal tradition as 'chthonic', as postulated by Glenn in his seminal work on the legal traditions of the world.[18] This, in his view, means that a people or community live in close harmony with the earth.[19] The significant implication of this viewpoint is that the tradition is described by its internal criteria and not by external or imposed criteria. Thus, according to Glenn, it is an attempt to examine traditions from within and, despite possible problems

11 Ibid. 381.

12 D. Kuwali, 'Decoding Afrocentrism: decolonizing legal theory' in O. Onazi (ed.), *African Legal Theory and Contemporary Problems: Critical Essays* (Ius Gentium: Comparative Perspectives on Law and Justice, 29) 71 at 72; See also Menski (n. 3) 380–381.

13 L. A. Ayinla, 'African philosophy of law: a critique' (2002) 6 *Journal of International and Comparative Law* 147.

14 A. N. Allott, 'African law' in J. D. M. Derrett (ed.), *An Introduction to Legal Systems* (Sweet & Maxwell, 1968) 131 at 132.

15 Ibid. 133.

16 Ibid. 135.

17 Ibid. 135.

18 *Supra*, Glenn, 62.

19 Ibid.

of language and perceptions, to see the traditions from a time prior to the emergence of 'colonial language'.[20] Chthonic legal traditions have no point of origin but emerged with growth of experience and through orality and memory. It is the oldest traditions that precede all modern traditions and its most evident features are its orality, communality and, largely, its informality.[21] It is preserved through human speech and human memory. Glenn went on to persuasively opine that such traditions are the way they are because they 'have been chthonic, for hundreds of thousands of years, though they also inevitably bear new designations since the colonial encounter of the last few hundreds'.[22] Commenting on the reliability and vulnerability of the tradition, Glenn observed that chthonic legal tradition,

> may appear highly unreliable and vulnerable to external influence, until we remember that the tradition appears to have preserved that which it says to preserve for most of the existence of humanity. So it is a tradition which is not overtly preoccupied with voluminous detail, which human memory really cannot master . . . The law is vested in a repository in which all, or most, share and in which all, or most, may participate.[23]

According to Menski, African law or African laws comprise of many different types of legal systems.[24] It may therefore be more accurate to refer to these as an 'African family of laws' or a 'family of systems' that may not necessarily have a common parent.[25] The administration of justice may vary from one tribe or society to another but there are certain commonalities that can be identified. Menski concluded that, 'African laws are as legal as other laws, but they may well have specific characteristics unique to them, defining their "identity postulates"'.[26] For ease of convenience and readability we shall refer to the concept as 'African law', while bearing in mind the generic nature of the concept.

Early scholars of African legal systems David and Brierley, commenting on the existence or otherwise of African law and in view of the disparate legal systems in the continent, observed:

> Does this mean, then, that there is no *legal* unity among these various communities, that there is no "African" law properly speaking? Opinions have in fact differed on this question. While acknowledging the great diversity of customs in a continent divided into so many communities, there is, however, now general agreement that certain characteristics common to all African laws do set them off from the laws of Europe.[27]

20 Ibid. 62.
21 Ibid. 62, 65, 66.
22 Ibid.
23 Ibid. 63, 64–67.
24 *Supra*, Menski, 308.
25 *Supra*, Allott, 131.
26 *Supra*, Menski, 381.
27 R. David and J. E. C. Brierley, *Major Legal Systems in the World Today* (Stevens & Sons, 1985) 549.

It is interesting to note that some early thinkers who influenced European legal thought, such as St Augustine, Plato and Aristotle, had some connection or contact with the continent of Africa that may have influenced their thoughts.[28]

A follow-up question then is that, if there is an African law, there must be an African theory of law. Indeed, this has been a key subject of debate for the past few decades. African legal theorists have consistently distanced African law from legal positivism and placed its foundation in natural law. This has informed the academic debate about the existence of an 'African theory of law'. According to Kuwali,

> [t]he hallmark of African Legal Theory is that is [sic] subscribed to natural law as opposed to legal positivism. In contrast to the positive law, natural law is universal, binding all people and all states. It is, therefore, a non-consensual law based upon the notion of the prevalence of right and justice.[29]

Kuwali went on to identify the theoretical underpinnings of African law, which include that it is rooted in culture, it is sometimes derived from proverbs, it seeks to maintain equilibrium in society, it provides the foundation for a theory of restorative and reconciliatory justice, it honours interdependence and collective responsibility and it provides for a consensus-based theory of decision making.[30] This book will explore how such theoretical underpinnings have influenced the emerging modern African Union law.

The nature of African law

As stated earlier in this chapter, it is true that in pre-colonial times there were no written codes of law in African societies. Nevertheless, laws were developed within the clan, tribe or family and applicable within the unit. Each unit had its own corpus of customary law. The law is directed towards maintaining the interests of the unit against outsiders.[31] Contacts between groups were minimal with each group developing its own customs and social habits.[32] Traditionally, 'law is an organic growth, inherent in the body politic and accepted just because it is organic, coherent and traditional'.[33] There was little inter-tribal or, in modern parlance, 'international law'. However, and significantly, there were rules that governed the making of war and peace and, in peace time, the rules that governed relations between neighbouring tribes.[34] In pre-colonial Africa, law comprised all

28 *Supra*, Menski, 386.
29 *Supra*, Kuwali, 72.
30 *Supra*, Kuwali, 7.
31 J. H. Driberg, 'The African conception of law' (1934) 16 (4) *Journal of Comparative Legislation and International Law* 231.
32 *Supra*, David and Brierley, 548.
33 *Supra*, Driberg, 231.
34 Ibid. 230.

'rules of conduct which regulate the behaviour of individuals and communities, and which by maintaining the equilibrium of society are necessary for its continuance as a corporate whole'.[35] This conception of law underscores the collectivist foundation of African law as opposed to the individualistic assumption in the mainstream Western approach.

In his seminal book, *The Nature of African Customary Law*, Elias (one of the earliest and foremost of African law theorists) posited that there is an 'African law', which does not stem from the Austinian theory 'as the command of a political sovereign over political subordinates', but a law that is an expression of the common consciousness of the people, that serves the purpose of social engineering.[36] The law, according to Elias, was based on the idea of the maintenance of social equilibrium.[37] Similar to customary international law, certain aspects of custom and practice developed into what he termed 'African customary law'.[38] The main difference with international law being that there were no international mechanisms to uphold these laws. African customary law, according to Elias, was meant to evolve slowly with society.[39] Elias asserted the basis of African customary law as follows:

> in large areas of Africa there had emerged broadly similar political and economic conditions and, therefore, similar rules of customary law, which makes it possible to speak of the existence of a universal body of principles of African law that is not essentially dissimilar to the broad principles of European Law.[40]

Max Glucksman, another early scholar of African law, was of similar sentiment when he said that:

> I have studied the work of African courts in Zululand and Rhodesia, and I found that they use the same basic doctrines as our courts do. African legal systems, like all legal systems, are founded on principles of the reasonable man, responsibility, negligence, direct and circumstantial and hear-say evidence, etc. African judges and laymen apply these principles skilfully and logically to a variety of situations in order to achieve justice.[41]

Allott was also of this opinion, stating that African laws 'reveal sufficient similarity in procedure, principles, institutions, and techniques for a common account

35 Ibid. 231.

36 T. O. Elias, *The Nature of African Law* (Manchester University Press, 1956) 294.

37 C. Landauer, 'Things fall together: the past and future Africas of T. O. Elias's *Africa and the Development of International Law*' (2008) 21 (2) *Leiden Journal of International Law* 351, 360.

38 Ibid.

39 Ibid.

40 Ibid. 367.

41 M. Gluckman, 'Letter to the *Observer*', 15 July 1951. Quoted in T. O. Elias, *The Nature of African Law* (Manchester University Press, 1956) 33.

to be given of them'.[42] Such a universal body of principles could be identified from the literature and practice and they include the following.

Purpose of law

The need to deliver substantial justice in the context of the wider community (as opposed to strict adherence to the letters of the law) and to all parties is at the heart of the law in Africa. According to Allott, in Africa a broader, more ambitious and humane approach dominated African law. The approach focuses on rendering essential justice in a 'particular case in conformity with the general principles and the appropriate patterns of behaviour recognised by custom for each relationship or transaction'.[43] For example, in relation to disputes about property, the law in this context is less about protecting private property and more about ensuring fair distribution of wealth in the community.

Reconciliation

Reconciliation is also an important feature of the law in Africa. Just as equity aims for fairness in the common law, African law seeks to achieve reconciliation at the expense of strict adherence to the letter of the law.[44] Allott identified this as one of the common themes in African law. According to him:

> At the heart of African adjudication lies the notion of reconciliation or the restoration of harmony. The job of the court or an arbitrator is less to find the facts, state the rules of law, and apply them to the facts than to set right a wrong in such a way as to restore harmony within the disturbed community.[45]

The rationale behind this concept is to ensure that disputes are resolved in ways that ensure harmony in the present and in the future for the community.[46]

Natural justice

Early scholars such as Gluckman recognised the fact that African societies have a conception of the idea of natural justice (and a rule of law) that was not developed in abstract terms.[47] As stated previously, reconciliation has been identified as one of the cardinal principles of African law and, according to Gluckman, a good example of the conception of natural law in Africa is the practice of reconciling parties in a dispute while at the same time maintaining the general

42 *Supra*, Allott, 131.
43 Ibid. 133.
44 M. Gluckman, *The Judicial Process Among the Barotse of Northern Rhodesia* (Manchester University Press, 1967) 357; *supra*, Allott, 144.
45 *Supra*, Allott, 145.
46 Ibid. 150.
47 M. Gluckman, 'Natural justice in Africa' (*Natural Law Forum*, Paper 81, 1964) 25.

principle of law.[48] In other words, in African tradition, the idea of natural law ensures that law is applied in ways that lead to reconciliation among parties.

Preservation of community and group concerns

Scholars of African law have always recognised the significance of group and community rights and powers in the African legal system, as opposed to the Western individualistic legal systems.[49] A person is regarded by nature to belong to a variety of communities, territory and family structures. By virtue of membership of the structure he has the right to access the resources of the community (economic and moral) with the corresponding obligation to respect 'the underlying and continuous needs of the rest of the community' and the authority of the community to control access to and use of the community resources.[50] This is not dissimilar to Maine's 'ancient law' in Europe, which he stated is not primarily concerned with individuals but families or not with single persons but groups.[51] Allott concluded that:

> African laws, with their strong organisation of tribe, family, locality, age-grades, societies, and other associations, undoubtedly emphasise the corporate and collective, at the expense of the individual element in social life and law; but the difference from western society is no more than one of degree, and there is, as in western society, a dialogue or tension between the collective and the individual principles in which now one, now the other, prevails.[52]

Ubuntu and its variants

This concept and its variants in societies in Africa is another important feature of African law. Ubuntu generally means 'humanity towards others'.[53] In the Yoruba land of Nigeria the concept is known as 'Omoluabi'. The concept generally translates to the notion that individual rights cannot be meaningfully exercised in isolation from broader community rights. The concept has striking similarity to the idea of restorative justice but with an emphasis on the collective. The concept recognises that humanness is shaped by interactions and, in order to sustain the community, human interactions must be nurtured.[54] Judicially the concept has been interpreted to include placing special value on life and human dignity.[55] According to Mapaure,

48 Ibid. 28.
49 *Supra*, Allott, 147; Glenn, 76.
50 Ibid. Allott, 150.
51 H. S. Maine, *Ancient Law: Its Connection to the History of Early Society* (JM Dent & Sons, 1917) 250.
52 *Supra*, Allott, 149.
53 C. Mapaure, 'Reinvigorating African values for SADC: the relevance of traditional African philosophy of law in a globalising world of competing perspectives' (2011) 1 *SADC Law Journal* 149, 160.
54 Ibid.
55 *S* v. *Makwanyana & Anor.* 1995 (2) SACR 1.

> This concept was born and bred and is evolving in Africa, thus it owes much to African traditional law[56]. . . in fact, the concept in itself embodies African traditional law principles which have to be enforced from an Afrocentric perspective in order to integrate societies divided by colonialism and apartheid.[57]

A belief in the supernatural/morality

African law is not a religious law strictly speaking but generally interwoven with a belief in the supernatural.[58] Approaching African law by attempting to separate the moral from the legal would not be the correct approach.[59] One needs to take a holistic view of the law in the African context. The society and the law are intertwined like subatomic particles, where one influences the other and vice versa constantly. In this interesting relationship, 'the law expressed the common moral code of the people; if the code changed, the law would automatically change as well'.[60] As Allott correctly observed, 'African society enjoyed an integrated culture, or set of institutions and beliefs, in which the law occupied a central position'.[61]

Subsequent chapters of this book will show how some of these universal principles have contributed to the emergence of AU law.

The role of Pan-Africanism and the ideas of the 'Union of African States' and the 'United States of Africa'

As stated earlier, in pre-colonial times the regions that comprised modern-day Africa were made of disparate tribal kingdoms and communities with the main commonality being the geographical contiguity of these entities. The colonial enterprise in Africa, however, changed the dynamics by fostering a sense of shared aspirations among the people of Africa, albeit within the artificially drawn boundaries of the colonial masters. One of the consequences of colonisation is the adoption of the concept of Pan-Africanism. The idea was originally conceived in the United States but became very popular in West Africa.[62] At the core of Pan-Africanism is integration.[63] The idea has its root in the 1920s with the emergence of Western-educated intellectuals from Africa who saw closer cooperation as an important strategy in the struggle for independence. The intellectuals involved in the continent at this early stage were mainly from the

56 *Supra*, Mapaure, 160.
57 Ibid. 161.
58 *Supra*, Allott, 131.
59 Ibid. 135.
60 Ibid. 135.
61 Ibid. 136.
62 P.-M. Henry, 'Pan-Africanism: a dream come true' (1959) 37 (3) *Foreign Affairs* 443, 445.
63 A. Jeng, *Peace Building in the African Union: Law, Philosophy and Practice* (Cambridge University Press, 2012) 138–143.

British colonies of West Africa, namely Nigeria, Ghana (then known as Gold Coast), Sierra Leone and Gambia. The thinking of these intellectuals gained significant momentum in the 1940s with a much broader agenda including a plan that was to start with the creation of a West African Federation and with the ultimate aim of creating a United States of Africa.[64] The project was planned to begin with the setting up of a permanent institution to be known as the 'West African National Secretariat'.[65]

A major landmark in the integration effort was the independence of Ghana (formerly Gold Coast) in 1957. Dr Nkrumah, one of the key drivers of Pan-Africanism, became the president of the newly independent country. One of his major ambitions was to use his new role as a platform for the actualisation of the integration idea of Pan-Africanism.[66] In Nkrumah's view, Ghana's independence would be complete and meaningful only within the context of the independence of other African states. In pursuit of his objective, Nkrumah called the first conference of independent African states in 1958. The attendee states were Ethiopia, Liberia, Libya, Sudan, Morocco, United Arab Republic (a short-lived union of modern-day Egypt and Syria) and Ghana.[67] In its final communiqué the meeting agreed to establish a joint Economic Research Council with the responsibility to promote trade, coordinate planning in economic matters and explore the possibility of an African common market.[68]

A follow-up conference in 1960 had an enlarged attendance because more states had gained independence by that time. Furthermore, six states that were not independent were invited to participate in the conference. The conference proposed the establishment of a joint African Development Bank, joint African Commercial Bank and a preferential trade area. Significantly, delegates from Ghana and Guinea called for a political union but no agreement was reached on this proposal. Delegates from Nigeria (which was yet to be independent at the time) and Liberia opposed the proposal on the ground that it was premature. This disagreement in approach laid the foundation of two schools of thought on African integration, the Casablanca and Monrovia groups and the subsequent ideological rivalry between the two groups. (The Casablanca group originally included Ghana, Guinea, Mali, Libya, Egypt, Morocco and Algeria while the Monrovia group included Cameroon, Liberia, Nigeria and Togo.) The Casablanca group was in favour of immediate political union and cooperation while the Monrovia group was in favour of functional cooperation at regional levels.[69] It is widely acknowledged that the idea behind

64 B. O. Fagbayigbo, A politico-legal framework for integration in Africa: exploring the attainability of a supranational African Union (Thesis submitted to the University of Pretoria, 2010) 39.

65 *Supra*, Henry, 444.

66 K. O. Kufuor, *African Unification: Law, Problems and Prospects* (Carolina Academic Press, 2016) 18.

67 *Supra*, Fagbayigbo, 40.

68 *Resolution of the Second Conference of Independent African States*, 24 June 1960.

69 A. Jeng, *Peace Building in the African Union: Law, Philosophy and Practice* (Cambridge University Press, 2012) 143; D. L. Badejo, *The African Union* (Chelsea House, 2008) 30.

the establishment of the OAU and the AU especially is the narrative of Pan-Africanism.[70] The notion that the AU has emerged as the expression of the Pan-Africanism idea is indeed compelling.

The Organisation of African Unity (OAU) and its role in the development of AU law

The divergence in approach to integration was somewhat overcome with the formation of the Organisation of African Unity in 1963. The OAU was established in the context of Article 53 of the UN Charter. Article 53 accommodates the establishment of such continental arrangements and other agencies. This development put an end to the old rivalry between the Casablanca and Monrovia groups. The OAU Charter did not create a political union or establish a 'United States of Africa' as advocated by Nkrumah and the Casablanca group. For example, Nkrumah and the Casablanca group had advocated the idea of an African continental army to liberate the Member States that were still under colonialism. This idea was rejected at the negotiations of the OAU Charter in 1964. The compromise reached was the establishment of a liberation committee based in Tanzania to assist liberation movements, especially in South Africa. This assistance to liberation movement in the process of decolonisation eventually turned out to be OAU's most notable achievement. Significantly, the OAU Charter did not involve transfer of sovereign power to a supranational body because Member States were not in favour of such a commitment. The configuration of the OAU limited its impact on the emergence of AU legal order.

The OAU may be regarded as a success as an instrument of intergovernmental cooperation. However, as an instrument for integration and unity the OAU had a dismal record. The OAU Charter itself became an obstacle to integration through its key principle of non-interference, which by implication affirms the absolute sovereignty of the Member States. This was inconsistent with the efforts to integrate the continent. According to Maluwa,

> With its emphasis on the related principles of sovereign equality of Member States, respect for the sovereignty, territorial integrity and independence of States and non-interference in the internal affairs of States, the OAU was clearly intended to be a loose organization for voluntary cooperation between African States, with no supra-national authority. As such, the OAU fell squarely within the typology of international organizations.[71]

70 R. K. Edozie and K. Gottschalk, *The African Union's Africa: New Pan-African Initiatives in Global Governance* (Michigan State University Press, 2014) 17.

71 T. Maluwa, 'The transition from the Organisation of African Unity to the African Union' in A. A. Yusuf and F. Ouguergouz (eds), *The African Union: Legal and Institutional Framework: A Manual on the Pan-African Organization* (Martinus Nijhoff, 2012), 28.

The OAU also did not achieve much in addressing the key challenges facing the continent such as alleviating poverty, promoting development and conflict resolution.[72] An attempt to review the Charter establishing the OAU to make it more functional and relevant to modern Africa was made with the establishment of the OAU Charter Review Committee in 1980. However, until it ceased to exist in 1996, the review exercise made no significant impact.[73] Nevertheless, the resolutions and treaties of the OAU form part of the corpus of African Union law.

It is important to bear in mind that the OAU was not conceived as a legislative body by its founding members.[74] However, it has been posited that through the adoption of multilateral treaties and resolutions it engaged in the creation of normative rules, some of which can be regarded as forming part of an emerging corpus of rules of international law and, in the context of this book, African Union law.[75] Maluwa further suggested that, in some areas, the OAU did not consciously mean to create new international law but it did so by 'purposely giving certain rules and principles a specifically regional African orientation'.[76] Maluwa contended that, from the 23 treaties that the OAU adopted in its 37 years of existence, one can deduce both contributions to international law and the addition of specific norms from an African perspective, thereby mapping new boundaries (incorporating some of the peculiar themes from Africa discussed previously). Maluwa made his point by referring to specific examples.[77] For example, in the area of environmental law, the African Convention on the Conservation of Nature and Natural Resources (1968) articulates, 'the principles of sustainable development and respect for the environment as a common heritage or public good' before these concepts were acknowledged commonly at the global level.[78] Furthermore, the recognition of a human right to a satisfactory environment under the African Charter on Human and Peoples' Rights (1981) was also a first of its kind. The African Charter also introduced the idea of peoples' rights, third generation rights and individual duties. (As will be shown later in this book, the rights under the African Charter have been further extended.) The Convention Governing the Specific Aspects of Refugee Problems in Africa (OAU 1969) has *inter alia* widened the definition of 'refugee' and broadened the scope of the principle of non-refoulement in this area of law.

It is pertinent to observe that in the OAU Statute establishing its Specialised Commission of Jurists, one of the purposes of the Commission in Article 1 (4) was:

72 Ibid. 30.

73 Ibid.

74 T. Maluwa, 'The OAU/African Union and international law: mapping new boundaries or revisiting old terrain', proceedings of the annual meeting (2004) 98 *American Society of International Law* 232, 233.

75 Ibid. 233.

76 Ibid.

77 Ibid. 234.

78 Ibid.

> to encourage the study of African Law, especially African customary law in the universities and institutions of legal studies in Africa and elsewhere, and its progressive development or codification by African Governments.[79]

This provision positively recognised the concept of African Law with a root in African customary traditions.

The formation of the African Union

The formation of the AU and its institutions shows a shift of focus from the long-standing idea of national sovereignty underpinning the OAU to a more radical integrationist approach. Jeng has argued that the African Union and its instruments largely reflect Kwame Nkrumah's visions of supranational continental government and a realisation of Pan-Africanism's desire to advance continental unity through a robust supranational body.[80] An unlikely figure that revived the idea of the 'United States of Africa' in the late 1990s was the late Libyan dictator Muammar Gaddafi at an extraordinary summit in Sirte, Libya, in 1999. He called for the establishment of African supranational bodies including an African Council (the supreme executive body), a federal executive council, specialised Federal Commissions, an African Congress (elected for four-year terms with responsibility for taking decisions on foreign policy, defence, economic matters, finance, external trade and consular matters), a Federal Supreme Court, an African Monetary Fund, an African Investment Bank and an African Central Bank.[81] However, the majority of the states at the summit rejected this idea. Nonetheless, Gaddafi's audacious idea influenced the emergence of the AU itself. The compromise that eventually emerged from Sirte was the creation of the AU to replace the OAU.[82] The African Union Treaty was adopted on 11 July 2000 at Lome in Togo by 27 African states. The inaugural session of the AU was held on 9–12 July 2002.

The formation of the AU was a significant milestone in the progress toward African integration and, as this book argues, it formally marks the emergence of an African Union legal order. In replacing the OAU with the AU, the Member States took a big step towards continent-wide legal order. The OAU did not establish or achieve a new legal order as it was an intergovernmental organisation

79 Z. Cervenka, *The Organisation of African Unity and Its Charter* (C. Hurst & Company, 1969) 75.

80 A. Jeng, *Peace Building in the African Union: Law, Philosophy and Practice* (Cambridge University Press, 2012) 178. See also, O. A. Boateng, 'Membership accession in the African Union: the relationship between enforcement and compliance, and the case for differential membership' (2017) 24 (1) *South African Journal of International Law* 21.

81 M. Bedjaoui, 'Brief historical overview of steps to African unity' in A. A. Yusuf and F. Ouguergouz (eds), *The African Union: Legal and Institutional Framework: A Manual on the Pan-African Organization* (Martinus Nijhoff, 2012) 9, 19.

82 See OAU, *The Sirte Declaration*, 9 September 1999, EAHG/Draft/Decl. (IV) Rev. 1, available at: http://webcache.googleusercontent.com/search?q=cache:LCW-pAx6zgYJ:www.chr.up.ac.za/chr_old/hr_docs/african/docs/ahsg/ahsg64.doc+&cd=5&hl=en&ct=clnk&gl=uk&client=safari accessed 27 November 2017.

within the structure of the existing international law architecture. In contrast, the AU paved the way for a legal order unique to the AU. This book further argues that it was this progressive, albeit small, step toward supranationalism that has made the emergence of the legal order possible.

This book takes the view that the creation of the African Union has engendered the emergence of a coherent African Union law. It is posited in this book that the establishment of institutions such as a continental-level court presupposes a move towards the establishment of a coherent legal order. However, it is noted that the ideas of an African legal order preceded the AU as previously discussed. This development has largely gone unnoticed or is under-explored within the academic discourse.

Integration theories and the creation of new legal orders

Regional integration has legal consequences both at the regional and the individual state's level. This is also true of the EU model, which greatly influenced the design of the AU.[83] In the case of the EU, the original idea behind the European Union or European Community (as it was previously known) was not to create a new legal order. Rather, the Treaties of Paris (1951)[84] and Rome (1957)[85] were accepted to be part of international law.[86] However, the European Court of Justice soon afterwards declared that the EU constituted 'a new legal order of international law'.[87] According to the Court, in contrast to ordinary international treaties, the treaties of the Union created its unique legal system, which became an integral part of the legal system of Member States and applicable by Member State courts. In Schutze's opinion, the EU 'assumed "statist" features and thus combined – like a chemical compound – international and national elements'.[88] This, in Schutze's view, represents a 'middle ground' between international and national law, a system considered *sui generis* and that the EU thinkers labelled 'supranationalism'.[89]

Similarly, the predecessor organisation of the AU, the Organisation of African Union, started out as treaty-based organisation and thus part of international law architecture. However, the decision to create a union to replace the OAU marks a significant shift. The legal order created and that is emerging from the African Union is assuming greater importance in Africa. There are strong indications that its structure and legal order will become increasingly '*sui generis*' in the same way that the EU has evolved. The decision of the ACHPR in *Falana* underscores this point.[90]

83 *Supra*, Edozie and Gottschalk, xiii; *supra*, T. Maluwa, 25, 38.
84 *Treaty Establishing the European Coal and Steel Community*, 18 April 1951, 261 U.N.T.S. 140.
85 *Treaty Establishing the European Economic Community*, 25 March 1957, 298 U.N.T.S. 11.
86 R. Schutze, *From Dual to Cooperative Federalism: The Changing Structure of European Law* (OUP, 2013) 3.
87 *Flaminio Costa* v. *ENEL* [1964] ECR 585 (6/64), 593.
88 *Supra*, Schutze, 3.
89 Ibid.
90 *Femi Falana* v. *African Union* (Application 001/2011). This decision is discussed in Chapter 3.

As Schutze correctly pointed out, the task of theory in science (or any other field for that matter) is to 'abstract' and thereby reduce complexity to a 'bearable size'.[91] A legal theory of integration focuses not only on explaining the evolution of a system but also on the implication of the process for relevant actors. Perhaps the best way to approach a discussion on integration theories and the AU is to examine the theories that have been used to explain European integration and see their relevance (if any) to the AU context. The European experiment provides a useful comparator for the study of the AU because of the similarities between the two regional systems.[92]

Craig and De Burca have observed that the theories of integration have been used to explain the various phases of European integration.[93] The various phases have led to the propounding of novel theoretical assumptions, which were later confirmed or challenged by later developments and theories. The first notable theory in the European context is functionalism, which emerged in the 1950s when the EU was a sectoral Coal and Steel Community. Functionalism focuses on the emergence of the EU as a means of preventing war or dispute over scarce resources through active cooperation.[94] Thus, by cooperating on economic matters that were previously within the remit of individual nation states, the EU provides a platform for interactions that ultimately prevented war.

When the European integration advanced to the wider Economic Community, the neofunctionalists took the theorisation further by suggesting that, from the cooperation on beneficial goals that produces economic prosperity, the process overtime transforms into one with a wider political consequence.[95] This has the effect of gradually reducing the powers of nation states' governments and increasing the political capacity of the centre. This viewpoint thus assumes that the emergence of the community's supranational institutions drove and still drives the integration process.

However, the 1970s saw a move towards a focus on individual states' self-interest promotion within the community, which challenged the assumptions of neofunctionalism. This development led to the emergence of neo-realist and neo-rational theories from which liberal intergovernmentalism emerged as the most prominent theory. The key contention of liberal intergovernmentalism is that state interests as opposed to supranational institutions are the key drivers

91 *Supra*, Schutze, 39.

92 D. Bach, 'The AU and the EU' in J. Akokpari, A. Ndinga-Muvumba and T. Murithi (eds), *The African Union and Its Institutions* (Fanele, 2008) 355; O. Babarinde, *The EU as a Model for the African Union: The Limits of Imitation*, Jean Monnet/Robert Schuman Papers Series Vol. 17, No. 2, April 2007, (University of Miami) 3–4; M. Paterson, 'The African Union at 10: problems, progress and prospects' (*International Colloquium Report*, Berlin, Germany, 30–31 August 2012).

93 P. Craig and G. de Burca, *EU Law: Text, Cases, and Materials*, 5th ed. (OUP, 2011) 2.

94 See generally, E. B. Hass, 'International integration: the European and the universal process' (1961) 15 (3) *International Organisation* 366; E. B. Haas, *Beyond the Nation State* (ECPR Press, 2008).

95 A. Moravcsik, 'Preferences and power in the European Community: a liberal intergovernmental approach (1993) 31 (4) *Journal of Common Market Studies* 474.

of the community integration process. According to Craig and De Burca, the state actors were essentially seeking 'to pursue their own respective preferences and to protect their sphere of power'.[96] These theories were used to explain developments in the 1980s and 1990s in relation to the Single European Act (SEA),[97] the various intergovernmental conferences that took place and the Maastricht Treaty.[98]

From the foregoing it is apparent that early theorisation on European integration was bifurcated along supranationalism versus intergovernmentalism lines. The relevance of this bifurcation was challenged in later years with the emergence of alternative theories that conceived of the emerging Community as a system of multi-level or network governance.[99] These theories acknowledge the involvement of a wider range of institutions and actors at different levels in the process of law making and policy making. These actors and institutions include national actors, supranational actors, subnational, infra-national, public and private entities.[100]

As discussed previously, in the aftermath of colonisation in Africa and the ensuing underdevelopment, there was the school of thought that was of the view that economic prosperity and development could be better achieved by the formation of a United States of Africa with a centralised administration under a Union Government. This school of thought rejected the idea of sub-regional integration mainly because of the fear that this might lead to fostering regional loyalties and balkanisation, ultimately leading to conflicts.[101] Originally, the United States of America's approach to unification of states was considered as the preferred model. This probably reflected the fact that some of the earliest proponents of the idea of integration, such as Nkrumah, studied in the USA. As Nkrumah envisaged, 'sovereignty' or independent authorities of the Member States will be maintained within the union with a Union Government exercising powers in fields reserved for 'common action in the interest of the security and orderly development of the whole continent'.[102] (In furtherance of his ambition and in the Ghanaian context, Nkrumah ensured that the nation's constitution after independence allowed for the partial or wholesale surrender of powers to the Union towards the attainment of unification.) Nkrumah suggested three objectives for the Union that included economic planning, unified military and defence and centralised foreign policy and diplomacy.[103] According to Nkrumah, the institutions of the Union should consist of an Assembly of Heads of States

96 *Supra*, Craig and de Burca, 3.
97 *Single European Act*, 1987 O.J. L 169/1 (amending Treaty Establishing the European Economic Community, 25 March 1957, 298 U.N.T.S. 11).
98 *Treaty on European Union* (Maastricht text), 29 July 1992, O.J. C 191/1.
99 G. Marks, L. Hooghe and K. Blank, 'European integration from the 1980s: state-centric v. multi-level governance' (1996) 34 (3) *Journal of Common Market Studies* 342.
100 *Supra*, Craig and de Burca, 3.
101 K. Nkrumah, *Africa Must Unite* (Praeger, 1963) 214–215.
102 Ibid. 218.
103 Ibid. 218–220.

and Government (headed by a President elected from among the Heads of States and Government assisted by a number of Vice Presidents), an executive arm (called a Cabinet or Council of Ministers headed by a Chancellor or Prime Minister) and a Federal House with two Chambers (the Senate and the House of Representatives).[104] As mentioned previously, this idea, in a modified form, was unsuccessfully revived by Muammar Gaddafi in 1999. Therefore, unlike the EU (in its entirety as an organisation), the idea of African integration originally started out with the aim of creating a supranational body.

A second school of thought that came out of the Casablanca bloc took a more pragmatic or functional approach and opined that subregional integration is the first and necessary step before a union at the continental level. The idea is that states will integrate at a faster pace at the subregional level and in less unwieldy fashion since states may have more in common with other states within the region than the whole continent in terms of culture, traditions, language and administrative set up. It was also argued that a subregional approach will make decision making easier because it will involve a lesser number of states at the discussion table. This approach to African integration is evidenced by the development in the economic sphere, which is discussed in Chapter 5. Continental economic integration was one of the purposes for the establishment of the OAU. Furthermore, states entered into various subregional treaties that put them on 'a path to economic integration',[105] leading to a situation that Oppong described as 'a bewildering array of economic integration processes'.[106] In each of the geographical regions of Africa there is an average of three or four economic organisations with a mandate for economic integration.[107] According to the AU itself, the regional economic communities (RECs) are increasingly active in the coordination of AU Member States' interests in other important areas such as peace and security, development and governance.[108] The aim of the AU is to use the major RECs as the basis for a wider African integration; moving from regional integration to an eventual continental integration.[109] Some of these RECs are already exhibiting some supranational characteristics.[110] The AU is engaging with the regional subgroupings with the ultimate aims of establishing a free trade and customs union in the regions by 2017; a continent-wide free trade and custom union by 2019; an African common market by 2023; and, by 2028, economic and monetary union and also a continent-wide parliament.

104 K. Nkrumah, *Revolutionary Path* (PANAF, 1973) 295–309.
105 R. F. Oppong, *Legal Aspects of Economic Integration in Africa* (CUP, 2011) 1.
106 Ibid. 14.
107 Ibid. 14.
108 *African Union Handbook* (African Union Commission and New Zealand Ministry of Foreign Affairs and Trade, 2014) 118.
109 Ibid.
110 B. Fagbayibo, 'Common problems affecting supranational attempts in Africa: an analytical overview' (2013) 16 (1) *Potchefstroom Electronic Law Journal/Potchefstroomse Elektroniese Regsblad* 32.

It would thus appear that the pragmatic/functional approach was more compelling in Africa, as evidenced by the subregional configuration that emerged between 1958 and 1963 and the establishment of the Organisation of African Unity. However, the significance of this should not be overstated. The evidence from the EU experience shows that a functional approach may achieve greater fusion in the long run. The emergence of the AU underscores the emergence of advancement in the integration agenda in Africa, which has led to a wider level of intergovernmental cooperation and shows positive signs of supranationalism in some spheres. As Edozie correctly argued,

> Compared to the EU, in institutional and organizational advancement and in its expansiveness and encroachment throughout the region in forging an integral network and movement toward integration, Africa's AU may justifiably be described as an emerging suprastate organization.[111]

African Union law: working definition

In the African Union's statute establishing the African Union Commission on International Law, an independent advisory organ of the AU, references were made to the 'laws of the Union'.[112] However, no attempt was made to define or explain what these terms mean. Furthermore, in the AU's decision expressing its willingness to collaborate with the State of Tanzania's offer to establish an African Institute of International Law, reference was also made to an 'African Union Law', again without providing a definition.[113] Also, in the Protocol on Amendments to the Protocol on the Statute of the African Court of Justice and Human Rights,[114] passing reference was made to the 'laws of the African Union' in Article 28G. Nevertheless, for the purpose of this book, the working definition of African Union law is the body of treaties, resolutions and decisions that have direct and indirect application to the Member States of the African Union (AU). It could be regarded in a simple sense as a 'subregional international law'.[115] Though currently not as advanced as the laws of the European Union (EU), this book will contend that AU law is evolving slowly and exhibiting traits similar to the development of European Union law. The book takes the position that the establishment of the AU to replace OAU was a significant step that has the effect of piercing national borders through transnational norms. The transnational norms form the basis for the evolvement or development of

111 *Supra*, Edozie and Gottschalk, 33.
112 Article 4(a), (e) Statute of the African Union Commission on International Law, EX.CL/478 (XIV) a (2009).
113 *Decision on the Establishment of an African Institute of International Law in Arusha*, The United Republic of Tanzania, Assembly/AU/14(XVIII) Add.5 (2012).
114 *Protocol on Amendments to the Protocol on the Statute of the African Court of Justice and Human Rights*, Assembly/AU/Dec.529(XXIII) (2014).
115 S. B. Ajulo, 'Sources of African law' (2001) 45 (1) *Journal of African Law*, 73, 74.

common legal rules, concepts and principles applicable to Member States.[116] As this book will show, further developments since the emergence of the AU have reinforced this viewpoint.

Conclusion

Africa has come a long way from the time it was considered a 'dark continent' with no conception of law. Scholars have, over time, recognised that Africa has always had its own conception of law, though different from the Eurocentric Western conception of law. African customary law may be considered its unwritten 'Magna Carta' with variations. Though there were many legal systems in pre-colonial Africa, there was a recognised universal body of principles running through these legal systems. These include the need to do substantial justice, natural justice, preservation of community and group concerns, a connection between law and morality, a belief in the supernatural, ubuntu and its variants and the idea of reconciliation. Colonisation, though disruptive of the traditional legal order, unwittingly advanced the development of African Union law on a continental basis. The idea of Pan-Africanism, which developed as a response to colonisation and the struggle for independence of African states, sowed the seed for integration in Africa. The formation of the OAU in 1963 moved the integration agenda forward to a limited extent and produced part of the corpus of African Union law. The emergence of the AU could be considered as the crystallisation of the integration agenda. Africa as a continent has much to gain from integration. These gains include improving cooperation and reduction in conflicts, internal trade creation, increased market size, setting continent-wide standards on important issues such as rule of law, democracy and human rights and stronger bargaining power on the international stage. However, arriving at the Union goal faces a lot more challenges than the European Union faced. Furthermore, integration has legal consequences for Member States, its citizens and the international community as a whole. The challenges and the legal consequences will be explored further in subsequent chapters.

116 See U. Scheuner, forward to C. J. Mann, *The Function of Judicial Decision in European Integration* (Nijhoff, 1971).

3 Ascertaining the sources of African Union law

A needle in a haystack?

Introduction

This chapter explores the constitutional basis of the African Union (AU) law and ascertains the boundary of the AU legal order by identifying its various sources. In addressing this task, the chapter engages in the analysis of the various sources of AU law and their relevance. For the purpose of clarity, the chapter adopts a practical categorisation of the identified sources. The African regional system has an evolving judicial/adjudicatory system. The system includes the African Commission on Human and Peoples' Rights, the African Court on Human and Peoples' Rights and the recently established African Court of Justice and Human Rights. The discussion also includes relevant significant issues such as the legal personality of the AU, the direct effect of AU law and its subsidiarity. Finally, the chapter discusses the potential contribution of the Pan-African Parliament (PAP) as a source of law. The PAP is the legislative body of the AU and was established in 2004. At present the PAP has only advisory and consultative powers. However, the ultimate aim of the AU is to progress the PAP into an institution with full legislative powers.

Legal personality of the African Union

According to Shaw, legal personality is important because it is required for the effective functioning of an institution.[1] Shaw observed that legal personality at the international level centres

> not so much upon the capacity of the entity as such to possess international rights and duties, as upon the actual attribution of rights and/or duties on the international plane as determined by a variety of factors ranging from claims made to prescribed functions.[2]

Legal personality is important in this context because it underscores the norm-generating capacity of such institutions as the AU. Although the AU was brought

1 M. N. Shaw, *International Law*, 6th ed. (CUP, 2013) 175.
2 Ibid. 194.

into existence by its Member States, it has a separate legal personality from the Member States. The AU has been described as endless in size and eternal in time, allowing for the admission of other members 'at any time after the entry into force' of its constitutive Act.[3] The Constitutive Act of the AU did not explicitly confer an international legal personality on the AU.[4] This is not unusual for an international organisation. As Abass observed, the reasons that constituent treaties of international organisations do not usually provide for their legal personality range from political to practical considerations.[5] In the case of the United Nations, for example, one of the reasons proffered for not conferring it with such personality is to avoid giving the impression that the body is a super-state. In the case of the EU, the reason was the uncertainty relating to the use of the word 'Union' to describe the organisation.[6] (The position has now changed under the 2008 Lisbon Treaty, which now provides legal personality for the EU.)[7] Commenting on the legal personality of the AU, Abass opined,

> As for the African Union, there is no indication that the legal personality of the Union was ever debated. One factor that might have contributed to this was the expectation, amongst African States, that since the Union was to succeed the Organization of African Unity (OAU), it would also automatically inherit the latter's legal personality. This expectation was ill-founded mainly because the OAU Charter, adopted in 1963, does not provide for the legal personality or capacity of the organization. Therefore, as far as legal personality is concerned, the African Union inherited nothing. The legal personality of the organization would therefore have to remain dependent on that conferred under customary international law.[8]

However, the African Court on Human and Peoples' Rights seems to have laid the debate to rest in its judgment in *Femi Falana* v. *African Union*,[9] in which it held (relying on the International Court of Justice's advisory opinion on 'Reparation for injuries suffered in the service of the United Nations')[10] that, as an international organisation, the African Union has a legal personality separate

3 N. J. Udombana, 'The institutional structure of the African Union: a legal analysis' (2002) 33 (1) *California Western International Law Journal* 69, 80.

4 A. Jeng, *Peace Building in the African Union: Law, Philosophy and Practice* (Cambridge University Press, 2012) 165–166; see also T. Murithi, 'Briefing – the African Union at ten: an appraisal' (2012) 111 *African Affairs* 1 at 2.

5 A. Abass, *Complete International Law* (OUP, 2012) 204.

6 Ibid. (n. 5) 205; J. W. de Zwaan, 'The legal personality of the European Communities and the European Union' (1999) 30 *Netherlands Yearbook of International Law* 75.

7 See European Union, *Consolidated Versions of the Treaty on European Union* 13 December 2007, 2008/C 115/01; European Union, *Consolidated Versions of the Functioning of the European Union*, 26 October 2012, OJ L.326/47-326/390.

8 *Supra*, Abass, 205.

9 *Femi Falana* v. *African Union*, Application No. 001/2011.

10 (Advisory Opinion) [1949] ICJ Reports 174.

from the legal personality of its Member States.[11] In that case, the Applicant had contended that the African Union can be sued as a corporate community on behalf of its Member States. The Applicant approached the court to hold the AU liable for the failure of Member States to ratify a treaty. The Court held that,

> In the present case, the African Union is not a party to the protocol. As a legal person, an international organization like the African Union will have the capacity to be party to a treaty between States if such a treaty allows an international organization to become a party. As far as an international organization is not a party to a treaty, it cannot be subject to legal obligations arising from that treaty. This is in line with Article 34 of the 1986 Vienna Convention on the Law of Treaties between States and International Organizations or between International Organizations.[12]

Categories of AU law

There is a level of complexity in the emerging corpus of African Union law because of the diversity of its sources and the multifarious factors or forces driving the emergent continent-wide legal order. Indeed, Watson, the legal historian, has described the endeavour to understand the forces behind changes in legal order as one of the most important legal tasks.[13] There is no doubt that the emerging AU legal order is reshaping the nature of the relationship between the law and society in the continent. The reshaping is occurring at the continental, Member-State and individual levels. However, to understand the change, it is essential to ascertain the sources of the changes. Watson has argued that the sources or causes are usually rooted in social, economic or political factors 'important to the life of the society or its leaders'.[14] However, Watson added that a significant part of the cause may be rooted in transnational aspects of the legal tradition that otherwise have little or nothing to do with the social, economic, or political conditions of the society.[15] Watson, credited with coining the term 'legal transplants', has also compellingly argued, and it is now widely acknowledged, that law in most jurisdictions borrows aspects of itself from elsewhere.[16] Transplants are not limited to legal systems; customs, for example, may also be transplanted.[17]

The idea of regionalisation has played a key role in Africa. Regionalisation is an aspect of the process of globalisation. Generally, increased globalisation has precipitated a move towards what Head described as 'multilateralisation', that is,

11 *Supra, Femi Falana* v. *African Union*, Paragraph 68.
12 Ibid.
13 A. Watson, 'Legal change: sources of law and legal culture' (1983) 131 (5) *University of Pennsylvania Law Review* 1121.
14 Ibid. 1135.
15 Ibid.
16 Ibid. 1146.
17 Ibid. 1147.

the 'attempts to deal with the frictions of an ever-shrinking world through the establishment of new legal regimes designed to apply globally, or nearly so.'[18] This development has, in Head's view, led to international law evolving into 'supranational law'. Head acknowledged that he used supranational law in his research paper in a broad sense. Such a usage may be contested, but it is more compelling to argue that the development has shaped the emergence of such organisations as the AU and the EU.

The legal system of the AU is based on several sources of law. The competence of the AU is determined by the powers attributed to it by the legal instruments and framework adopted by its constituent Member States. Laws of supranational organisations evolve progressively with the institutions. The AU, similar to the EU, is no different in this regard. In the case of the EU, for example, the scope and application of its laws have been widened and the powers of the EU institutions increased through successive treaties and the interpretation of community powers by the European Court of Justice.[19]

Similar to the EU, the emergent AU law is distinct and separate from international law and the domestic laws of Member States. This legal order emanates from sources that have developed along with the emergence of the AU and its institutions. The legal order is partly based on the continent's unique normative values, as discussed in Chapter 2.[20] Preliminarily, the various sources can be hierarchically categorised into primary sources, i.e., primary treaties, secondary legislation made under the treaties, international agreements concluded by the AU/OAU, 'soft laws' that are not legally binding but may be useful in the interpretation and application of AU law, regional courts' decisions and the future laws to be made by the Pan-African Parliament.

There was no attempt to state the sources of AU law in the AU Constitutive Act itself. However, as mentioned in Chapter 2, references were made in the statute establishing the African Union Commission on International Law (AUCIL) to 'African Law'. More significantly, the statute unwittingly identified, albeit indirectly and vaguely, certain key sources of AU law. In Article 4, the objectives of the AUCIL are stated as follows:

> The AUCIL shall act at the instance of the Policy and other Organs of the Union. It shall have the following specific objectives:
>
> a) to undertake activities relating to codification and progressive development of international law in the African continent with particular attention to the *laws of the Union* as embodied in the *treaties of the Union*, in the *decisions of the policy organs of the Union* and in *African customary international law arising from the practice of Member States*;

18 J. W. Head, 'Supranational law: how the move toward multilateral solutions is changing the character of "international" law' (1993) 42 (3) *Kansas Law Review* 606.

19 See, generally, M. Horspool and M. Humphreys, *European Union Law* (OUP, 2008).

20 A. Jeng, *Peace Building in the African Union: Law Philosophy and Practice* (Cambridge University Press, 2012) 137.

b) to propose draft framework agreements, model regulations, formulations and analyses of *emerging trends in States' practice* to facilitate the codification and progressive development of international law;

[. . .]

e) to encourage the teaching, study, publication and dissemination of literature on international law in particular the *laws of the Union* with a view to promoting acceptance of and respect for the principles of international law, the peaceful resolution of conflicts, respect for the Union and recourse to its Organs, when necessary. (Emphasis added.)[21]

A careful reading of the text above thus shows an implicit recognition of particular sources of AU law in Article 4(a), which are Treaties of the AU, decisions of the policy organs of the AU and African customary international law arising from the practice of member states. Though these law sources were merely stated as the focus for the objectives of the AUCIL in its task of codification and the progressive development of international law, it is observed that these sources have immediate relevance as a statutory framework that impacts Member States. Significantly, the Protocol on the Statute of the African Court of Justice and Human Rights took a similar approach when it outlined the applicable law of the court. Article 31 provides the following:

In carrying out its functions, the Court shall have regard to

a) The Constitutive Act;
b) International treaties, whether general or particular, ratified by the contesting States;
c) International custom, as evidence of a general practice accepted as law;
d) The general principles of law recognised universally or by African States;
e) Subject to the provisions of paragraph 1, of Article 46 of the present Statute, judicial decisions and writings of the most highly qualified publicists of various nations as well as the regulations, directives and decisions of the Union, as subsidiary means for the determination of the rules of law;
f) Any other law relevant to the determination of the case.[22]

Article 31(1) is similar to Articles 38(1)–(2) of the Statute of the International Court of Justice (ICJ), which has led to the generally accepted view that the Statute of the ICJ did not enumerate a formal hierarchy of sources. This view may be applicable to Article 31 in relation to the sources it outlined.[23] However,

21 African Union, *The Statute of the African Union Commission on International Law*, EX.CL/478 (XIV) a, 4 February 2009.

22 Ibid. Article 31(2).

23 K. D. Magliverals and G. J. Naldi, 'The African Court of Justice' (2006) 66 *Heidelberg Journal of International Law* 187–213.

there are two significant differences due to the nature of the AU itself. In the first place, the AU Constitutive Act is a constitutional instrument, and it lies at the foundation of the AU legal order. Its provisions have constitutional status and thus will have supremacy within its legal order. Second, paragraph 31 (d) specifically classified judicial decisions, writings by eminent experts, and regulations, directives of the AU as 'subsidiary' sources, which indicates that they are lower in the hierarchy compared with other sources in Article 31.

OAU contributions to the primary sources of AU law

The OAU was effectively disbanded on the 9 July 2002 with the creation of the AU. However, despite its demise, the OAU footprint is evident in the corpus of AU law. As noted in Chapter 2, the OAU founding members did not conceive the organisation as a legislative body.[24] However, through the adoption of treaties, resolutions and declarations, and similar instruments, the OAU inevitably assumed a quasi-legislative role. The adoption of multilateral treaties, resolutions and declarations were the primary contributions of the institution as a source of law. The OAU contributions were primarily driven by the political/policy organs of the institution.[25] These were the Assembly of Heads of State and Government (Assembly) and the Council of Ministers. The functions of the Assembly under the OAU Charter and the Assembly's practice suggest that it was mainly a forum for discussion and deliberations. However, as Cervanka correctly observed, the Assembly discussions usually reached conclusions.[26] More importantly, under Article X of the OAU Charter, the conclusions reached by the Assembly must be registered as resolutions except where they relate to appointments, elections or procedural or organisational matters. Furthermore, under Article X(2) of the OAU Charter, the Assembly can adopt a resolution by a two-thirds majority of members. The Charter itself was silent on the legal status of these resolutions. However, they were generally accepted as recommendations to the Member States.[27] Cervanka concluded that resolutions do not impose any legal obligations.[28] Similarly, Maluwa argued that the OAU resolutions were not legally binding as such and had the nature of 'hortatory soft law only'.[29] Nevertheless, Cervanka stated two strong caveats for this conclusion. First, he argued that although resolutions addressed to Member States were not legally binding, they provided an important avenue for bringing the weight of public opinion from the continent and the world to bear upon the Member States. In particular, the right of discussion and consequent recommendations on matters of common concern

24 T. Maluwa, 'International law-making in post-colonial Africa: the role of the Organization of African Unity' (2002) 41 (1) *Netherlands International Law Review* 81 at 84.

25 Ibid. 85.

26 Z. Cervenka, *The Organisation of African Unity and Its Charter* (C. Hurst & Company, 1969) 44.

27 Ibid. 45.

28 Ibid.

29 *Supra*, Maluwa, 99.

to Africa gives the Assembly '*carte blanche* to tackle matters of far-reaching consequences in the political, military and economic spheres of Africa'.[30]

Second, Cervanka identified important exceptions to the non-binding nature of OAU resolutions. The exceptions include three situations where resolutions and the decisions of the Assembly organs could have binding effect. These situations include the power of the Assembly to decide on questions relating to the interpretation of the OAU Charter (by two-thirds majority), the power to decide on admission of new Members (by a simple majority) and the power to approve amendments to the OAU Charter (by two-thirds majority). Cervanka noted that 'decisions on these matters are clearly legally binding on all Members, including those casting dissenting votes'.[31] The legally binding nature of these exceptions underscores the limited norm-creating capability of the OAU Assembly in practice.

This capability can be contrasted with resolutions from the Council of Ministers of the OAU. The primary responsibility of the Council, which comprised the foreign ministers from Member States or such ministers designated to act in that capacity, was to implement the decisions of the Assembly. The Assembly's deliberations usually resulted in resolutions determined by a simple majority. Resolutions of the Council of Ministers were required to be submitted to the Assembly for approval under Article XIII of the Charter. According to Cervanka, '[t]he limited powers of the Council indicate clearly that its resolutions are mere recommendations, imposing no legal obligations on the Members of the Council'.[32] However, one may argue that once these resolutions were approved by the Assembly, and if they fell within the exceptions discussed in relation to the Assembly, they became legally binding.

The OAU treaties that have survived the OAU itself and are part of the corpus of AU law are:

General Convention on the Privileges and Immunities of the Organisation of African Unity, adopted on 25 October 1965 and entered into force on 25 October 1965.

Phyto-Sanitary Convention for Africa, adopted on 13 September 1967 and entered into force on 6 October 1992.

African Convention on the Conservation of Nature and Natural Resources, adopted on 15 September 1968 and entered into force on 16 June 1969.

(continued)

30 *Supra*, Cervenka, 46.
31 Ibid. 46.
32 Ibid. 51.

(continued)

African Civil Aviation Commission Constitution, adopted on 17 January 1969 and entered into force on 15 March 1972. (The Constitution has since been revised, and the revised version was adopted in July 2003.)

The OAU Convention Governing the Specific Aspects of Refugee Problems in Africa, adopted on 10 September 1969 and entered into force on 20 January 1974.

Constitution of the Association of African Trade Promotion Organisations, adopted on 18 January 1974 and entered into force on 1 February 2010.

Inter-African Convention Establishing an African Technical Co-operation Programme, adopted on 1 August 1975.

Cultural Charter for Africa, adopted on 5 July 1976 and entered into force on 19 September 1990. (To be replaced by the Charter for African Cultural Renaissance, adopted in January 2006, when the latter came into force.)

Convention for the Elimination of Mercenarism in Africa, adopted on 3 July 1977 and came into force on 22 April 1985.

Additional Protocol to the OAU General Convention on Privileges and Immunities, adopted on 1 July 1980.

African Charter on Human and Peoples' Rights, adopted on 1 July 1981 and entered into force on 21 October 1986.

Convention for the Establishment of the African Centre for Fertilizer Development, adopted on 1 July 1985.

Agreement for the Establishment of the African Rehabilitation Institute (ARI), adopted on 17 July 1985 and entered into force on 2 December 1991.

African Charter on the Rights and Welfare of the Child, adopted on 1 July 1990 and entered into force on 29 November 1999.

Bamako Convention on the Ban of the Import into Africa and the Control of Transboundary Movement and Management of Hazardous Wastes within Africa, adopted on 30 January 1991 and entered into force on 22 April 1998.

Treaty Establishing the African Economic Community, adopted on 3 June 1991 and entered into force on 12 May 1994.

African Maritime Transport Charter, adopted on 11 June 1994. (A revised version of this Charter was adopted in 2010 and it replaced the 1994 Charter when it came into force.)

The African Nuclear-Weapon-Free Zone Treaty (Pelindaba Treaty), adopted on 11 April 1996 and entered into force on 15 July 2001.

Protocol to the African Charter on Human and Peoples' Rights on the Establishment of an African Court on Human and Peoples' Rights, adopted on 10 June 1998 and entered into force on 25 January 2004. (This was replaced by the Protocol on the Statute of the African Court of Justice and Human Rights of 2008 when it came into force.)

The OAU Convention on the Prevention and Combating of Terrorism, adopted on 1 July 1999 and entered into force on 6 December 2002.

Constitutive Act of the African Union, adopted on 7 November 2000 and entered into force on 26 May 2001.

Norms and law creation in the AU: decisions and the treaty-making process

The AU Constitution empowers the institution to govern wider areas of activities within the continent that affect Member States and their citizens at large. The AU Constitutive Act entered into force as a binding legal instrument on the 26 May 2001, after its ratification by two-thirds of the Member States, as required by Article 28. This act effectively replaced and superseded the OAU Charter.[33] The Constitutive Act is significant because it has constitutional status. The act represents the organic written constitution of the AU. It not only established the AU as an institution but also provides for the fundamental principles governing the Union. According to Edozie, the AU Constitutive Act is the social contract and legal code that now underlies the AU's political profile and the continent's will for collective action.[34] The ultimate aim of the AU Constitution is the ambitious goal of achieving political integration in the continent, which is a far cry from the limited ambition of the OAU Charter, which aimed only at fostering cooperation. Interestingly, Maluwa has argued that there is a direct link between the concept of Pan-Africanism and the Constitutive Act of the AU. According to him,

> the adoption of the Constitutive Act is but an aspect of the historic quest for a united Africa, whose origin can be traced back to the pioneers of the Pan-Africanist movement in the pre-independence era.[35]

33 African Union, *Constitutive Act of the African Union*, 1 July 2001, Article 33(1), available at: https://au.int/en/constitutive-act, accessed 6 December 2017.

34 R. K. Edozie and K. Gottschalk, *The African Union's Africa: New Pan-African Initiatives in Global Governance* (Michigan State University Press, 2014) xxxxix.

35 T. Maluwa, 'The transition from the Organisation of African Unity to the African Union' in A. A. Yusuf and F. Ouguergouz, *The African Union: Legal and Institutional Framework: A Manual on the Pan-African Organization* (Martinus Nijhoff, 2012) 35.

Even though the Constitutive Act accommodated some of the principles of the OAU Charter, at the same time it marked a significant change in direction for the legal framework of the Union.[36] Article 3 of the Constitutive Act (as amended)[37] states the objectives of the AU, and it is notable that the objectives geared towards the ultimate goal of the AU are more extensive than similar provisions under the OAU Charter. However, apart from changing the underlying objectives of the continental organisation, the Constitutive Act also dispenses with obsolete objectives contained in the OAU Charter. An example is the provision relating to the eradication of all forms of colonialism in Africa. That provision is no longer relevant because all African States are now independent nations.

A look at certain of the key provisions of the AU Constitutive Act shows how the instrument underscores the emergence of a new legal order. A majority of the objectives of the AU are directly or indirectly linked with integration and collectivism (Article 3(a), (c)–(m)). The principles set out in Article 4 also signify a new approach to the underlying principles of African approaches to norm and standard setting. These principles include popular participation (4c), common defence policy (4d), peaceful conflict resolution (4e), right of the Union to intervene in Member States (4g and j), self-reliance (4k), gender-equality (4l), social justice in economic matters (4n), rejection of terrorism (4o) and rejection of unconstitutional change of government (4p). These expanded objectives and additional principles play significant roles in the normative underpinning of the emerging AU law.

It has been opined that the AU is playing a continental role as a 'norm entrepreneur' and 'a normative leader who encourages Member States to uphold a range of norms and standards for the improvement of the livelihood of people within their jurisdiction or authority'.[38] According to Murithi, the evidence for this assertion includes the AU's active role in advancing norms relating to peace, security and stability, norms relating to the rights to intervene in Member States and human rights norms. The norm relating to the rights to intervene in Member States is recognised widely as the AU's potential ability to set global standards due to its clarification on when an international organisation can interfere in the affairs of Member States. It is noteworthy that the AU is the first international organisation to provide a legal basis for such in its constitution.[39]

Two principal organs are responsible for decision making in the AU. These are the Executive Council and the Assembly of the Union. Each organ has the responsibility for making decisions on particular issues. The Assembly is composed of the heads of state and government, and it is the supreme organ of the Union. It meets

36 Ibid. 50.

37 Protocol on the Amendments to the Constitutive Act of the African Union, available at: https://au.int/en/treaties/protocol-amendments-constitutive-act-african-union, accessed 6 December 2017.

38 T. Murithi, 'Briefing – the African Union at ten: an appraisal' (2012) 111 (445) *African Affairs* 1 at 2.

39 *Supra*, Edozie and Gottschalk, 25.

twice a year, usually in January and July. The powers and functions of the Assembly are stated in the Rules of Procedure of the Assembly of the Union.[40] These are wide ranging and include policy and decision making, implementation and compliance by Member States, decisions on intervention in Member States' affairs, power to impose sanctions, membership, and appointment of judges. It may convene an extraordinary session if such a session is requested by a Member State. Its decisions are taken by consensus and, failing that, by a two-thirds majority of Member States that are eligible to vote. The Executive Council is composed of ministers of foreign affairs of all Member States. It meets twice a year in ordinary sessions. The Executive Council makes decisions on the budget, proposals with financial implications, decisions on legal instruments and appointment of elected officers. The decision of the executive council requires the endorsement of the Assembly.

Usually, the decision-making process commences as a policy proposal from the AU Commission or from a Member State(s) or another organ of the AU. In the case of proposals originating from the Commission, its power to initiate such a proposal is provided in Article 3(2)(b) of the Statute of the African Commission.[41] In practice, the Commission usually calls a meeting of experts from AU Member States to discuss new policy proposals that it has decided to take forward. The meeting of experts makes recommendations, which are delivered to the Ministers from Member States for the relevant sector under consideration. If the ministerial meeting approves the recommendations, it reports to the Executive Council, which may approve the recommendations.

It may be observed that certain proposals with implications for the budget go through the Permanent Representative Council for consideration. The Permanent Representative Council consists of permanent representatives from all AU Member States and acts in an advisory capacity to the Executive Council. After its deliberations, the Executive Council tables the recommendation before the Assembly. If the recommendation is one that can be decided by the Executive Council, the recommendation becomes a decision if it is approved by the Executive Council. The Executive Council reaches its decisions by consensus and, where there is no consensus, by a two-thirds majority of Member States eligible to vote. Prior to publication, the decisions are authenticated by the chairperson of the Assembly or the Council, as the case may be. The decisions of the Assembly and the Executive Council are published in the official journal of the AU in its official languages (Arabic, English, French and Portuguese) within 15 days of authentication. The decisions are transmitted to all Member States, organs of the AU, and regional economic communities (REC).

It is the responsibility of the AU Commission, as the administrative branch, to implement the decisions. African Union decisions can result in Charters,

40 Rule 4, *Rules of Procedure of the Assembly of the Union*, available at: https://oldsite.issafrica.org/uploads/rules_AssemblyJuly2002.pdf, accessed 6 December 2017.

41 *Statute of the Commission of the African Union*, ASS/AU/2(I) - d (2002), available at: https://issafrica.s3.amazonaws.com/site/uploads/STATCOMMISSION.PDF, accessed 11 December 2017.

Treaties, Conventions and Protocols that are legally binding on Member States after ratification. Usually, any instrument created in the process requires ratification by a number of Member States, normally 15, before it enters into force. Other decisions made by the Assembly and Executive that do not fall into the above categories are only binding on all Member States or individuals and organs of the AU affected by the decision. For the purpose of implementing AU decisions, regulations may be put in place to govern the implementation. The regulations consist of rules and procedures for implementation of particular decisions. All Member States that are obliged to implement the decision are bound by such regulations.

The AU institutions regularly issue resolutions and declarations. These instruments have no obvious legal standing. It has been suggested that these resolutions and declarations are not binding because they are intended to guide and harmonise viewpoints of Member States.[42] However, the resolutions may lead to the creation of new treaties, conventions or protocols.

Enforcement of obligations under binding instruments is an area where the AU significantly differs from the OAU. The OAU Charter does not provide for any procedure to enforce decisions made by its institutions. However, Article 23 of the AU Constitutive Act gives the Assembly the power to impose sanctions on erring Member States, and Article 30 empowers the Assembly to suspend a member in the case of unconstitutional change of government.[43] Failure of any Member State to comply with their obligation under AU instruments may attract sanctions. Specific scenarios that could attract sanctions include failure to pay contributions, occurrence of unconstitutional change of government and failure to comply with AU policies.[44]

Categorising AU treaties

Similar to that of the OAU, the AU's primary approach towards achieving its policy objectives is through the adoption of treaties.[45] The AU has not arranged its treaties into specific categories.[46] However, for ease of discussion, the classification suggested by Maluwa will be adopted for the purposes of this book.[47] It is important to note, as Maluwa himself conceded, that these are not mutually exclusive categories, and certain treaties may overlap. Nonetheless, Maluwa organised the treaties based on the policy areas to which he concluded they were substantially related. The categories, with the addition of 'soft law' and judicial decisions, are as follows:

42 OXFAM International, *African Union Compendium*, 2nd ed. (AMEYIB Communications & Marketing Plc, 2014) 54, available at: www.oxfam.org/en/research/african-union-compendium, accessed 5 December 2017.

43 This is discussed in Chapter 6.

44 *Supra*, OXFAM International, 52–56.

45 T. Maluwa, 'Ratification of African Union treaties by Member States: law, policy and practice' (2012) 13 (2) *Melbourne Journal of International Law* 1.

46 Ibid. 17.

47 Ibid.

Foundational legal instruments and institutions (the AU's basic documents)

These documents are underlying treaties of the Union with constitutional implications, and they establish the main organs of the Union. The instruments are the main pillars of the Union and spell out its overall framework. Treaties in this category include: the Constitutive Act of the African Union;[48] Treaty Establishing the African Economic Community;[49] Protocol to the Treaty Establishing the African Economic Community relating to the Pan-African Parliament;[50] Peace and Security Council Protocol;[51] Protocol on the Statute of the African Court of Justice and Human Rights;[52] and the Statute of the African Union Commission on International Law.[53] The African Charter on Human and Peoples' Rights[54] should also be included here because of its wide-ranging legal implications but it is included in the human rights section because of its subject matter.

Trade, economic and technical cooperation

These are sector-specific agreements in trade-related matters. These include: the Revised Constitution of the African Civil Aviation Commission;[55] Rehabilitation Institute Agreement;[56] and the Convention of the African Energy Commission.[57]

48 *Supra*, African Union, *Constitutive Act of the African Union*, 1 July 2001.

49 African Union, *Treaty Establishing the African Economic Community*, 12 May 1994, available at: https://au.int/en/treaties/treaty-establishing-african-economic-community, accessed 24 November 2017.

50 African Union, *Protocol to the Treaty Establishing the African Economic Community relating to the Pan-African Parliament*, 14 December 2003, available at: https://au.int/en/treaties/protocol-treaty-establishing-african-economic-community-relating-pan-african-parliament, accessed 24 November 2017.

51 African Union, *Protocol Relating to the Establishment of the Peace and Security Council of the African Union*, 9 July 2002, available at: www.peaceau.org/uploads/psc-protocol-en.pdf, accessed 24 November 2017.

52 African Union, *Protocol on the Statute of the African Court of Justice and Human Rights*, 1 July 2008, available at: https://au.int/en/treaties/protocol-statute-african-court-justice-and-human-rights, accessed 24 November 2017.

53 African Union, *The Statute of the African Union Commission on International Law*, EX.CL/478 (XIV) a, 4 February 2009, available at: https://au.int/en/treaties/statute-african-union-commission-international-law-aucil, accessed 24 November 2017.

54 OAU, *African Charter on Human and Peoples' Rights*, 27 June 1981, CAB/LEG/67/3 rev. 5, 21 I.L.M 58 (1982), available at: www.achpr.org/files/instruments/achpr/banjul_charter.pdf, accessed 24 November 2017.

55 African Union, *Revised Constitution of the African Civil Aviation Commission*, available at: https://au.int/en/treaties/revised-constitution-african-civil-aviation-commission, accessed 12 December 2017.

56 African Union, *Agreement for the Establishment of the African Rehabilitation Institute*, 2 December 1991, available at: https://au.int/en/treaties/agreement-establishment-african-rehabilitation-institute-ari, accessed 24 November 2017.

57 Organisation of African Unity, *Convention of the African Energy Commission*, 13 December 2006, available at: https://au.int/en/treaties/convention-african-energy-commission, accessed 24 November 2017.

Privileges and immunities of the organisation

These include the General Convention on the Privileges and Immunities of the OAU[58] and the Additional Protocol to the OAU General Convention on Privileges and Immunities.[59]

Human rights (including women's rights and children's rights) and refugees

These are instruments relating to various aspects of human rights. These include: the OAU Convention Governing the Specific Aspects of Refugee Problems in Africa;[60] African Charter on Human and Peoples' Rights;[61] African Charter on the Rights and Welfare of the Child;[62] Protocol to the African Charter on Human and Peoples' Rights on the Establishment of an African Court on Human and Peoples' Rights;[63] Protocol to the African Charter on Human and Peoples' Rights Relating to the Rights of Women in Africa;[64] and the Protocol to the African Charter on Human and Peoples' Rights on the Rights of Older Persons.[65]

Environment

These are instruments underscoring the concern for environmental issues. These include the African Convention on the Conservation of Nature and

58 Organisation of African Unity, *General Convention on the Privileges and Immunities of the Organisation of African Unity*, 25 October 1985, U.N.T.S. Vol. 1000, 1–14688, available at: https://treaties.un.org/doc/Publication/UNTS/Volume%201000/volume-1000-I-14688-English.pdf, accessed 24 November 2017.

59 Organisation of African Unity, *Additional Protocol to the OAU General Convention on Privileges and Immunities*, 1 June 1980, CM/103(XXXV) Rev. 3, Annex 1, available at: www.refworld.org/docid/514ae7232.html, accessed 24 November 2017.

60 Organisation of African Unity, *Convention Governing the Specific Aspects of Refugee Problems in Africa*, 10 September 1969, U.N.T.S. No. 14691, available at: www.unhcr.org/uk/about-us/background/45dc1a682/oau-convention-governing-specific-aspects-refugee-problems-africa-adopted.html, accessed 24 November 2017.

61 OAU, *African Charter on Human and Peoples' Rights*, 27 June 1981, CAB/LEG/67/3 rev. 5, 21 I.L.M. 58 (1982), available at: www.achpr.org/files/instruments/achpr/banjul_charter.pdf, accessed 24 November 2017.

62 African Union, *African Charter on the Rights and Welfare of the Child*, 11 July 1990, CAB/LEG/153/Rev. 2 (1990), available at: https://au.int/en/treaties/african-charter-rights-and-welfare-child, accessed 25 November 2017.

63 African Union, *Protocol to the African Charter on Human and Peoples' Rights on the Establishment of an African Court on Human and Peoples' Rights*, 10 June 1998, available at: https://au.int/en/treaties/protocol-african-charter-human-and-peoples-rights-establishment-african-court-human-and, accessed 25 November 2017.

64 African Union, *Protocol to the African Charter on Human and Peoples' Rights relating to the Rights of Women in Africa*, 1 July 2003, available at: https://au.int/en/treaties/protocol-african-charter-human-and-peoples-rights-rights-women-africa, accessed 25 November 2017.

65 African Union, *Protocol to the African Charter on Human and Peoples' Rights on the Rights of Older Persons*, 2016, available at: https://au.int/en/treaties/protocol-african-charter-human-and-peoples%E2%80%99-rights-rights-older-persons, accessed 12 December 2017.

Natural Resources[66] and the Bamako Convention on the Ban of the Import into Africa and the Control of Transboundary Movement and Management of Hazardous Wastes within Africa.[67]

International security and crimes

These include the OAU Convention for the Elimination of Mercenarism in Africa;[68] the African Nuclear-Weapon-Free Zone Treaty;[69] the OAU Convention on the Prevention and Combating of Terrorism;[70] the African Union Convention on Preventing and Combating Corruption;[71] and the African Union Non-Aggression and Common Defence Pact.[72]

Culture

This category is related to culture and includes the Cultural Charter for Africa[73] and the African Youth Charter.[74]

Soft law

The AU, similarly to other international actors, also acts through soft laws in a wide range of areas. These are instruments that are non-binding but have

66 Organisation of African Unity, *African Convention on the Conservation of Nature and Natural Resources*, 15 September 1968, U.N.T.S. Vol. 1001, 1–14689, available at: https://treaties.un.org/doc/Publication/UNTS/Volume%201001/volume-1001-I-14689-English.pdf, accessed 25 November 2017.

67 OAU, *Bamako Convention on the Ban of the Import into Africa and the Control of Transboundary Movement and Management of Hazardous Wastes within Africa*, 30 January 1991, U.N.T.S. Vol. 2101, 1–36508, available at: https://treaties.un.org/doc/Publication/UNTS/Volume%20 2101/v2101.pdf, accessed 25 November 2017.

68 Organisation of African Unity, *OAU Convention for the Elimination of Mercenarism in Africa*, 3 July 1977, CM/817 (XXIX) Annex II Rev. 1, available at: https://au.int/sites/default/files/treaties/7768-treaty-0009_-_oau_convention_for_the_elimination_of_mercenarism_in_africa_e.pdf, accessed 25 November 2017.

69 African Union, *African Nuclear-Weapon-Free Zone Treaty*, 11 April 1996, available at: https://au.int/sites/default/files/treaties/7777-treaty-0018_-_the_african_nuclear-weapon-free_zone_treaty_the_treaty_of_pelindaba_e.pdf, accessed 25 November 2017.

70 Organisation of African Unity, *OAU Convention on the Prevention and Combating of Terrorism*, 1 July 1999, available at: https://au.int/sites/default/files/treaties/7779-treaty-0020_-_oau_convention_on_the_prevention_and_combating_of_terrorism_e.pdf, accessed 25 November 2017.

71 African Union, *African Union Convention on Preventing and Combating Corruption*, 1 July 2003, available at: https://au.int/en/treaties/african-union-convention-preventing-and-combating-corruption, accessed 25 November 2017.

72 African Union, *African Union Non-Aggression and Common Defence Pact*, 1 January 2005, available at: https://au.int/en/treaties/african-union-non-aggression-and-common-defence-pact, accessed 25 November 2017.

73 African Union, *Cultural Charter for Africa*, 5 July 1976, available at: https://au.int/en/treaties/cultural-charter-africa, accessed 25 November 2017.

74 African Union, *African Youth Charter*, 2 July 2006, available at: https://au.int/en/treaties/african-youth-charter accessed 25 November 2017.

quasi-legal character. Such instruments are useful in areas in which regulation is desirable but agreements are difficult to reach.[75] Soft law instruments are issued by AU/OAU institutions from time to time and occur in various forms. Examples of such instruments include the Lomé Declaration of July 2000 on the framework for an OAU response to unconstitutional changes of government,[76] which provides guidance for responding to unconstitutional change of government. Other examples are the New Partnership for Africa's Development;[77] the African Peer Review Mechanism;[78] Guidelines on the Conditions of Arrest, Police Custody and Pre-Trial Detention in Africa[79]; Guidelines and Principles on Economic, Social and Cultural Rights in the African Charter on Human and Peoples' Rights;[80] Guidelines for African Union Electoral Observations and Monitoring Missions,[81] etc. Model laws could also be included in this category. The AU is developing notable expertise in these areas, and a number of such laws have been developed under the AU/OAU auspices. These include the African Model Legislation for the Protection of the Rights of Local Communities (2000),[82] The African Model Anti-Terrorism Law (2011),[83] The Model Law on Access to Information for Africa[84] and the African Union (AU) Model Law on Medical Products Regulation (2016).[85]

Judicial decisions

The African Commission, which was originally the main mechanism for ensuring compliance with the provisions of the African Charter on Human and Peoples' Rights (African Charter), was established under the African Charter as

75 A. T. Guzman and T. L. Meyer, 'International soft law' (2010) 2 *Journal of Legal Analysis* 171, 172.

76 *Lomé Declaration on the Framework for an OAU Response to Unconstitutional Changes of Government*, AHG/Decl.5 (XXXVI), July 2000, available at: www2.ohchr.org/english/law/compilation_democracy/lomedec.htm, accessed 25 November 2017.

77 African Union, *New Partnership for Africa's Development*, 9–11 July 2001, AHG/Dec. 1–11 (XXXVII), AHG/Decl. 1–2 (XXXVII), available at: http://archive.au.int/collect/auassemb/import/English/2001%20AHG%20Dec%20160-170%20(XXXVII)%20_E.pdf, accessed 26 November 2017.

78 African Union, *African Peer Review Mechanism*, 2013, available at: http://aprm-au.org/index, accessed 26 November 2017.

79 ACHPR, *Guidelines on the Conditions of Arrest, Police Custody and Pre-Trial Detention in Africa*, adopted by the ACPHR during its 55th Ordinary Session, Angola, 28 April–12 May 2014, available at: www.achpr.org/files/instruments/guidelines_arrest_detention/guidelines_on_arrest_police_custody_detention.pdf, accessed 26 November 2017.

80 ACPHR, *Guidelines and Principles on Economic, Social and Cultural Rights in the African Charter on Human and Peoples' Rights*, 24 October 2011, available at: www.achpr.org/files/instruments/guidelines_arrest_detention/guidelines_on_arrest_police_custody_detention.pdf, accessed 26 November 2017.

81 ACPHR, *Guidelines for African Union Electoral Observations and Monitoring Missions*, 8 July 2002, EX.CL/91 (V), Annex II, available at: www.achpr.org/instruments/guide-elections, accessed 26 November 2017.

82 www.wipo.int/wipolex/en/text.jsp?file_id=252153, accessed 22 November 2017.

83 www.peaceau.org/en/article/the-african-model-anti-terrorism-law-2, accessed 22 November 2017.

84 www.achpr.org/instruments/access-information, accessed 22 November 2017.

85 www.nepad.org/resource/african-union-au-model-law-medical-products-regulation, accessed 22 November 2017.

a quasi-judicial body.[86] The Commission was modelled on the European Human Rights Commission (since abolished)[87] and the Inter-American Commission on Human Rights.[88] The Commission's functions are stated in Article 45 of the Charter and include the promotion of human rights, the protection of human rights under the African Charter, the interpretation of the African Charter, and any other functions assigned to the Commission by the Assembly of Heads of State. The Commission also has the task of preparing cases for submission to the African Court on Human and Peoples' Rights and, in the future, the African Court of Justice and Human Rights.[89] The Commission thus has both protective and promotional responsibilities. Its protective responsibility involves receiving communications on violations of rights protected under the Charter, communicating them to States and investigating them, with the view towards reconciling the parties. The Commission's decisions are included in the Commission's yearly activity report.

Although the African Charter directly refers only to communications from states, the Commission also accepts communications from non-state actors under the provision for 'Other Communications'.[90] This makes it possible for individuals and NGOs to bring complaints before the Commission. This is an expression of the vertical direct effect of AU human rights law. However, a communication can only be brought against a State Party to the Charter and not against private persons or individuals, thereby preventing a horizontal direct effect.[91] Hence, a private person or individual can only be implicated where a State is held liable for the violation of human rights.

There has been a debate on the question of whether the decisions of the Commission are binding.[92] The African Commission itself has been ambiguous in stating the legal status of its decisions.[93] As noted by Murray and Long, the Commission has sometimes referred to its decisions as non-binding because of the quasi-judicial nature of its mandate.[94] Nevertheless, the Commission has also suggested that its decisions are authoritative interpretations of the Charter.

86 Article 30 of the African Charter.

87 The European Commission on Human Rights was abolished by *Protocol 11 to the European Convention for the Protection of Human Rights and Fundamental Freedoms* (213 U.N.T.S. 222 as amended).

88 The Inter-American Commission on Human Rights is an autonomous organ of the Organization of American States (OAS). It was created in 1959 to promote and protect human rights in the Americas pursuant to the OAS Charter (119 U.N.T.S. 3 as amended) and the American Convention on Human Rights (O.A.S. Treaty Series No. 36, 1144 U.N.T.S. 123).

89 Article 5 of the *Protocol to the African Charter on Human and Peoples' Rights on the Establishment of an African Court on Human and Peoples' Rights*, 1998, OAU Doc. OAU/LEG/EXP/AFCHPR/PROT (III).

90 Articles 55–59, *African Charter*.

91 Ibid. Article 47. This is discussed further in Chapter 10.

92 R. Murray and D. Long, *The Implementation of the Findings of the African Commission on Human and Peoples' Rights* (Cambridge University Press, 2015) 24, 50.

93 Ibid. 50.

94 Ibid. 53.

Furthermore, it has been argued that since the Commission's recommendations are included in its activity report, they should become binding upon adoption.[95] However, irrespective of this debate, as shown in Chapters 7 and 8, the Commission's jurisprudence has been a key building block in shaping the AU legal order, especially in the human rights sphere and in the development of key underlying principles of the AU legal order. The Commission occasionally grants interim or provisional measures to avoid irredeemable harm.[96] In *International Pen and Others (on behalf of Saro-Wiwa)* v. *Nigeria*, the Commission held that such provisional measures are binding and should be respected by Member States.[97]

The Commission has produced world-leading decisions in areas such as economic, social and cultural rights, thereby refuting the widely canvassed argument that such rights cannot be dealt with through a judicial process.[98] The Commission is also leading the way in translating collective rights (such as the right to development, the right of people to dispose of their wealth and natural resources freely, the right to peace and security, the right to self-determination and cultural rights) into enforceable rights.[99]

To strengthen the mechanism for the protection of human rights and to address the limitations of the African Commission's procedure, there was a push towards the creation of a court for human rights within the African system. This led to the establishment of the African Court on Human and Peoples' Rights (African Court).[100] However, the lifespan of the Court will be short because it will soon be replaced by the African Court of Justice and Human Rights,[101] once the protocol establishing the latter comes into force. The African Court was established by an additional protocol to the African Charter adopted by the Assembly of Heads of State and Governments of the OAU in 1998.[102] The Protocol came

95 Ibid. 53.

96 Rule 111 of the *Rules of Procedures of the African Commission on Human and Peoples' Rights* adopted on 6 October 1995 allows the Commission to grant interim provisional orders. See U. O. Umozorike, 'The African Charter on Human and Peoples' Rights: suggestions for more effectiveness' (2007) 13 (1) *Annual Survey of International & Comparative Law* 179 at 186.

97 See *International Pen and Others (on behalf of Saro-Wiwa)* v. *Nigeria*, Communication Nos 137/94, 139/94, 154/96 and 161/97 (1998). See also R. Wright, 'Finding an impetus for institutional change at the African Court on Human and Peoples' Rights' 24 (2) *Berkeley Journal of International Law* 463 at 471.

98 S. Sceats, 'Africa's new Human Rights Court: whistling in the wind?' Chatham House Briefing Paper (IL BP 09/01), March 2009, p. 7, available at: www.chathamhouse.org/sites/files/chathamhouse/public/Research/International%20Law/bp0309sceats.pdf, accessed 27 November 2017.

99 *Social and Economic Rights Action Centre (SERAC) and The Centre for Economic and Social Rights (CESR)* v. *Nigeria*, Communication No. 155/96, 2001; *Democratic Republic of Congo v. Burundi, Rwanda and Uganda*, Communication No. 227/99, 2006.

100 *Supra*, African Union, *Protocol to the African Charter on Human and Peoples' Rights on the Establishment of an African Court on Human and Peoples' Rights.*

101 African Union, *Protocol on the Statute of the African Court of Justice and Human Rights*, 1 July 2008, available at: https://au.int/en/treaties/protocol-statute-african-court-justice-and-human-rights, accessed 27 November 2017.

102 *Supra*, African Union, *Protocol to the African Charter on Human and Peoples' Rights on the Establishment of an African Court on Human and Peoples' Rights.*

into force in 2004. Under the Protocol, the African Court is empowered to exercise jurisdiction over all human rights instruments 'ratified by the States concerned'.[103] It has been suggested that this may include regional, subregional, bilateral and multilateral international treaties.[104] This means that where rights are not adequately protected under the African Charter, recourse could be had to other treaties signed by Member States.[105] This process is in contrast to the jurisdiction of the Commission, which is limited to the interpretation and application of the African Charter only.

The jurisdiction of the African Court covers a wide range of human rights areas, including violations of civil and political rights, socio-economic rights and the collective rights of the people. The Court has both advisory and contentious jurisdiction. The Court is generally empowered to receive complaints alleging violations of human rights submitted by States, the African Commission on Human and Peoples' Rights, African intergovernmental organisations and (subject to certain restrictions) NGOs and individuals.[106] It has jurisdiction to entertain requests for advisory opinion on any legal matter relating to the Charter or any other relevant human rights instrument from Member States, the AU and its organs or any other organisation recognised by the regional body.[107] The contribution of the court's jurisprudence to the evolving AU law is discussed further in Chapters 8, 9 and 10.

The Court of Justice of the African Union is one of the organs of the AU specified under Article 5(1) of the Constitutive Act of the AU. At the AU's 3rd ordinary session in July 2004, the Assembly of Heads of State and Government of the African Union adopted a resolution to the effect 'that the African Court of Human and Peoples' Rights and the Court of Justice should be integrated into one Court'.[108] At the African Union Summit in July 2008, the Court of Justice was officially merged with the African Court and renamed the 'African Court of Justice and Human Rights'.[109] When it becomes operational, the Court will take over the adjudicatory duties of the African Commission on Human and Peoples' Rights. The merger of the Court of Justice and the African Court

103 Ibid. Article 3(1).

104 R. W. Eno, 'The jurisdiction of the African Court on Human and Peoples' Rights' (2002) 2 (2) *African Human Rights Law Journal* 223 at 226: N. J. Udombana, 'Towards the African Court on Human and Peoples' Rights: better late than never' (2000) 3 (1) *Yale Human Rights and Development Law Journal* 45.

105 *Supra*, Eno, 226.

106 *Supra*, African Union, *Protocol to the African Charter on Human and Peoples' Rights on the Establishment of an African Court on Human and Peoples' Rights*, Article 5.

107 Ibid. Article 4.

108 See African Union, *Decision on the Seats of the Organs of the African Union*, Assembly/AU/Dec. 45 (III) Rev.1, adopted in Addis Ababa, Ethiopia, 6–8 July 2004, available at: https://au.int/sites/default/files/decisions/9550-assembly_en_30_31_january_2005_auc_third_ordinary_session.pdf, accessed 27 November 2017; African Union, *Decision on the Merger of the African Court on Human and Peoples' Rights and the Court of Justice of the African Union*, Assembly/AU/Dec. 83(V), adopted in Sirte, Libya, 4–5 July 2005, available at: http://archive.au.int/collect/auassemb/import/English/Assembly%20AU%20Dec%2083%20(V)%20_E.PDF, accessed 27 November 2017.

109 *Supra, Protocol to the Statute of the African Court of Justice and Human Rights.*

and its incorporation of the adjudicatory functions of the African Commission are significant going forward because these changes will affect certain key issues, including access to the court, scope of jurisdiction and enforcement of decisions. The Protocol establishing the Court requires the ratifications of 15 Member States for the Court to become operational. As of the time of writing, only six Member States have ratified the protocol.

Significantly, in 2014, amendments were introduced to the Protocol establishing the African Court of Justice and Human Rights with the adoption of the Malabo Protocol on Amendments to the Protocol on the Statute of the African Court of Justice and Human Rights (Malabo Protocol).[110] The Malabo Protocol changed the name of the Court to the African Court of Justice and Human and Peoples' Rights. The Malabo Protocol significantly extended the jurisdiction of the Court over crimes under international law including aggression, piracy, genocide, crimes against humanity, war crimes and various forms of transnational crimes. It also criminalises unconstitutional change of government. One of the most controversial aspects of the Malabo Protocol is the inclusion of immunity from prosecution for serving African Union Heads of State or government and other State senior officials or anyone acting in those capacities. This is a significant departure from other international courts. It would make it impossible to hold serving Heads of State and senior officials accountable in a continent where impunity and abuse of office is rife. It is doubtful if this approach is consistent with the founding principle of the AU as expressed in the Constitutive Act, and it is obviously inconsistent with international standards. Other concerns have been raised in relation to the Malabo Protocol, including its broad definition of crimes such as terrorism and the crime of unconstitutional change of government.[111] It has also been argued that by expanding the jurisdiction of the court and reducing the number of judges available to address human rights matters in order to cater to the additional jurisdiction, the Malabo Protocol would adversely impact human rights enforcement.[112] The Protocol will come into force after ratification by 15 Member States. As of the time of writing, only nine Member States have appended their signatures and no ratification has been effected.

Principles of subsidiarity and proportionality

The African Union legal order borrows principles from other legal orders, especially from the EU. Examples of these are the principles of subsidiarity,

110 African Union, *Malabo Protocol on Amendments to the Protocol on the Statute of the African Court of Justice and Human Rights*, 27 June 2014, available at: https://au.int/en/treaties/protocol-amendments-protocol-statute-african-court-justice-and-human-rights, accessed 27 November, 2017.

111 Ibid. Article 28G and Article 28E.

112 Amnesty International, *Malabo Protocol: Legal and Institutional Implications of the Merged and Expanded African Court Snapshots*, published 2 May 2017, Index No. AFR 01/6137/2017, available at: www.amnesty.org/en/documents/afr01/6137/2017/en, accessed 27 November 2017.

proportionality and direct effect. There is no universal definition of the principle of subsidiarity. In fact, the principle has been described as 'a notoriously vague and multi-faceted term'.[113] Jachtenfuchs and Krisch described the principle as 'a presumption for local-level decision making, which allows for the centralisation of powers only for particular, good reasons'.[114] The principle is enshrined in international law in relation to the definition of certain roles for regional organisations under Chapter VIII of the UN Charter.[115] The principle of subsidiarity is one of the central principles of European Union Law and is defined in Article 5 of the Treaty on the European Union. Article 5(3) provides that

> Under the principle of subsidiarity, in areas which do not fall within its exclusive competence, the Union shall act only if and in so far as the objectives of the proposed action cannot be sufficiently achieved by the Member States, either at central level or at regional and local level but can rather, by reason of the scale or effects of the proposed action, be better achieved at Union level.

In the context of the EU, the aims of the subsidiarity principle are twofold. One is to ensure that decisions are made as closely as possible to the citizens in Member States. The second is to ensure that there is justification for taking action at the EU level that outweighs the possibilities available at domestic or national level. The Court of Justice of the European Union has jurisdiction over any allegation of breach of the principle. In the AU context, the principles of subsidiarity are relevant to understanding the relationship between the AU and the RECs. It is also relevant to the relationship between the AU and its Member States.

Closely linked with the principle of subsidiarity is the principle of proportionality, which requires that any action by the EU should not extend beyond what is necessary to achieve the objectives of the EU Treaties. Article 4(3) provides that, 'Under the principle of proportionality, the content and form of Union action shall not exceed what is necessary to achieve the objectives of the Treaties'. This concept has also found its way into AU law, especially in judicial decisions.[116]

Direct effect

Direct effect has its origin in EU law and is a fundamental principle of the EU legal order. The principle is not stated explicitly in EU treaties but

113 A. Wolman, 'National human rights institutions and their sub-national counterparts: the question of decentralisation' (2017) 6 (1) *International Human Rights Law Review* 8.

114 M. Jachtenfuchs and N. Krisch, 'Subsidiarity in global governance' (2016) 79 (2) *Law and Contemporary Problems* 1, 5.

115 United Nations, *Charter of the United Nations*, 24 October 1945, 1 U.N.T.S. XVI, (Chapter VIII), available at: www.un.org/en/sections/un-charter/chapter-viii/index.html, accessed 27 November 2017.

116 B. Møller, *The Pros and Cons of Subsidiarity: The Role of African Regional and Subregional Organisations in Ensuring Peace and Security in Africa* (Danish Institute for International Studies (DIIS), 2005).

was established by the European Court of Justice in *Van Gend en Loos* v. *Nederlandse Administratie der Belastingen*.[117] The doctrine allows or enables individuals to invoke and rely upon EU law before national or EU courts. The ability of individuals to do this does not depend on a test by national law; it is completely dependent on EU law. The consequence of this is that individuals may challenge actions in Member States or violations of EU law, thereby bringing the individual within the EU legal order.[118] The direct effect characteristic is one of the key differences between EU law and other international agreements. Generally, international agreements usually bind States at the intergovernmental level and not individuals directly, unless implemented by national law (the exception to these are monist States that allow for direct applicability of international agreements in varying degrees). However, according to the Court in *Van Gend en Loos* v. *Nederlandse Administratie der Belastingen*, for EU law to apply, certain conditions must be met: the relevant provision(s) must be clear, unambiguous, and unconditional, and implementation must not be dependent on any further action by national authority or the EU.[119] The European Court of Justice generally accepts that individuals may invoke EU law against Member States (vertical direct effect), but the application of the law between individuals is limited (horizontal direct effect).

In the context of AU law, an example of direct effect is provided by the ability of the African Commission to accept communications. As mentioned above, even though the African Charter directly refers only to communications from States, the Commission also accepts communications from non-State actors under the provision for 'Other Communications'.[120] This makes it possible for individuals and NGOs to bring complaints before the Commission. This is an expression of the vertical direct effect of AU law. However, a communication can only be brought against a State Party to the Charter and not against private persons or individuals, thereby precluding horizontal direct effect.[121] This approach has been adopted by the African Court.

Pan-African Parliament

Notable evidence of the AU's supranational ambition is the provision for the establishment of a parliament in the Constitutive Act. The Pan-African Parliament (PAP) was originally proposed in the 1991 Treaty establishing the African Economic Community (Abuja Treaty) as one of the nine African Economic Community's (AEC) organs and was meant to be established at the sixth stage of the AEC planned process. It was envisaged that the PAP would be at the heart

117 *Van Gend en Loos* v. *Nederlandse Administratie der Belastingen* (1963) Case 26/62.
118 P. Craig and G. de Burca, *EU Law: Text, Cases and Materials*, 5th ed. (OUP, 2011) 181.
119 T. C. Hartley, *The Foundations of European Community Law*, 6th ed. (OUP, 2007) 193.
120 *Supra*, *African Charter*, Articles 55–59.
121 Ibid. Article 47.

of the new legal order at the continental level. The Sirte Declaration of 1999[122] reiterated this proposal and called for the establishment of the PAP within the continental framework. Following this call, the Protocol Establishing the Pan-African Parliament was adopted in 2001 and entered into force in 2003.[123] According to Article 17 of the AU Constitutive Act, the purpose of the PAP is 'to ensure the full participation of African peoples in the development and economic integration of the continent'. Furthermore, Article 2 of the Protocol Establishing the Pan-African Parliament provides that the PAP established under the Abuja Treaty 'is hereby continued in existence and shall have the functions and powers provided for in the present Protocol'.[124] The Parliament's first session occurred in March 2004. In June 2014 the AU Assembly adopted an additional Protocol, the Protocol to the Constitutive Act of the African Union on the Pan-African Parliament.[125] Significantly, the Protocol *inter alia* provides that, after it comes into force, the PAP can make proposals on issues or areas on which it may submit or recommend draft model laws to the Assembly for its consideration and approval.[126] In the future, such laws will form part of the corpus of AU law and would be expected to have direct effect on Member States. This protocol further underscores the supranational leaning of the AU legal order.

Currently, members of the PAP are elected by the legislatures of Member States, not directly elected by citizens in Member States.[127] This system obviously creates a democratic and legitimacy deficit on the part of the institution. However, it must be noted that the ultimate aim of the AU is to have members elected directly by universal suffrage down the line. Presently, the PAP has only advisory and consultative powers, responsibilities suited to its current status. Nonetheless, the goal of the AU is to progress the PAP into an institution with full legislative powers in future. There is no indication of when and what will prompt Member States to vest the PAP with full legislative powers. This places the PAP in limbo regarding its future role. However, it must be observed that although the PAP currently has only an advisory and consultative role, such a limitation may not be that significant, judging from the experience of the European Parliament. The European Parliament started out as a consultative assembly when it was established in 1952. Its opinion was non-binding on

122 OAU, *The Sirte Declaration*, 9 September 1999, EAHG/Draft/Decl. (IV) Rev. 1, available at: http://webcache.googleusercontent.com/search?q=cache:LCW-pAx6zgYJ:www.chr.up.ac.za/chr_old/hr_docs/african/docs/ahsg/ahsg64.doc+&cd=5&hl=en&ct=clnk&gl=uk&client=safari, accessed 27 November 2017.

123 African Union, *Protocol to the Treaty Establishing the African Economic Community Relating to the Pan-African Parliament*, available at https://au.int/en/treaties/protocol-treaty-establishing-african-economic-community-relating-pan-african-parliament, accessed 12 December 2017.

124 Ibid.

125 African Union, *Protocol to the Constitutive Act of the African Union on the Pan-African Parliament*, 27 June 2014, Assembly/AU/Dec.529(XXIII), available at: https://au.int/en/treaties/protocol-constitutive-act-african-union-relating-pan-african-parliament, accessed 27 November 2017.

126 Ibid. Article 8.

127 Ibid. Article 5(3).

the decision makers in the EU. Nonetheless, over time, it gradually achieved more supervisory and legislative powers within the EU Treaty framework. Currently, the European Parliament has legislative, budgetary and supervisory powers. Although it cannot initiate legislation, it can put forward amendments to proposals and veto policy proposals in many areas, especially through the 'co-decision' procedure of the EU.[128]

The functions of the PAP are set out in the Protocol to the Abuja Treaty relating to the Pan-African Parliament and in its Rules of Procedure.[129] These functions include:

- Facilitating and overseeing implementation of AU policies, objectives and programmes.
- Promoting human rights and consolidating democratic institutions and culture, good governance transparency and the rule of law by all AU organs, regional economic communities (RECs) and Member States.
- Participating in creating awareness among the peoples of Africa on the AU's objectives, policy aims and programmes; strengthening of continental solidarity, cooperation and development; promotion of peace, security and stability; and pursuit of a common economic recovery strategy.
- Contributing to the harmonisation and coordination of Member States' legislation.
- Promoting the coordination of RECs' policies, measures, programmes and activities.
- Preparing and adopting its budget and Rules of Procedure.
- Electing its Bureau members.
- Making recommendations on the AU budget.

The full PAP Assembly is the main decision-making body and is called the Plenary. The Plenary is chaired by the President of PAP. Under Rule 3 of the PAP Rules of Procedure,[130] the PAP has two organs: the Bureau and the Permanent Committees. The Bureau is responsible for the management of the parliament and all of its organs. There are 11 Committees, including ten permanent and one ad hoc Committee. The functions and mandate of the committees are contained in the PAP Rules of Procedure and are similar to the AU Specialised Technical Committees.[131] The Parliament meets at least two times annually in its ordinary session. A Parliamentary session can last for up to one month.[132] It also has the ability to meet in extraordinary sessions, which is provided for in Rule 29.

128 G. M. Musila, 'United State of Africa: positioning the Pan-African Parliament and Court in the political union debate', ISS Paper 142, (June 2007) 7.

129 *Supra*, African Union, *Protocol to the Treaty Establishing the AEC Relating to the Pan-African Parliament and in Its Rules of Procedure* (most recently amended in 2011).

130 Ibid. Rule 3.

131 Ibid. Rules 22 to 27.

132 Ibid. Rule 28.

Conclusions

African Union law has emerged gradually over a long period of time, with the establishment of various and sometimes overlapping institutions and through a variety of diverse instruments. Identifying the sources and their implications for the African Union legal order is thus a complex task. However, certain instruments stand out, which helps to elucidate the sources. The Constitutive Act of the AU is fundamental in this regard because it has constitutional status and has far-reaching implications when compared with the OAU Charter. It therefore sits at the heart of the AU legal order. Treaties agreed upon from the time of the OAU to the present time have also generated important norms at the continental level. The judicial and quasi-judicial jurisprudence at the continental level also play an important role as a source of law. Similarly, soft law instruments contribute to the emergence of standards, especially in areas where it is difficult to reach an agreement.

4 Membership of the African Union

Introduction

Complete integration is the overarching ambition of the African Union (AU), and this is reflected in its emergent legal order.[1] The strategies put in place to achieve this have implications not only for Member States but also for citizens. The AU currently has 55 Member States (52 republics and three monarchies) spanning the entirety of the continent, including numbering over 1 billion citizens. This chapter examines the requirements for membership and accession to the AU by a non-Member State. The chapter considers how the accession process could moderate the behaviour of Member States. The chapter further examines provisions for withdrawal/renunciation of membership. The chapter analyses the legal implications of membership for States and citizens. The issue of citizenship and nationality is important because it has been at the root of some of the major conflicts in the continent. The AU legal order has the potential to reform and harmonise Member States' rules and laws regarding citizenship and nationality.

Accession to the OAU and AU membership

It has been contended that the high level of non-compliance with membership obligations (mainly in relation to payment of dues and implementation of policies) in the predecessor organisation, the OAU, and in the AU is partly due to the failure to put in place strict membership accession conditionalities and to enforce such conditionalities.[2] Having such a strict regime has the added advantage of adequately preparing States for membership and using the process as a quality assurance mechanism. It could shape the behaviour of members and align the values of the AU with those of its membership. This is exemplified by the impact the accession process had in the case of the EU in relation to the admission of

1 O. A. Boateng, 'Membership accession in the African Union: the relationship between enforcement and compliance, and the case for differential membership' (2017) 24 (1) *South African Journal of International Law* 21.

2 Ibid. 22.

Baltic and Central European countries in the 1990s.[3] A merit-based admission process could also help deepen cooperation among Member States.[4]

Historically, the predecessor organisation, the OAU, started out with 32 Member States at its establishment in 1963. The enlargement of the OAU was mainly driven by decolonisation, which gradually extended the reach of the organisation across the continent. The nature of the OAU's origin had an impact on its approach to membership. As discussed in Chapter 2, the OAU itself was a product of two groups of countries, the Casablanca and Monrovia groups, which took different approaches to continental integration.[5] To foster a compromise between the two groups, the OAU took an inclusive and broadly accommodating approach to membership. Therefore, the membership accession criteria in the OAU Charter was not strict in any sense. The relevant provisions of the Charter are Article I (2) on the establishment of the OAU and Article IV on membership. Article I (2) provides that '[t]he Organisation shall include the Continental African States, Madagascar and other Islands surrounding Africa'. Article IV states that '[e]ach independent sovereign African State shall be entitled to become a Member of the Organisation'. Consequently, the accession to membership under the Charter was treated as an 'entitlement' to all sovereign States in the continent. Hence, the only criterion for admission under Article IV is independent statehood.[6] This singular focus on statehood is reflected by the pace of the enlargement under the OAU. As stated previously, the OAU began with the 32 States that were independent when it was established in May 1963. It admitted new Member States almost on a yearly basis between 1963 and 1994. In 1994, when South Africa ended the apartheid system and joined the OAU, the OAU achieved universal membership, with the exception of Morocco, which had withdrawn its membership in 1984. With the accession of South Africa to membership, the OAU declared an end to its project of liberation, thereby paving the way for its integration agenda.

Morocco, which was a founding Member State, withdrew its membership in 1984 because of its objection to the admittance of the Sahrawi Arab Democratic Republic to OAU membership. Historically, Morocco disputes the sovereignty of the Sahrawi Arab Democratic Republic, a partially recognised State on its border that lays claim to territories within Morocco itself. However, Morocco re-joined the AU in January 2017. Currently, the only parts of the continent that are not

3 J. Kelly, 'International actors in the domestic scene: membership conditionality and socialization by international institutions' (2004) 58 (3) *International Organization*, 426.

4 *Supra*, Boateng, 24.

5 Ibid. 25.

6 Ibid.

7 Note that the AU also grants observer status to Non-Governmental Organisations and International Governmental Organisations. See Executive Council, *Decision on the Criteria for Granting Observer Status and a System of Accreditation*, EX.CL/Dec.168(VI) (2005), available at: https://au.int/sites/default/files/decisions/9627-council_en_24_28_january_2005_executive_council_sixth_ordinary_session_session.pdf, accessed 12 December 2017.

within the AU are dependencies and minor territories of the United Kingdom, France, Italy, Portugal, Spain and Yemen.

Articles 27 and 29 are fundamental to the legal requirement for membership under the AU legal order. Article 27 (1) of the Constitutive Act states that the Act is open to signature and accession by the Member States of the OAU, the predecessor organisation. That provision allowed for a smooth transition of membership from the OAU era to the AU by providing for a mechanism for automatic transfer of membership. More importantly, Article 29 of the Constitutive Act provides for the admission of new States to membership. Subsection 1 of the Article states that any African State may notify the Chairperson of the Commission of its intention to accede to the Constitutive Act and be admitted into membership of the Union. Implicit in Article 29 is the idea that only African States may apply to join the Union. This has led to the suggestion that the AU can be regarded as a 'closed organisation' because of its geographical restriction, which does not allow non-African States to join its membership. However, it is observed that the AU has granted observer status to countries outside of the continent. Currently, observer status has been granted to non-African countries including Haiti, Kazakhstan, Latvia, Palestine, Serbia and Turkey.[7]

The case of Haiti's attempt to join the AU is instructive in this regard. In February 2012 the Caribbean state, 95% of whose population is of African descent and which already had observer status with the AU, indicated its ambition to upgrade its observer status to associate membership. The basis for Haiti's attempt at membership is based on Article 3(q) of the Constitutive Act, which declares that the AU 'invite and encourage the full participation of the African Diaspora as an important part of our continent, in the building of the African Union'.[8] In support of Article 3(q), the AU established a Diaspora Division to coordinate its link with the Diaspora. The division defines the Diaspora as 'the communities throughout the world that are descended from the historic movement of peoples from Africa, predominantly from the Americas, Europe and Middle East, among other areas around the globe'.[9] In fact, the Diaspora is regarded by the AU as the sixth region of the African continent. The Diaspora currently has 20 seats on the Economic Social and Cultural Council (ECOSOC), a permanent organ of the AU. The AU initially sent out positive signals regarding Haiti's intention, and it was expected that Haiti's move might be approved at the AU Summit in 2013. However, this approval was not forthcoming. In May 2016 the AU issued a statement to the effect that, under Article 29(1), only African States can join the AU membership. This decision raises the question of whether membership in the Union should be delimited by geography or heritage or both.

8 The provision was introduced by the *Protocol on the Amendments to the Constitutive Act of the African Union* (2003), available at: https://au.int/en/treaties/protocol-amendments-constitutive-act-african-union, accessed 12 December 2017.

9 CIDO, The Diaspora Division of the AU, available at: https://au.int/en/diaspora-division, accessed 12 December 2017.

It must be observed that the process for membership under Article 29 is different from the automatic membership that was available to founding Member States under Article IV of the OAU Charter. It departs from the entitlement paradigm under the OAU to a marginally merit-based paradigm.[10] The application to join is by 'notification', which is in itself a form of application. According to Boateng, the application process allows prospective Member States to demonstrate genuine interest in joining the AU.[11] Furthermore, for the application by notification to succeed, it needs the support of a simple majority of Member States. The Chairperson of the AU Commission has the responsibility to send copies of the membership application to all Member States. Each Member State is required to provide the Chairperson of the Commission with their individual decision on the application. The Chairperson of the Commission informs the Applicant State of the final outcome. This process has been regarded as an attempt to introduce a form of quality assurance into the admission process.[12] However, there are no standard criteria for Member States to consider when assessing applications. Instead, each State is left to its own discretion. This means that, in practice, little has changed.

It is notable that the Article is forward-looking, as it envisaged the emergence of new States in the continent. A case in point is the recently created Republic of South Sudan. After an independence referendum in 2011, the Republic of South Sudan was created from the Republic of Sudan. The procedure under Article 29 was followed in the admission to membership of the Republic of South Sudan. Following notification, 33 Member States of the Union, including the existing Republic of Sudan, submitted written communications to the African Commission in support of the membership application, which is more than the simple majority required under Article 29.[13] There was strong support for the admittance of the new State, mainly because this was seen as a way to support the peace process following the protracted civil war that led to the creation of the Republic of South Sudan.

The requirement for accession into membership under the Constitutive Act, although different from that of the OAU, still appears to be lax, especially when compared with the EU, where there are strict requirements for membership. However, this raises the important question of whether the provisions of the Constitutive Act are adequate. At the very least, a new Member State should be in a position to fulfil membership obligations and have the capacity to do so upon admission.[14] As observed by Magliveras and Naldi, it is arguable that Sudan, at

10 *Supra*, Boateng, 32.
11 Ibid.
12 Ibid.
13 African Union, Press Release N79/2011 'African Union welcomes South Sudan as the 54th Member State of the Union', available at: https://au.int/en/pressreleases/20110727-1, accessed 12 December 2017; K. D. Magliveras and G. J. Naldi, *The African Union (AU)* (Wolters Kluwer, 2013) 93.
14 Ibid, Magliveras and Naldi, 93.

the time of its admission and as a newly created State, may not be in a position to fulfil all of its obligations.[15] For example, the Republic of South Sudan did not have in place at the time of its admission into membership the procedure for signing and ratifying key AU instruments such as the African Charter on Human and Peoples' Rights and the African Charter on the Rights and Welfare of the Child. Nevertheless, its accession to the AU took three weeks from achieving statehood and two weeks from its application for membership.[16] If the goal of integration, which is at the heart of AU law, is to be achieved, Member States must at the very least be in a position to sign and ratify AU key instruments and be able to internalise AU norms.

In a similar vein, it has been argued that the lax rules of admission made it easy for Morocco to rejoin the AU after several years of absence. Morocco met the current criteria for joining the AU, i.e., it is geographically located in Africa and it was able to secure a favourable vote by a simple majority of existing members. This easy access has been argued to be a weakness for two reasons.[17] The first reason is that Morocco has not changed its hostile attitude towards Western Sahara, a position at odds with the AU's position. Western Sahara is a full member of the AU and is recognised by the AU. Therefore, readmitting Morocco without securing at least a commitment to a peaceful resolution of the Western Sahara dispute was a missed opportunity. Second, the AU did not consider Morocco's commitment to AU's ideals, such as rule of law, democracy and human rights. Even though, compared with South Sudan, Morocco is a largely stable country, it nonetheless has a deficient record regarding democracy, rule of law and human rights.

There is, therefore, a need to reform the admission criteria to establish much more robust pre-conditions that recognise and reflect AU values and norms. The absence of stringent membership criteria has contributed to the inability of the AU to hold members to account. Members often dispute their obligations within the AU and challenge the interpretation of their commitments as Member States. For example, Fagbayigbo has proposed including the 'adherence to democratic norms', as expressed in Article 3 and 4 of the Constitutive Act, as a pre-requisite for membership.[18]

Sanctions of Member States

As stated previously, one of the key challenges facing the AU is the high level of non-compliance with membership obligations (mainly in relation to payment of dues and implementation of policies in the predecessor organisation, the OAU, and the AU). The constitution of the AU attempts to address this issue and

15 Ibid.

16 *Supra*, Boateng, 27.

17 B. Fagbayigbo, 'Why the African Union needs to revisit its admission criteria', *The Conversation*, 5 April 2017, available at: https://theconversation.com/why-the-african-union-needs-to-revisit-its-admission-criteria-75479, accessed 12 December 2017.

18 Ibid.

takes a proactive approach by introducing a sanction regime. Three provisions of the Constitutive Act address the issue of sanctions. These include Article 23(1), which empowers the Assembly of the AU to impose sanctions on Member States if they default in the payment of their contributions to the AU budget. Second, Article 23(2) provides that a Member State that fails to comply with AU decisions or policies may be subject to further sanctions, such as denial of transport and communication links to other Member States. The Assembly may also impose other measures of a political or economic nature pursuant to the provision. In addition, Article 30 provides that a Member State shall be suspended from the organisation where there has been an unconstitutional change of government in the Member State concerned.[19]

In recent times the AU has taken steps through its Executive Council to sanction erring members under Article 23(1), and the sanctions are only lifted after compliance with the obligation in question.[20] This provision is considered to be stricter when compared with similar provisions of other international organisations such as the United Nations.[21] This is because the usual practice is that sanctions are employed where a Member State has been in arrears for approximately two years. However, under Article 23(1), the Assembly of the AU is mandated to impose sanctions for any amount of contributions that is in arrears. The range of measures that could be imposed include denial of right to speak at AU meetings, denial of right to vote, and denial of the right to present candidates for AU positions or posts or to benefit in any way from the AU. The provision in Article 23(1) is augmented by Rule 35 of the Rules of Procedure of the Assembly, which provides the procedure for the implementation of the Article and expounds on its content. It must be noted, however, that the provision in the rules cannot derogate from the substantive provision of the Constitutive Act. It is notable that, unlike the Treaty Establishing the African Economic Community,[22] which considers the economic fragility of many African States that may affect their ability to meet their financial obligations, the AU regime does not appear to accommodate such extenuating circumstances. Because this problem is common and pervasive in Africa, there may be a need to create a legal mechanism to accommodate such extenuating circumstances when they are legitimate.[23] It is notable that in its practice, the AU, through its Executive Council, tends to give exemptions where there are genuine reasons why a Member State could not meet its obligation.[24]

19 This is discussed in Chapter 6.

20 K. D. Magliveras, 'The sanctioning system of the African Union: part success, part failure', revised version of a paper presented at an Expert Roundtable on 'The African Union: The First Ten Years', Institute of Security Studies, Addis Ababa, Ethiopia (2011).

21 Ibid.

22 African Union, *Treaty Establishing the African Economic Community*, 12 May 1994, available at: https://au.int/en/treaties/treaty-establishing-african-economic-community, accessed 24 November 2017.

23 Ibid. Magliveras, 7.

24 Ibid. 7.

Article 23(2) offers wide latitude to the AU Assembly to impose sanctions of a political or an economic nature where a Member State fails to comply with AU policies and decisions. Such sanctions could also include the denial of transport and communication links with other Member States of the AU. The procedure for the application of this section is provided for in Rule 36 of the Rules of Procedure of the Assembly. However, as of the time of writing, no Member State has been sanctioned for non-implementation of AU policies under Article 23(2), even though this non-implementation is a widespread practice. The low level of ratification of AU's normative and policy instruments by Member States demonstrates the apathy towards compliance by many Member States.[25]

Article 30, on sanctions for unconstitutional change of government in Member States, is discussed in detail in Chapter 6. However, it is worth noting at this juncture that the Constitutive Act itself does not define what constitutes 'unconstitutional change of government' for the purposes of the Act. Nevertheless, Rule 37 of the Rules of Procedure of the African Union Assembly provides key examples of situations that may fall within this category. These include military coup d'état, intervention by mercenaries or armed dissident and rebel groups, refusal to relinquish power and change of government by the use of mercenaries.[26] In a case of unconstitutional change of government, Rule 37 requires the Chairperson of the Assembly and the Chairperson of the AU Commission to, among other steps, officially condemn the development and call for a speedy return to constitutional order. The concerned Member State is also suspended immediately, and a meeting of the Peace and Security Council is called to discuss the matter. It must be observed that Rule 37(4)(e) placed a rider on the suspension stating that the suspension does not affect the State's membership status and the State's obligations to the Union. The suspension only excludes the concerned State from participation in the activities of the Union. Rule 37(5) provides for sanctions that should be applied to any regime that refuses to restore a Member State to constitutional order. The provision mandates the Assembly to impose sanctions such as visa denials, restriction on government-to-government contacts, and trade restrictions, as well as sanctions provided under Article 23(2).

Cessation/termination of membership status

Article 31 of the Constitutive Act provides a method for voluntary withdrawal from the Union by Member States. It provides that a Member State may renounce its membership by written notification to the Chairperson of the AU Commission. The renunciation takes effect automatically one year from the date of the notification, if it is not withdrawn by the departing State. The withdrawing State is obliged to discharge its duties and obligations under the Constitutive Act

25 *Supra*, Boateng, 30.

26 See also Article 28E of the Malabo Protocol in relation to the defining of the 'Crime of unconstitutional change of government'.

in the 12-month period from notification.[27] It is arguable that having such a provision offers a level of clarity in the case of withdrawal from membership that has been problematic in the EU context in relation to the United Kingdom's attempt to withdraw from the European Union. Article 50 of the Treaty of the EU created a complexity and lack of clarity that arguably is absent from Article 31.

However, Article 31 was technically deleted by Article 12 of the Protocol on Amendments to the Constitutive Act of the African Union for no apparent reason.[28] To date, the protocol has not received the required number of ratifications for it to come into force. Therefore, at the present moment, a Member State can withdraw its membership following the procedure in Article 31. Nonetheless, the introduction of Article 12 under the Protocol raises the pertinent question of why the mechanism was deleted and the implication of that deletion if the Protocol comes into force. As Magliveras and Naldi noted, this development is puzzling because its utility is not clear.[29] One can argue that this was done to strengthen the supranational credentials of the AU by restricting the ability to withdraw from the Union. However, even without a provision for withdrawal, a Member State that has decided to leave the Union cannot, practically, be stopped. Potentially, the absence of such a provision could lead to protracted negotiation on the terms of exit, similar to the EU–UK negotiations on Brexit.

A related question is whether the AU could expel a member that has refused, neglected or failed to meet their obligations or to comply with any measure imposed on them by the AU. There is no express provision for expulsion from membership in the AU Constitutive Act. However, the question is whether a member could potentially be expelled pursuant to Article 23(2) of the Constitutive Act as a measure of 'political nature'. Magliveras and Naldi have argued that this should not be possible. Their argument is that 'political', as used in that section, should not be read to include measures that would have impact on membership status. This argument is also in line with the OAU Secretariat's opinion in 2002, that since the Constitutive Act does not include a provision for the expulsion of members, the AU Assembly has no legal capacity to expel members.[30]

Implication of membership for citizens

This section considers the impact of the AU legal order on the citizenship/nationality of individuals in the Member States of the AU. It is important to note that citizenship or nationality in the African context is unique because of the continent's peculiar history, colonial intervention and large populations of

27 Article 31(2).

28 *Protocol on the Amendments to the Constitutive Act of the African Union*, available at: https://au.int/en/treaties/protocol-amendments-constitutive-act-african-union, accessed 6 December 2017.

29 *Supra*, Magliveras and Naldi, 95.

30 Ibid. 101.

traditionally nomadic peoples. As a starting point, it will be useful to note the ambiguity in the usage of 'nationality' and 'citizenship'. Notably, the terms are used interchangeably in many cases, especially in AU instruments and decisions.[31] In the *Nottebohm* case (*Liechtenstein* v. *Guatemala*),[32] the International Court of Justice, while restating the long-standing rule that States decide under their own laws the question of nationality, defines nationality in the following terms:

> According to the practice of States, to arbitral and judicial decisions and to the opinions of writers, nationality is a legal bond having as its basis a social fact of attachment, a genuine connection of existence, interests and sentiments, together with the existence of reciprocal rights and duties. It may be said to constitute the juridical expression of the fact that the individual upon whom it is conferred, either directly by the law or as the result of an act of the authorities, is in fact more closely connected with the population of the State conferring nationality than with that of any other State. Conferred by a State, it only entitles that State to exercise protection vis-a-vis another State, if it constitutes a translation into juridical terms of the individual's connection with the State which has made him its national.

Therefore, when addressing the issue of nationality at the international level, it involves rights and duties of the State concerned in relation to other States.[33] In contrast, under domestic law, nationality and citizenship denote the relationship between that State and the individual citizen and the ensuing rights and responsibility emanating from that relationship. According to Boll, the terms nationality and citizenship are so often confused because they are closely connected.[34] Therefore, in most cases, the terms are used interchangeably, 'depending on the language in which a text is written, an author's concept of the underlying relationship or status being described, and the legal system within which a particular commentator works'.[35] Boll argued that, despite the widespread interchangeable use of the concepts, it is important to maintain a theoretical distinction because the practical legal consequences of these statuses can still be distinguished.[36] He went on to differentiate 'the relationship between nationality and citizenship on the municipal plane, where the terms may be thought as identical or convergent, from that on the plane of international law', where this is not the case

31 African Commission on Human and Peoples' Rights, 'The Right to Nationality in Africa' study undertaken by the Special Rapporteur on the Rights of Refugees, Asylum Seekers and Internally Displaced Persons, pursuant to Resolution 234 of April 2013 and approved by the Commission at its 55th Ordinary Session, May 2014 (African Commission's nationality study).

32 *Liechtenstein v. Guatemala* [1955] ICJ 1.

33 A. M. Boll, *Multiple Nationality in International Law* (Martinus Nijhoff Publishers, 2007), Chapter 3.

34 Ibid. 57–58.

35 *Supra*, African Commission's nationality study, paragraph 35.

36 *Supra*, Boll, 58.

and they are, according to him, clearly distinguished.[37] Boll held the view that, under domestic or municipal law, 'nationality gives rise to a bundle of individual rights and obligations, which is typically conceptualised as the status of citizenship, whereas under international law, nationality largely entails some rights and duties of the state involved in relation to other states'.[38] However, other authors have found it more prudent to use the terms interchangeably since, in practice, State institutions use them interchangeably.[39] This is why Close defines nationality as 'the external face of a complex concept which also possesses an internal face, which is citizenship'.[40] This definition is reflective of the use of the concepts in the context of the African Union and its Member States.

AU law and citizenship

The pursuant question regards the impact of the AU legal order on the nationality/citizenship question. Despite the attainment of independence across the African continent, the concept of citizenship or nationality remains a contentious concept, often with violent and calamitous consequences, as tragically exemplified by the Rwanda genocide. Primordial identity derived from communal, ethnic and ancestral origins persists in various forms and manifestations and in direct conflict with the notion of citizenship and nationality in modern States. Colonial practices and laws are also contributing factors to what Dorman has aptly described as 'citizenship conflict'.[41] The colonial authorities created 'artificial' nations and ascribed citizenship arbitrarily in many instances, dividing up communities in the process. The European colonialist powers defined the citizenship/nationality of Africans based on European legal traditions.[42] For instance, in British Colonial territories, the inhabitants were classified as either British subjects or British protected persons. Furthermore, under the British Nationality Act of 1948, the British created the 'commonwealth citizenship' that applied to its colonies and, later, to former colonies in Africa. Similarly, in the French territories, inhabitants

37 H. U. J. D'Oliveira, '*Multiple Nationality and International Law* by Alfred M. Boll. Leiden, Boston: Martinus Nijhoff Publishers, 2007. Pp. xix, 626, $201, €149', (2007) 101 (4) *The American Journal of International Law* 922–928.

38 *Supra*, Boll, Chapter 3.

39 See, for example, S. O'Leary, *The Evolving Concept of Community Citizenship – From the Free Movement of Persons to Union Citizenship* (Kluwer Law International, 1996); R. Donner, *The Regulation of Nationality in International Law*, 2nd ed. (Transnational Publishers Inc, 1994); D. Heater, What Is Citizenship (Polity Press, 1999); E. Guild 'The legal framework of citizenship of the European Union', in D. Cesarani and M. Fulbrook (eds), *Citizenship, Nationality and Migration in Europe* (Routledge, 1996) 32.

40 G. Close, 'Definitions of citizenship', in P. Gardner, *Hallmarks of Citizenship – A Green Paper* (British Institute of International and Comparative Law, 1994) 6.

41 S. Rice Dorman, 'Citizenship in Africa: the politics of belonging' in E. F. Isin and P. Nyers (eds), *Routledge Handbook of Global Citizenship Study* (Routledge, 2014) 161.

42 B. Manby, 'Trends in citizenship law and politics in Africa since the colonial era' in E. F. Isin and P. Nyers (eds), *Routledge Handbook of Global Citizenship Study* (Routledge, 2014) 173.

were divided into French citizens, French subjects, French-administered persons and French protected persons.[43]

As Manby correctly observed, the Western conception of nationality is generally based on the principle of *jus soli* (citizenship based on birth place) and *jus sanguinis* (based on parents' citizenship, including by acquisition, e.g., naturalisation).[44] In colonial times, the UK imposed the *jus soli* principle on its territories, as reflected in its Nationality Act of 1948. With independence, the constitutional arrangements in most African States incorporated the two principles in varying degrees but with less restrictive provisions on citizenship by birth and registration and more restrictive provisions in relation to citizenship by acquisition.[45] However, the general trend post-independence was to tighten laws on citizenship, with countries taking different approaches to the issue of citizenship.[46]

The OAU's decision to incorporate State structures and approaches to nationality from the colonialist enterprise as a basis for its territorial integrity norms incorporated the ambiguity created during that era into post-independence Africa, with adverse consequences including statelessness.[47] To complicate matters, domestic laws in most African countries tend to muddy the waters. According to Adejumobi, there is a tendency towards 'the institutionalization of ethnic entitlements, rights and privileges, which creates differentiated and unequal status of citizenship'.[48] For example, under the Nigerian constitution, sections 223(2)(b) and 318(1), citizenship rights were supposedly accorded to all Nigerians without discrimination. However, other provisions in the Nigerian constitution appear to recognise two classes of citizens – indigenes and settlers.[49] This provision means that a Nigerian could be treated as a first- or second-class citizen depending on this classification as either an indigene or settler, with the consequence that, in most cases, the rights of an indigene citizen would trump those of a settler. These apparently conflicting provisions have led to significant violence in the Nigerian context.[50] The problem is not limited to Nigeria and may be found in various forms across Africa. It takes various dimensions, including tribal, racial, religious, gender, circumstances of birth or class distinctions.[51] Commenting on the Nigerian scenario, Adejumobi observed:

43 B. Manby, *Citizenship Law in Africa: A Comparative Study*, 3rd ed. (Open Society Foundation, 2016) 39.

44 *Supra*, Manby (2014), 176.

45 See, for example, Part 2 of the *Constitution of the Federation of Nigeria*, 1960; K. C. Okoli, 'Nigerian citizenship law: a current perspective' (1990) 34 (1) *Journal of African Law* 27.

46 *Supra*, Manby (2016).

47 *Supra*, Manby (2014), 172.

48 S. Adejumobi, 'Citizenship, rights and the problem of internal conflicts and civil war in Africa' (2001) 6 (2) *African Journal of Political Science* 77.

49 See, for example, Section 147 (3) *Constitution of the Federal Republic of Nigeria*, 1999.

50 O. Onazi, 'Before rights and responsibilities: an African ethos of citizenship' in O. Onazi (ed.) *African Legal Theory and Contemporary Problems: Critical Essays* (Ius Gentium: Comparative Perspectives on Law and Justice, 29) 154–158.

51 Ibid. 155.

> in the localities, there is usually a clear distinction between the 'natives' or 'indigenes' of those areas who are considered as the 'local citizens' and the 'immigrants' or 'settlers' who are considered as 'non-citizens' (in spite of the fact that they are all nationals of the same country).[52]

Also apposite is the situation of Zimbabwe, where there is an apparent distinction between 'white settlers', who are considered to be a different class of citizens, and those who are considered 'natives'.[53] This distinction played a significant role in the controversial 'land reform' that led to the seizure of farms from settlers.[54] As Dorman noted, the attempts in the continent to adopt and implement democratic electioneering systems has also unwittingly exacerbated citizenship conflicts. In many States the citizenship of ethnic groups is routinely challenged in run-ups to elections, with the consequence that these groups may be denied voting or participation rights. The highest-profile case in this regard is the attempt by the Zambian State to withdraw the nationality of its former President Kenneth Kaunda and declare him stateless. Similar problems have occurred in Cameroon, the Democratic Republic of Congo, Côte d'Ivoire, Mauritania, Uganda, Zanzibar, Zambia, Botswana, Zimbabwe, and others.[55]

The conflict of citizenship also has inter-State dimensions. From the 1950s to the 1980s en masse deportation was common across the continent.[56] Many post-colonial African States deported people en masse on the basis of their citizenship or lack thereof. Examples abound, including the deportation of Asians from Uganda in 1973 and Nigeria's expulsion of over 1 million workers from neighbouring Member States in 1983.

The myriad problems surrounding the issue of citizenship and nationality, especially for individuals, has thus made it a key focus for the AU and its legal order. This topic is important because of its implications, not only for individuals but also for Member States.[57] Manby has argued that the OAU and its successor, the AU, have failed to take effective steps against the widespread abuse of citizenship, especially for political purposes.[58] However, it is contended in this book that while this may largely be the case in relation to the OAU, the emergence of the AU and its legal framework has significant legal ramifications with consequential implications on the question of citizenship going forward.

Harmonising citizenship law under the AU legal order

The AU approach to the citizenship/nationality challenge is rooted in its ambitions of integration. The African Union and its institutions have been taking

52 *Supra*, Adejumobi, 86.
53 Ibid. 87.
54 *Supra*, Dorman, 165.
55 Ibid. 161, 163.
56 *Supra*, Dorman, 163.
57 A. M. Boll, *Multiple Nationality in International Law* (Martinus Nijhoff Publishers, 2007) 13.
58 *Supra*, Manby (2014), 172–173.

incremental steps to assist the harmonisation of standards and laws on citizenship and nationality. The steps are aptly summarised in the study on the right to nationality by the African Commission.[59] The African Commission, exercising its power under the African Charter to 'undertake studies and research on African problems in the field of human and peoples' rights' and to 'formulate and lay down, principles and rules aimed at solving legal problems relating to human and peoples' rights and fundamental freedoms upon which African Governments may base their legislations', commissioned this extensive research in 2014.

According to the study, the first significant step towards addressing problems related to citizenship and nationality was the recommendations in the African Union's Migration Policy Framework, adopted in 2006.[60] The framework includes the recommendation that Member States incorporate key guidelines recommended in the longstanding 1954 and 1961 Statelessness Conventions in their legislation and policy frameworks and that they reform national citizenship legislation to achieve this. This recommendation was echoed at the meeting of experts under the African Union Border Programme in June 2007 in the context of State boundary disputes and the impact the resolution of such disputes may have on populations. The meeting urged Member States to 'take the necessary steps to protect the rights of the affected populations, notably where there is a risk of loss of nationality [statelessness], of real property or of forced displacement'.[61] In the context of the problem of stateless persons, refugees and internally displaced persons, the African National Human Rights Institutions recommended at their meeting in 2007 that Member States evaluate and review existing legislation on citizenship and nationality to address these issues. This approach was widely endorsed by the meeting of Member States in 2009.

A public debate held at the 47th ordinary session of the African Commission in 2010 focused on the right of nationality within the African regional human rights system. This was followed by further and expanded discourse facilitated by the African Commission at its 9th extraordinary meeting in 2011. The 2011 meeting expanded the scope of the enquiry to include a reflection on the nationality question from an international comparative law perspective. In the same year, the first substantive decision of the African Committee of Experts on the Rights and Welfare of the Child (ACERWC) considered the question of the status and nationality of children with Nubian descent that were born in Kenya. The Committee applied the provisions of Article 8 of the African Charter and held that the Kenyan State had violated its obligation under Article 6 regarding the right of a child to a name, birth registration and a nationality. This decision prompted the ACERWC to convene a debate in 2012 on Article 6 and its implications for the nationality of a child. The debate resulted in the formulation of a

59 *Supra*, African Commission's nationality study.

60 Available at: www.unhcr.org/uk/protection/migration/4d5258ab9/african-union-migration-policy-framework-africa.html, accessed 13 December 2017.

61 *Supra*, African Commission's nationality study.

draft General Comment that seeks to clarify the issues relating to nationality and birth registration of children in the continent.

In 2012 the AU Commission held a symposium on the themes of citizenship, statelessness and conflicts. The symposium recommended *inter alia* that the Member States should develop a continent-wide 'instrument on statelessness that reflects African realities and contexts such as nomadic, historical migrations and border dimensions of the phenomenon'.[62] The African Commission mandated its Special Rapporteur on Refugees, Asylum Seekers, Migrants and Internally Displaced Persons in Africa to conduct an in-depth study on the nationality question in 2013. This study later fed into the work of the Committee on the Rights of the Child through its technical committee mentioned above. The Committee undertook the task of drafting the General Comment, with the aim of clarifying the relevant provisions of the African Children's Charter and providing explanations on issues such as birth registration and acquisition of nationality. The General Comment was adopted in 2014 and it explains the scope of Member States' duties in the implementation of the obligations stated in Article 6 of the African Children's Charter in relation to the right of all children to a name, birth registration and a nationality.[63]

Following the report of the extensive study on nationality in Africa, at its 18th extraordinary session held in Nairobi, Kenya, the Commission adopted the draft *Protocol to the African Charter on the Right to a Nationality*.[64] The Executive Council of the African Union approved the proposal from the Commission that the draft protocol enter the procedures for elaboration as a legal instrument for adoption at a later stage by the African Union.

African Charter on Human and Peoples' Rights and the citizenship/nationality question

The ACHPR does not have any specific provision on the right to citizenship or nationality. This is surprising considering the multifarious problems linked to this issue across the continent and its impact on human rights. However, the provisions of the Charter have been invoked on cases implicating citizenship issues.[65] According to the African Commission,

> Although the right to a nationality was not included in the list of rights protected under the African Charter, the African States alluded to the concept of nationality through the adoption of provisions referring to the rights

62 Ibid.

63 See African Committee of Experts on the Rights and Welfare of the Child, available at: www.acerwc.org/general-comments, accessed 13 December 2017.

64 *Resolution on the drafting of a Protocol to the African Charter on Human and Peoples' Rights on the Right to Nationality in Africa*, available at: www.achpr.org/sessions/55th/resolutions/277, accessed 13 December 2017.

65 *Supra*, Manby (2014), 181.

> of the 'citizen', compared to those of the 'non-national' or the duty of the individual 'to serve his national community', to protect 'the security of the State whose national [. . .] he is' and to 'preserve and strengthen social and national solidarity'. Notably, the Charter strictly forbade mass expulsion of non-nationals, i.e., 'that which is aimed at national, racial, ethnic or religious groups'.[66]

In recognition of this implied aim of the African Charter, the African Commission has treated cases raising the issue of nationality/citizenship with a creative interpretation of specific articles of the African Charter with a view to making the right implicit in the continental treaty.[67] The articles employed in these cases include Articles 2 (freedom from discrimination), 3 (equality), 5 (human dignity), 7 (fair trial), 12 (freedom of movement), 13 (right of participation in government) and 18 (family and the rights of women and children).[68] The attempt to fill the gap in the African Charter was partly influenced by the adoption of the United Nations Convention on the Rights of the Child in 1989, which was effectuated in the African Charter on the Rights and Welfare of the Child (ACERWC) in 1999. As stated previously, the ACERWC[69] is designed to have significant implications for citizenship rights from birth across the continent. Article 6 of the Charter provides as follows:

> **Name and Nationality**
>
> 1 Every child shall have the right from his birth to a name.
> 2 Every child shall be registered immediately after birth.
> 3 Every child has the right to acquire a nationality.
> 4 State Parties to the present Charter shall undertake to ensure that their Constitutional legislation recognise the principles according to which a child shall acquire the nationality of the State in the territory of which he has been born if, at the time of the child's birth he is not granted nationality by any other State in accordance with its laws.

The inclusion of this right in the ACERWC was subsequently reflected in the Protocol to the African Charter on Human and Peoples' Rights on the Rights of Women in Africa of 2003 (Maputo Protocol).[70] The Maputo Protocol provides *inter alia* for the right of women to a nationality and, if they get married,

66 African Commission nationality study, 11.

67 Ibid. 12, paragraph 27.

68 These cases are discussed in Chapter 7.

69 *African Charter on the Rights and Welfare of the Child*, OAU Doc. CAB/LEG/24.9/49 (1990), entered into force 29 November 1999.

70 *Protocol to the African Charter on Human and Peoples' Rights on the Rights of Women in Africa*, adopted by the 2nd Ordinary Session of the Assembly of the Union, Maputo, CAB/LEG/66.6 (Sept. 13, 2000), entered into force 25 November 2005.

to acquire the nationality of their husband. However, it is disappointing that it includes exceptions in Article 6(g) and (h) restricting the ability of a man to acquire citizenship through his wife's nationality and that of a child to acquire his/her mother's nationality.

Conclusions

Although membership in the AU for States in the continent of Africa is universal, the provisions on membership are still relevant for two key reasons. In the first place, the AU did not foreclose the emergence of new nations that could seek membership in the Union. The recent case of the emergence of the Republic of South Sudan is a case in point. Second, despite the disappointing approach of the AU to the attempt of Haiti to seek membership in the AU, there is still the possibility that the AU may revisit the geographical limitation placed on membership in the AU. The AU sanctions regime is significant because it underscores the AU's supranational ambitions. The practice and procedure of the sanction regime is developing gradually and will become more coherent with time. Membership in the AU also has positive implications for the over one billion citizens of the Member States. Developments at the continental level show a determination on the part of the AU to engage with critical issues affecting individual citizens. The challenge for the AU is to ensure that its policies and laws are implemented by Member States at the domestic level.

5 African economic and business law

Green shoots in the new economic legal order

Introduction

The level of poverty in Africa and its impact on citizens across the continent has made economic development a major focal point within the AU and its emerging legal order. Since independence, African states have struggled to develop and broaden their economies. Poor economic performance across the continent has been attributed to a number of internal and external factors. Internal factors include deficient economic policies, insufficient financial resources, deficient institutional infrastructures, weak managerial capacity, corruption and political instability. External factors include adverse international trade terms, overreliance on natural resources and high debt problems.[1] African leaders have viewed integration as an important tool for promoting economic growth, improving citizens' standard of living and fostering sustainable development.[2] However, the challenge of integration is daunting due to the diversity of language, traditions, culture and, more importantly, legal systems across the continent. At the domestic level, the legal systems of Member States of the AU are mostly vestiges of colonisation, which accounts for their diversity. The laws of former French and Portuguese colonies are based on the Napoleonic code. The laws of former British colonies are based on the common law legal system, while South Africa, Namibia, Botswana, Zimbabwe, Lesotho and Swaziland have a mix of Roman-Dutch and common law. In addition, Islamic law plays a significant role in the laws of some of the Member States. Apart from these, each Member State also has traditional customary laws with peculiar legal traditions. Nevertheless, it is widely acknowledged that for meaningful development to occur, a level of integration and harmonisation or uniformisation of business laws must be undertaken within the continent. The experience of the European Union shows that it is possible to bring diverse systems of law together within the framework of a harmonised legal system.[3]

1 K. D. Magliveras and G. J. Naldi, *The African Union (AU)* (Wolters Kluwer, 2013) 322.

2 United Nations Economic Commission for Africa, *Assessing Regional Integration in Africa, Volume IV* (2010) 7, available at: www.uneca.org/sites/default/files/PublicationFiles/aria4full.pdf, accessed 14 December 2017.

3 S. Mancuso, 'The new African law: beyond the difference between common law and civil law' (2008) *Annual Survey of International & Comparative Law* 14, 39.

The advantages of integration in the context of the AU are patently obvious. International and cross-border businesses have had to navigate different standards, laws and tariffs, among other challenges, in doing business in the continent. In comparison, within the European Union, harmonisation of laws has increasingly created common standards of doing business across the EU internal market. Harmonisation facilitates consistency of laws, regulations, standards and practices, so that similar rules apply to businesses that operate across borders. In addition, harmonisation reduces transaction costs, regulatory arbitrage and time constraints, and facilitates faster development of economic activities. It also reduces compliance and regulatory burdens for businesses operating across borders.[4] Moreover, the adoption of harmonised and modern laws in the area of commercial law would benefit AU Member States' commercial partners. An improved legal system would further fuel African integration into the global economy and significantly aid its economic development.[5]

Thus, this chapter examines the emerging economic and business law in the continent against the backdrop of efforts at integration through harmonisation and uniformisation of standards.[6] The chapter focuses on the legal dimensions of the economic integration process. It is conceded that, compared with norm development in the human rights sphere, development in the business and economic sphere has been slow and with lesser overall impact; however, there exists significant potential that could shape developments in the AU legal order in the future.

Background

African Union Member States' governments have long recognised the need for closer regional and continental economic ties for development.[7] According to Allott, the move towards integration or unification of laws in the continent is a

4 W. Menski, *Comparative Law in a Global Context* (Cambridge University Press, 2005) 39; M. Hesselink, 'The ideal of codification and the dynamics of Europeanisation: the Dutch experience' in S. Vogenauer and S. Weatherill (eds), *The Harmonisation of European Contract Law: Implications for European Private Laws, Business and Legal Practice* (Hart Publishing, 2006) 49, 50.

5 S. Mancuso, 'China in Africa and the law' (2012) *Annual Survey of International & Comparative Law* 18, 243.

6 C. Lopes, 'Regional Integration and Monetary Unions in Africa', a speech delivered at the Africa Training Institute of the International Monetary Fund on 8 March 2016 in Mauritius, available at: www.uneca.org/es-blog/regional-integration-and-monetary-unions-africa, accessed 14 December 2017; G. Bamodu, 'Transnational law, unification and harmonisation of international commercial law in Africa' (1994) 38 (2) *Journal of African Law* 125, 143; L. H. Hayes, 'A modern *lex mercatoria*: political rhetoric or substantive progress?' (1977) 3 (2) *Brooklyn Journal of International Law* 210; B. M. Cremades and S. L. Plehn, 'The new *lex mercatoria* and the harmonisation of the laws of international commercial transactions' (1984) 2 (3) *Boston University International Law Journal* 317; D. A. Walsh and K. W. Ryan, 'Harmonisation and standardisation of legal aspects of international trade' (1977) 51 *Australian Law Journal* 608.

7 M. Ndulo, 'Harmonisation of trade laws in the African Economic Community' (1993) 42 *International and Comparative Law Quarterly* 101–118.

'consequence of independence, the desire to build a nation, to guide the different communities with their different laws to a common destiny'.[8] This viewpoint is also true in relation to the AU approach to economic integration. Economic integration is recognised as a vehicle for advancing economic and social development in Member States. This perception is reinforced by the relatively successful experiences of integration of the European Union. For instance, the AU and all eight of its recognised regional economic communities consider the free movement of goods and services to be a priority area for integrating Member States. Trade integration is also one of the key elements included in the African Union Minimum Integration Programme (discussed below).[9]

The origin of the integration effort in the economic and business sphere is traceable to the Lagos Plan of Action for Economic Development of Africa, which was a special initiative of the predecessor organisation, the OAU.[10] The ultimate economic integration of the continent was a central theme of the plan. The plan was one of the key drivers that led to the adoption of the Treaty Establishing the African Economic Community (Abuja Treaty) in June 1991. The Treaty entered into force on 12 May 1994. The Abuja Treaty aimed to unify the continent's economy through the establishment of free trade and monetary union, ultimately leading to the establishment of the African economic community.[11] The introduction of the African Economic Community (AEC) has been described as one of the most ambitious developments in Africa's economic sphere.[12] According to Magliveras and Naldi, '[n]ot unlike the EU, the AEC has the features of a supranational organisation and foresees a role beyond the economic sphere, in the social political worlds, leading to political union, since achieved with the creation of the AU'.[13] The AEC framework is the central mechanism for promoting and implementing integration strategies in the continent's economic sphere. It is important to note that even though the Treaty stated that it established the 'African Economic Community', the Treaty did no more than establish a framework or interim agreement that will facilitate the formation of a continent-wide economic community,[14] since the Treaty did not comprehensively address the substantive issues of integration. Rather, the strategy behind the Treaty was to

8 A. N. Allott, 'Towards the unification of laws in Africa' (1965) 14 (2) *International and Comparative Law Quarterly* 366, 378.

9 *Supra*, United Nations Economic Commission for Africa, Assessing Regional Integration in Africa, 13.

10 OAU, *Lagos Plan of Action for the Economic Development of Africa* 1980–2000, available at: file://smbhome.uscs.susx.ac.uk/oa288/Downloads/Lagos-Plan-of-Action.pdf, accessed 14 December 2017; E. Dickson, 'African perspectives on democracy and the dilemmas of postcolonial intellectuals in African affairs' (1998) 45 (3–4) *Africa Today* 281–306; *supra*, Ndulo, 101–118.

11 T. Ricks, 'From the Abuja Treaty to the Sustainable Development Goals: realizing economic integration in Africa' (2016) 42 (1) *North Carolina Journal of International Law* 250.

12 *Supra*, Magliveras and Naldi, 322.

13 Ibid. 323.

14 S. Koroma *et al.*, *Towards an African Common Market for Agricultural Products* (Food and Agricultural Organisation of the United Nations, 2008) 24.

use selected regional economic communities (RECs) as the building blocks in a process that would lead to the establishment of a continental trading community. To this end, Article 88(2) of the Treaty provides *inter alia* that:

> Member States undertake to promote the co-ordination and harmonisation of the integration activities of regional economic communities of which they are members with the activities of the Community.

Eight RECs have been recognised by the AU for this purpose. These are the Arab Maghreb Union (AMU/UMA) in the north of the continent; the Common Market for Eastern and Southern Africa (COMESA) in the southeast; the Community of Sahel-Saharan States (CEN-SAD), which includes countries to the north of the Democratic Republic of the Congo, Comoros, and São Tomé and Príncipe, excluding Algeria and Ethiopia; the East African Community (EAC) and the Intergovernmental Authority on Development (IGAD) in the east; the Economic Community of Central African States (ECCAS) in the middle of the continent; the Economic Community of West African States (ECOWAS) in the west; and the Southern African Development Community in the south. The consequence of this arrangement is that Member States have the obligation to comply with the Abuja Treaty alongside the Treaty establishing the relevant RECs in their region. There is an ongoing negotiation of a Tripartite FTA (TFTA), which has the aim of uniting three major RECs, i.e., the SADC, the EAC and COMESA. Twenty-six countries are involved in the project, which is approximately half of the AU membership. It also represents 56% of the continent's population (approximately 625 million people) and 50% of the GDP (USD 1 trillion). It is expected that the TFTA will serve as one of the pillars for creating a continental free trade area in the near future.

In a significant move to advance the objectives of integration in the Abuja Treaty and the AU Constitutive Act and to increase the speed of integration in the continent, a Minimum Integration Programme (MIP) was agreed upon in 2009.[15] The MIP was a product of collaboration between the African Union Commission, the RECs and the Conferences of African Ministers in Charge of Integration (COMAIs). According to the AU report, 'the minimum integration programme is the missing link in the big loop for the implementation of the Treaty establishing the African Economic Community animated by Member States, the regional economic communities (RECs), the African Union Commission (AUC) and development partners'. The MIP lists the priority areas that are to be pursued in the actualisation of the integration objective. Most of the priority areas would have consequences for the emerging legal order. For example, the first phase of the MIP includes the progressive elimination of tariff and non-tariff barriers in RECs, simplification and harmonisation of rules of origin, creation of custom unions in

15 African Union, Minimum Integration Programme, available at: https://au.int/en/ea/ric/mip, accessed 14 December 2017.

RECs, and free movement of persons, goods and services, among others. In addition, the second phase of the MIP is designed to build on the first phase but also to focus on additional tasks, including harmonisation of fiscal policies, establishment of regional payment systems, development of capital markets, development of a legal and statutory framework on the free movement of capital, harmonisation of monetary policies, adoption of a continental common external tariff, monitoring of the macroeconomic convergence of countries, harmonisation of statistics on national accounts and monitoring of the macroeconomic convergence, and investment promotion and improvement of the investment climate.

Economic integration and norm creation

The integration of standards and laws leads to changes in the legal environment and order. In certain cases, such as in the EU, these changes may produce a new legal order. Integration takes many forms. For example, it could occur by harmonisation or uniformisation of norms.[16] Harmonisation is a less radical technique as compared with uniformisation. Harmonisation consists of changing the provisions of domestic law from various countries in order to make them more similar. Therefore, while respecting the peculiarities of the various national legal systems, harmonisation gives the opportunity to reduce differences in selected areas and to enhance legal cooperation between countries. In the European Union, harmonisation is achieved through the mechanisms of directives adopted at the EU level and thereafter passed on to Member States for implementation.[17] Furthermore, harmonisation processes can take different forms at the domestic, continental and international levels. For instance, such a process can be embodied in (1) the revision of a national code, (2) the creation of an international code (such as the Convention on the International Sales of Goods),[18] (3) an international restatement (such as the UNIDROIT Principles of International Commercial Contracts),[19] (4) the adoption of regional choice of law conventions (such as the Rome Convention on the Law Applicable to Contractual Obligations)[20] and (5) the adoption of uniform

16 G. Conway, *The Limits of Legal Reasoning and the European Court of Justice* (Cambridge University Press, 2014) 86, 175.

17 A. Rosett, 'UNIDROIT Principles and harmonisation of international commercial law: focus on Chapter Seven' (1997) 2 (3) *Uniform Law Review* 441; A. Rosett, 'Unification, harmonization, restatement, codification, and reform in international commercial law' (1992) 40 (3) *American Journal of Comparative Law* 683–697.

18 *United Nations Convention on Contracts for the International Sale of Goods*, Vienna, 11 April 1980, S.Treaty Document Number 98–9 (1984), UN Document Number A/CONF 97/19, 1489 UNTS 3.

19 *UNIDROIT Principles of International Commercial Contracts*, available at: www.unidroit.org/instruments/commercial-contracts/unidroit-principles-2016, accessed 14 December 2017.

20 *1980 Rome Convention on the Law Applicable to Contractual Obligations* (consolidated version), Official Journal C 027, 26/01/1998 P. 0034–0046.

private rules (such as the Uniform Customs and Practices on Documentary Credits-UCP).[21] A more radical form of legal integration is 'uniformisation'. Uniformisation is a technique aimed at eliminating the differences between national provisions by replacing them with a unique and identical text for all the States involved in the legal integration process.[22] This process can be pursued either by the adoption of the same legal text by Member States or the text contains the principle of supranationality, by which the uniform norm is directly integrated into the domestic legal order.

Procedurally, the process of integration usually starts with countries forming a Free Trade Area (FTA), which enables the removal of most trade barriers, such as quotas and tariffs. Once the FTA is well established, the next step is to move to the formation of a Customs Union that facilitates the introduction of common external tariffs or imports from non-Member States. Further deepening of integration leads to the creation of a Common Market, which facilitates free movement of factors of production including labour and capital. The common market also facilitates the establishment of common financial institutions. The ultimate stage in the integration process is the establishment of an Economic Union, which allows for the harmonisation of fiscal and monetary policies and the introduction of common currency.

As the EU experience has shown, economic integration requires a certain level of legal unification to thrive. International legal instruments developed within multilateral institutions and applicable to certain cross-border transactions have become increasingly important to the development of what is sometimes described as transnational commercial law. The term 'transnational commercial law' refers to all kinds of principles and rules, not restricted to domestic use, relevant in international and cross-border business practices or that provide an alternative to domestic laws.[23] The transnational commercial legal framework was developed through several intergovernmental institutions, international business organisations and legal research centres, such as the International Institute for the Unification of Private Law (UNIDROIT), the United Nations Commission on International Trade Law (UNCITRAL), and the International Chamber of Commerce (ICC). These developments reinforce the trend of seeking harmonised solutions to cross-border business-related issues. The developments within the emerging AU legal order discussed in this chapter could be considered to be the continent's contribution to transnational commercial law.

21 *ICC Uniform Customs and Practice for Documentary Credits* – UCP 600, available at: http://store.iccwbo.org/icc-uniform-customs-and-practice-for-documentary-credits, accessed 14 December 2017.

22 See S. Mancuso, 'Trends on the harmonisation of contract law in Africa' (2007) 13 *Annual Survey of International & Comparative Law* 157.

23 Ibid. Mancuso; M. J. Bonell, 'The UNIDROIT Principles and transnational law' (2000) 5 (2) *Uniform Law Review* 199.

Foundation of AU economic and business law and the African Economic Community

As stated previously, the harmonisation of business laws has been pursued primarily through the establishment of the AEC and RECs. These institutions are tasked with the promotion of legal homogeneity in an attempt to achieve eventual economic integration at the continental level. As expressed in Articles 3 and 4 of the Abuja Treaty, cooperation on integration and harmonisation is at the heart of the AEC ambitions. Article 3 set out the principles underpinning the Community. These include inter-state cooperation, policy harmonisation, integration of programmes and the promotion of harmonious development of economic activities among Member States. The objectives of the Community, set out in Article 4, are as follows: (a) to promote economic, social and cultural development and the integration of African economies in order to increase economic self-reliance, indigenous and self-sustained development; (b) to establish, on a continental scale, a framework for the development, mobilisation and utilisation of the human and material resources of Africa in order to achieve a self-reliant development; (c) to promote cooperation in all fields of human endeavour in order to raise the standard of living of African peoples, maintain and enhance economic stability, foster close and peaceful relations among Member States and contribute to the progress, development and the economic integration of the continent; and (d) to coordinate and harmonise policies among existing economic communities in order to foster the gradual establishment of the Community.

Member States are required to create favourable conditions for the development of the economic community.[24] Furthermore, each Member State is required to take all necessary measures to ensure the enactment and dissemination of such legislation as may be necessary for the implementation of the provisions of the Treaty. Under Articles 29 and 30, Member States of each REC are required to progressively eliminate customs duties, other restrictions or prohibitions, and administrative trade barriers, as well as all other non-tariff barriers. In addition, Article 43 underscores the commitment of Member States to progressively secure free movement of persons and the rights of residence and establishment in other Member States. Furthermore, under Article 44, Member States are to harmonise monetary, financial and payment policies. This would lay the foundation for the ultimate aim of establishing the African Monetary Union.[25] The Treaty also addresses other areas in which integration is desirable, including agricultural development, food production, science and technology, natural resources and energy, transport, communications, tourism, education, culture, human resources, social affairs, health and population management.

24 *Supra*, Abuja Treaty, Article 5.

25 *Supra*, Magliveras and Naldi, 319.

As stated in Article 6 of the Treaty, the Community is scheduled to be established over a 34-year period and in six stages, beginning with the creation of regional blocs, followed by the strengthening of intra-regional integration and the harmonisation of the activities of the RECs. The other stages include the establishment of free trade areas and customs unions in each REC, the creation of a continental customs union, the creation of an African common market and, lastly, the establishment of an African economic monetary union and a parliament. The first stage has been largely completed. However, the second stage, which was originally planned to be completed in 2007, is still ongoing due to the different pace of progress within RECs and their Member States.[26] The third stage, which involves the establishment of free trade areas and customs unions in each REC, was to be completed in 2017. However, the speed of progress at the REC level varies significantly, although five of the RECs have launched free trade areas as of the time of writing. More problematic, in this respect, is the fact that some Member States have not even joined an FTA, which has negative consequences for the flow of intra-regional trade. The Treaty empowers the Assembly of Heads of State and Government to determine, at the end of each stage, whether expectations have been met to enable progression. The Treaty further provides that any of the stages may be extended beyond the initial period established, provided that all six transitional periods do not exceed a total period of 40 years.[27]

It is notable that Article 25 of the Abuja Treaty, which addresses the establishment of specialised technical committees, includes committees that can play significant roles in the harmonisation process. These committees include the committee on rural economy and agricultural matters; the committee on monetary and financial affairs; the committee on trade, customs and immigration; the committee on industry, science and technology, energy, natural resources and environment; the committee on transport, communications and tourism; the committee on health, labour and social affairs; and the committee on education, culture and human resources. The specialised technical committees are designed to play important roles in the implementation of the objectives of the Community. They are tasked with, among other things, the preparation of projects and programmes for the Community; the supervision, follow-up and evaluation of the implementation of decisions made by the organs of the Community; ensuring the coordination and harmonisation of projects and programmes; and submitting reports and recommendations on the implementation of the provisions of the Treaty.

Notably missing from the list of committees is a legal committee that could be specifically charged with the responsibility of drawing up legal texts for the

26 A. Sy, 'Hearing on "Will there be an African Economic Community?"', available at: www.brookings.edu/testimonies/hearing-on-will-there-be-an-african-economic-community, accessed 14 December 2017.

27 Article 6(4)(5); *supra*, Ndulo, 101, 118.

several protocols under the treaty, or for advancing cooperation with regard to the development of trade law and commercial practices within the community. This is a glaring omission in view of the ambitions of the AEC. The inclusion of such a committee would be useful in nurturing and fostering harmonisation and standardisation of norms. The functions of the committee could include the preparation of studies and recommendations on challenges in the process of harmonisation and unification, comparative analyses of national legislation, studies and research on particular topics at the request of relevant AU institutions, preparation of trade conventions, model laws and uniform laws, promotion of the codification and wider acceptance of regional trade terms, customs and practices and the promotion of a uniform interpretation and application of regional conventions. In addition, the committee could also serve as a forum for Member States in which to consider and debate proposals for the harmonisation of laws on a universal scale and for developing, if possible, a common African strategy towards such initiatives. It could also serve as a forum for consideration of the legal aspects of other international developments affecting the global economic order.

A significant development that enhanced the AEC capacity for norm generation is the provision in relation to the Court of Justice.[28] Article 18 of the Treaty provides that parties to the Treaty may refer disputes to a Court of Justice. The Court was to be charged with ensuring adherence to the law in the implementation of the Treaty. It had the power to decide on disputes that may emanate from the Treaty, brought by any Member State or the Assembly on grounds of violation of the Treaty or on grounds of competence, abuse of powers by an organ, an authority or a Member State. In addition, it may, at the request of the Assembly of Heads of State and Government or Council of Ministers, give advisory opinions. The Assembly further conferred on the Court the power to assume jurisdiction over disputes other than those in Article 18 (3)(a).[29] Notably, Article 19 of the Abuja Treaty states that the decisions of the Court of Justice are binding on Member States and organs of the Community. Importantly, the Court of Justice was the only judicial organ mentioned in the AU Constitutive Act.[30] A protocol to establish the Court as the Court of Justice of the African Union and as the principal judicial organ of the AU was adopted in 2003.[31] However, that Court did not become operational because of the AU Assembly's decision to merge it with the African Court on Human and Peoples' Rights to create the African Court of Justice and Human Rights.[32]

28 *Supra*, Abuja Treaty, Article 7.

29 *Supra*, Ndulo.

30 Article 18.

31 *Protocol of the Court of Justice of the African Union* (2003), available at: https://au.int/en/treaties/protocol-court-justice-african-union, accessed 14 December 2017.

32 See Chapter 10.

Establishing the pillars for the continental economic community at the REC level

As stated previously, the speed of progress within each REC on the different aspects and objectives of integration differs significantly. Five of the RECs appear to have made noteworthy progress, with the ECOWAS and the EAC making the most progress. Similarly, the progress of individual Member States within the RECs in achieving REC objectives has been uneven for many reasons, including differences in legal systems, historical factors, levels of development and political priorities. A related problem is the overlapping membership of certain Member States, which affects how individual Member States make their priority choices. Nevertheless, some progress has been made in the area of free movement, currency unification and reduction of trade tariff barriers.

Trade and tariff

The EAC, with its six Member States, has established a Common Market and Monetary Union. This development has helped to streamline border clearances, simplify work permit issuance and ensure mutual recognition of professional agreements. Member States of the EAC are making progress towards forming a single currency by 2024. Against this backdrop, intra-regional trade has significantly increased in recent years. In the case of COMESA, it has established an FTA to which 17 of its 19 Member States have acceded. In 2009 COMESA launched its Customs Union. However, the Union is not yet operational, as Member States are still finalising legislation for the domestication of the objectives. The legislation under negotiation includes the Common Tariff Nomenclature, Common External Tariff and the Common Market Customs Management Regulations. With respect to ECOWAS, it has established a Customs Union among its 19 Member States and is making progress towards establishing a Common Market. The SADC, for its part, established its free trade area in 2009. This has led to more than 80% of intra-regional trade among the Member States becoming free of import tariffs. However, seven of its 15 Member States are yet to fully implement the free trade area agreements. One customs union, the Southern African Customs Union, has existed in the Southern African Region since 1910. All members of the SADC are also members of the Customs Union. The ECCAS, consisting of 11 Member States, has established an FTA but has made slow progress in achieving its objectives. CEN-SAD, IGAD and AMU are also behind schedule and remain at stage two of the Abuja Treaty. Despite the varied progress, in 2012 the Assembly of Heads of State and Government of the AU adopted a decision to establish the Continental Free Trade Area (CFTA), negotiation regarding which was completed in 2018.[33] The aim of the CFTA

33 African Union, CFTA – Continental Free Trade Area, available at: https://au.int/en/ti/cfta/about, accessed 15 December 2017. See also African Continental Free Trade Area (AfCFTA) Legal Texts and Policy Documents, available at https://www.tralac.org/resources/by-region/cfta.html, accessed 16 May 2018.

is to create a single continental market for goods and services in the continent, with free movement of persons, business and investments, with the aim to accelerate the establishment of a continental Customs Union.

Currency unification and the African Monetary Union

The focus of the sixth stage of the Abuja Treaty is the establishment of an African Monetary Union with a single African Central Bank and a single currency, to be called the 'afro'.[34] The building block towards achieving this is the creation of similar frameworks at the REC level. Unification of currency is seen as a necessary step towards the eventual creation of a continent-wide monetary union. Monetary union is a particular type of monetary integration that facilitates a group of countries sharing a common currency and central banking. According to UNCTAD, this could:

> enhance regional trade because it saves on the transaction costs of exchanging currencies, synchronizes business cycles, and enhances exchange rate and macroeconomic stability. In addition, a common currency increases price transparency and facilitates movement of capital between members, thereby fostering investment and trade.[35]

The main reason for increased interest in this idea is the creation of the Eurozone in 1999 and the subsequent introduction of the euro currency in 2002.[36] It is notable that there is historical precedent for the use of single currency in the continent that dates back to the colonial period. For example, the Eastern African countries colonised by the United Kingdom (Kenya, Uganda, Tanganyika and Zanzibar) used East African Shillings as their single currency. This historical precedent explains why areas in which single currencies were introduced during the colonial period have made the most progress in this respect.

One of the objectives of the ECOWAS from its inception was the creation of a single currency union. However, its failure to make progress on this front led to a subset of ECOWAS Member States forming a different monetary union. The West African Economic and Monetary Union (UEMOA)[37] was formed in 1994 and shares the CFA franc among eight West African countries. The UEMOA is not only a currency union but also a monetary union. The members, with the exception of Guinea-Bissau, are francophone Member States of ECOWAS. The monetary union was established to promote

34 *Supra*, Ricks, 249, 253.

35 UNCTAD, 'Monetary unions and regional trade in Africa' (2014), available at: http://unctad.org/meetings/en/SessionalDocuments/tdbex59d3_en.pdf, accessed 15 December 2017.

36 P. R. Masson and C. Pattillo, *The Monetary Geography of Africa* (Brookings Institution Press, 2005), 1–11; *supra*, Ricks, 254.

37 The acronym is based on its French name, Union Économique et Monétaire Ouest-Africaine.

economic integration among the Member States. The exchange rate of the monetary Union's currency, the CFA franc, is tied to that of the euro and is guaranteed by the French Treasury. A related development is the establishment of the West African Monetary Zone (WAMZ) in 2000 by another group of countries within ECOWAS that plans to introduce a common currency called the eco. This group originally comprised five countries: Gambia, Ghana, Guinea, Nigeria and Sierra Leone. Liberia joined in 2010. With the exception of Guinea, all the Member States are English-speaking countries. There is an ambition to merge the CFA and the eco in the future, thereby introducing a single currency that covers West and Central Africa. The ECOWAS and UEMOA have also worked jointly on a common plan of action in the area of trade and macroeconomic policy convergence.

Apart from the above, there is also the Economic and Monetary Community of Central Africa, a customs and monetary union among former French Central African countries that also use the CFA franc pegged to the euro. In 2013 the EAC signed a protocol to start the process of setting up a monetary union within 10 years. The SADC has an ongoing plan to establish a monetary union and introduce a single currency. The COMESA also has similar plans. It is expected that these initiatives will feed into the establishment of an African economic and monetary union as envisaged in the Abuja Treaty. In addition, there is the Common Monetary Area, within which the domestic currencies of Lesotho, Namibia and Swaziland have pegged their currencies to the South African rand, in effect sharing the same monetary policy with South Africa.

The EU's Economic Monetary Union (EMU) is a model that could serve as a useful template for the AU effort. Similar to the African continent, it covers a large geographical area and has faced significant challenges, including the 2008/9 financial crises. The EU had consolidated its single market and had already achieved a high level of economic and trade integration before establishing the EMU. The Eurozone Member States have, over time, built an impressive architecture of processes, institutions and regulations that could feed into the EMU. A key lesson for Africa from the EU's experience is that the institutional environment must be favourable to integration at the level of both Member States and the continent as a whole.

The advancement of the EU in the area of rule of law is also a lesson for the AU in the process of creating a stable environment for the creation of a continental monetary union. The relationship between trade and the rule of law has been generally acknowledged. Adherence to the rule of law is necessary to ensure predictability in trade and investment regulation and protection. Rule of law may also, in turn, increase trade and investment through a reliable legal framework. This relationship indicates that the move towards uniform business law would contribute to other initiatives that could potentially improve the rule of law and stability in the continent.

A stable macroeconomic policy is also important in this context. As the Eurozone experience has shown, wide differences in the degree of fiscal discipline among Member States could lead to instability.[38] It is notable that in order to address this issue, RECs have imposed macroeconomic convergence criteria modelled after the approach of the EMU Member States. However, this may not be a perfect solution because the criteria may limit the policy options available to Member States to respond to peculiar development challenges going forward. The EMU experience has also demonstrated the need for Member States to have credible and feasible mechanisms in place to respond to asymmetric shocks that may occur within a union.

Freedom of movement

The African Union, through the Abuja Treaty, has a longstanding ambition to create a free movement regime similar to that of the EU. There is a plan to increasingly improve mobility of labour and the ability of citizens to establish businesses in any Member States that they may wish. Free movement of persons, it is envisaged, will benefit the continent socio-economically and will strengthen cross-border trade and investment. It will also boost the creation of new opportunities and will simplify basic travel.

The RECs have the initial responsibility to develop region-wide mobility protocols. The strategy is that the regional effort would ultimately pave the way for continental integration under the AU. Again, the progress made by the RECs has been varied. While progress has been made in most RECs in establishing a framework to facilitate freedom of movement, major challenges such as insecurity and conflicts have hampered implementation. It is widely acknowledged that ECOWAS and the East African Community (EAC) have made the most progress in this area.[39] Under the ECOWAS regime, citizens may obtain a regional passport, which allows visa-free cross-border travel for 90 days. Seven Member States have converted their national passport to the ECOWAS passport: Benin, Ghana, Guinea, Liberia, Niger, Nigeria and Senegal. The East African Community (EAC) is in the process of introducing a common travel passport in 2018. Current national passports are expected to be phased out between 1 January 2017 and 31 December 2018. The new common passport will guarantee citizens of the six Member States visa-free cross-border travel. The SADC and COMESA currently have a regime that allows 90-day visas to citizens of Member States. The CEMAC has a plan in the offing to introduce a similar regime.

38 M. Dabrowski, *Monetary Union and Fiscal and Macroeconomic Governance* (2015), available at: https://ec.europa.eu/info/sites/info/files/file_import/dp013_en_2.pdf, accessed 15 December 2017.

39 P. Kagame, *The Imperative to Strengthen Our Union. Report on the Proposed Recommendations for the Institutional Reform of the African Union*, 29 January 2017, available at: https://au.int/sites/default/files/pages/32777-file-report-20institutional20reform20of20the20au-2.pdf, accessed 11 December 2017.

A decision was made at the AU summit in Johannesburg, South Africa, in 2015 to start work on drafting a Protocol on Free Movement of Persons for the entire continent.[40] The task was assigned to the African Commission and is scheduled to be completed by January 2018. The legal basis for the free movement protocol is Article 43 of the Abuja Treaty, which provides as follows:

1 Member States agree to adopt, individually, at bilateral or regional levels, the necessary measures in order to achieve progressively the free movement of persons and to ensure the enjoyment of the right of residence and the right of establishment by their nationals within the Community.
2 For this purpose, Member States agree to conclude a Protocol on the Free Movement of Persons, Right of Residence and Right of Establishment.

Furthermore, the AU has launched an AU passport under its Agenda 2063 that is expected to be fully implemented by 2020. It is envisaged that the passport will replace the national passports of Member States and grant visa exemption in all Member States.

Road-testing supranationality: the case of OHADA

The Organisation for the Harmonisation of African Business Laws (OHADA) is generally seen as a model and a potential driver for the continental efforts at harmonisation and uniformisation of legal standards and norms. Though not technically a trade bloc or one of the recognised RECs, OHADA has played a leading role in regional integration and harmonisation of laws in West and Central Africa.[41] The OHADA was created by a treaty between certain members of the AU, primarily in the French-speaking areas.[42] The treaty was signed in Port Louis, Mauritius, on 7 October 1993 and entered into force in July 1995. The original Member States were Benin, Burkina Faso, Central African Republic, Chad, Cameroon, Comoros, Congo, Côte d'Ivoire, Equatorial Guinea, Gabon, Mali, Niger, Senegal and Togo. Guinea, Guinea-Bissau and the Democratic Republic of Congo subsequently joined the organisation. The OHADA is a system of law with implementing institutions. Its main goal is to create and establish legal and judicial certainty in Member States through the introduction of codified uniform laws. The OHADA framework was created to harmonise

40 African Union, *Draft Protocol to the Treaty Establishing the African Economic Community Relating to Free Movement of Persons, Right of Residence and Right of Establishment*, available at: https://au.int/sites/default/files/newsevents/workingdocuments/33023-wd-pa20330_e_original_free_movement_protocol.pdf, accessed 15 December 2017.

41 OHADA is the acronym for the name of the organisation in French, 'Organisation pour l'Harmonisation en Afrique du Droit des Affaires'.

42 The amended Treaty on the Harmonisation of Business Law in Africa (1993 and 2008) is available at: www.droit-afrique.com/uploads/OHADA-Treaty-2008-harmonization-business-law.pdf, accessed 15 December 2017.

business laws, promote investment and develop economic growth in the participating countries. Additionally, it was envisaged that the framework would help make Member States more attractive to foreign investments by providing a modern legal structure that increases the predictability of commercial transactions.[43] It is notable that even though the treaty talks about harmonisation, the ultimate ambition of OHADA, based on interpretation of its provisions, is to make the law of Member States uniform.[44] It is also important to note that under Articles 1 and 2 of the OHADA Treaty, the organisation's jurisdiction is limited to business matters.

The OHADA framework introduced five principal supranational institutions to facilitate the achievement of its objectives.[45] These include a Council of Ministers, which acts as the legislature and is assisted by a Permanent Secretary (the executive);[46] a Common Court of Justice and Arbitration (*Cour Commune de Justice et d'Arbitrage*, 'CCJA'), which is the court of final appeal;[47] and a training school for judicial personnel and lawyers (*Ecole Rigionale Superieure de Magistrature*, 'ERSUMA').[48] Following a revision of the Treaty in 2010, a Conference of Heads of State and Government was added to the institutions. The conference is a political forum for deliberating on national concerns related to the organisation.

Statutes enacted under the OHADA framework are known as 'Uniform Acts'. The Uniform Acts have been described as 'the most powerful aspect' of OHADA[49] because, under the Treaty, the Acts automatically become part of the internal laws of Member States 90 days after their adoption.[50] The Acts are directly applicable in all Member States, in the same way as the European Union (EU) Regulations are directly applicable in EU Member States. The Acts are prepared by the Permanent Secretariat of the OHADA in consultation with the governments of participating Member States. The Council of Ministers, which acts as the legislature, discusses and adopts the Acts on the advice of the Common Court of Justice and Arbitration (CCJA). Parliaments of Member States are excluded from the process of making and adopting Uniform Acts. The Council of Ministers has sole competence in this area, making it possible to avoid the drawbacks of different procedures that could lead to the adoption of conflicting legal texts.

43 N. Enonchong, 'The harmonisation of business law in Africa: is Article 42 of the OHADA Treaty a problem?' (2007) 51 (1) *Journal of African Law* 51, 95.
44 C. M. Dickerson (ed.), *Unified Business Laws for Africa* (IEDP, 2012) 1.
45 Ibid. 63.
46 Based in Yaoundé, Cameroon.
47 This Court is based in Abidjan, Ivory Coast.
48 *Supra*, OHADA Treaty.
49 C. M. Dickerson, 'Harmonizing business laws in Africa: OHADA calls the tune' (2005) 44 (1) *Columbia Journal of Transnational Law* 17; C. M. Dickerson, 'The OHADA Common Court of Justice and Arbitration: exogenous forces contributing to its influence' (2016) 79 (1) *Law and Contemporary Problems* 62.
50 *Supra*, OHADA Treaty, Article 10.

As stated above, the Acts are designed to have direct effect. The Acts become effective without the need for additional domestic legislation from the parliament of participating Member States. They are directly applicable and binding in all participating Member States, notwithstanding any contrary provisions in existing or future national laws. Domestic legislation incompatible with the OHADA Uniform Acts is automatically repealed by the enactment of a Uniform Act. To date, nine Uniform Acts have been introduced pursuant to Articles 5–12 of the OHADA Treaty.[51] These acts include the Uniform Act on bankruptcy proceedings, Uniform Act on general commercial law, Uniform Act organising securities, Uniform Act on contracts for the carriage of goods by road, Uniform Act on commercial companies and economic interest groupings, Uniform Act on cooperatives, Uniform Act organising simplified recovery procedures and measures of execution, organisation and harmonisation of business accounting and Uniform Act on arbitration law.[52]

It is important to reiterate that not only do the Uniform Acts automatically repeal contradictory legislation, but also, once a matter is within the competence of OHADA, under the provisions of Article 10 of the OHADA Treaty, any domestic legislation on the same issue would be null and void. Moreover, the Uniform Acts can only be modified under the conditions provided for at their adoption, and any intervention at the national level to modify them is not permitted. In this respect, the Common Court of Justice and Arbitration (CCJA) has clarified that the repealing effect set forth in Article 10 of the OHADA Treaty refers to the abrogation and prohibition against enacting any internal norm of law or regulation (regardless of whether it is an article of the text, a paragraph or a sentence of it), either present or future, contradicting a rule from the Uniform Act.[53] However, any Member State may veto a draft of the Uniform Act before adoption.[54]

The OHADA framework also provides a legal mechanism for the settlement of disputes. The CCJA is the supranational apex court for OHADA for all matters relating to the application of the Treaty, as well as the Uniform Acts.[55] It has jurisdiction over judicial (ruling on decisions rendered by the penultimate courts of Member States) and arbitration matters (holding a supervisory role over the appointed arbitrators and granting enforceable status to awards), thereby ensuring the uniform interpretation of the Treaty, Uniform Acts and relevant regulations and arbitration agreements. With reference to the authority of the CCJA jurisprudence, Article 20 states:

51 *Supra*, Dickerson, *Unified Business Laws for Africa*.

52 www.ohada.org/index.php/en, accessed 15 December 2017.

53 *Supra*, Dickerson, 'The OHADA Common Court of Justice and Arbitration: exogenous forces contributing to its influence', 62.

54 Articles 8 and 12 of the OHADA Treaty.

55 *Supra*, Dickerson, 'The OHADA Common Court of Justice and Arbitration: exogenous forces contributing to its influence', 62; K. O. Kufuor, *African Unification: Law, Problems and Prospects* (Carolina Academic Press, 2016) 96.

> [T]he judgments of the Common Court of Justice and Arbitration are final and conclusive. [. . .] In no case may a decision contrary to a judgment of the Common Court of Justice and Arbitration be lawfully executed in a territory of a Contracting State.

Therefore, a decision of the CCJA has the same effect as those of national appellate courts and cannot be contravened by subsequent decisions of lower courts or national courts on the same matter.

The OHADA has the ambition to extend its economic legal order across Africa. Thus, in the preamble of the OHADA Treaty, Member States reaffirm their commitment to the establishment of an African Economic Community and that, ultimately, integration must be realised within a larger African framework. In keeping with this objective, Article 53 states that the Treaty is open to all Member States of the African Union.[56] Therefore, other African countries may join through Article 53.

Interestingly, in *Kevin Mgwanga Gunme* et al. v. *Cameroon*,[57] the African Commission had to consider whether the adoption of the OHADA Treaty could lead to a violation of a Member State's obligation under the African Charter. In that case, the Complainants alleged that the accession of Cameroon as a State Party to the OHADA was discriminatory against the people of Southern Cameroon on the basis of language. This is because OHADA stipulates that the language of interpretation and settlement of disputes in relation to the OHADA treaty shall be French. The people of Southern Cameroon are historically largely English speakers due to their colonial history. This complaint was lodged against the backdrop of Cameroon's bijural system, with English Common Law applicable in its anglophone regions and French Civil Law applicable in its eight francophone regions. The Complainants further argued that the ratification and implementation of the OHADA Treaty was discriminatory to businesses and individuals involved in businesses in Southern Cameroon. This argument was exemplified by the allegation that companies not registered under OHADA law could not open bank accounts in Cameroon. The Complainants thus argued that the Cameroonian State had violated Article 2 of the African Charter.

In response, Cameroon argued that OHADA is not designed to promote the superiority of French civil law but to harmonise business law in the OHADA Member States 'by elaborating simple, modern, common rules aimed at encouraging regional development and growth, setting up appropriate judicial procedures and encouraging arbitration for the settlement of contractual disputes'.[58] The Cameroonian State further argued that the fact that some non-French speaking countries, such as Nigeria and Ghana, were in the process of acceding to the Treaty demonstrates that the Treaty is not discriminatory. The Cameroonian

56 *Supra*, Enonchong, 51, 95.

57 *Kevin Mgwanga Gunme* et al. v. *Cameroon*, ACHPR, Comm. No. 266/03 (2009).

58 Ibid. paragraph 105.

State also argued that it had introduced several measures to mitigate any negative impact the implementation of the Treaty might have on the people of Southern Cameroon. These include the translation of the OHADA laws into English and the training of anglophone and francophone judicial officers on the laws of OHADA.

The Commission was particularly persuaded by the measures that Cameroon put in place to address the discriminatory effects of the ratification of OHADA on the people of Southern Cameroon. According to the Commission, had those measures not been put in place, the Commission would be inclined to find a violation of Article 2. According to the Commission,

> The mere accession or ratification of OHADA should not be deemed a violation of Article 2, unless the Respondent State had manifestly failed to take any steps to ameliorate the effects of the linguistic differences. The Respondent State has shown that it took measures, such as the training of magistrates, and translation of texts to address the discriminatory concerns.

Notably, the Commission found that the ratification of OHADA has led to discrimination against companies and businesses in Southern Cameroon. This finding was made based on evidence placed before the Commission that companies and businesses could not open bank accounts unless they registered under OHADA law and translated their basic documents into French. The evidence was not challenged by Cameroon, and Cameroon did not show that it had taken any measure to address this issue. According to the Commission,

> Notwithstanding the translation of OHADA into English, it was wrong for institutions such as banks to force Southern Cameroon-based companies to change their basic documents into French. The banks and other institutions could have dealt with the companies without imposing the language conditionality. Banking documents should have been translated into English. The Commission finds that the Respondent State failed to address the concerns of Southern Cameroonian businesses, which were forced to re-register under OHADA, and as such violated Article 2 of the African Charter.[59]

A major significance of the finding of discrimination is that it indirectly demonstrates the superiority of AU law to OHADA law. Although OHADA law is superior to the laws of Member States and cannot be contradicted by domestic law, its application must be consistent with AU legal instruments such as the African Charter.

59 Ibid. paragraph 108.

Conclusions

Despite the longstanding recognition that the harmonisation of business norms and standards is a necessary prerequisite for development in the African continent, limited progress has been made to date. Several factors militate against the integration of business and economic laws in Africa. The strong economic nationalism among Member States following independence from colonial rule still lingers. The differences in linguistic, political, legal and administrative systems also pose significant challenges to integration. The existence of border conflicts, linguistic rivalries (especially between English and French regions), compounded by racial suspicion, also hamper economic integration.[60] The Abuja Treaty sets out a bold agenda for the continent in the economic sphere, with the ultimate aim of achieving a continent-wide economic community. The strategy of engaging eight selected RECs as building blocks to achieve the integration objective has led to some notable progress in areas such as trade and tariffs, currency unification and monetary union, and freedom of movement. However, the pace of progress has been slow and patchy. Nonetheless, the progress made by OHADA in introducing supranational norms and implementing the norms in its Member States is evidence that the aim of the Abuja Treaty and, indeed, the AU, is achievable in the long run.

60 *Supra*, Ndulo, 101, 118.

6 Peace, security, the rule of law and African Union law

Introduction

This chapter discusses the AU legal framework for ensuring peace, security and respect for rule of law in Member States and across the continent. The chapter will be less focused on the political and historical aspects of these issues, which have been widely covered in the literature over the years.[1] The long history of dictatorships, authoritarian governments and conflicts in many Member States have caused the AU to prioritise the areas of rule of law, peace and security in its legal order. This focus is also necessary because critical issues such as economic development and human rights cannot be properly addressed without sustained peace, security and rule of law. There is recognition that these areas are crucial to the overall success of the legal order emerging from closer integration in the African Union. The steps taken to improve peace, security and the rule of law have led to the emergence of new norms and standards with significant implications for Member States. These norms and standards are reflected in major instruments of the AU. The main norms in this respect include the norm of non-indifference, democratic constitutionalism, human rights, right to protect and prevention of unconstitutional change of government. The chapter also discusses the significant role of the African Peace and Security Architecture (APSA) in this context.[2] The APSA provides the broad legal basis for AU involvement in peace building and post-conflict reconstruction across the continent.

Background: the OAU and the non-interference norm

As stated in Chapter 2, the predecessor organisation to the AU, the OAU, was established with the aim of safeguarding African States' interests in the process

1 See, for example, A. Jeng, *Peacebuilding in the African Union: Law, Philosophy and Practice* (Cambridge University Press, 2012); I. Badmus, *The African Union's Role in Peacekeeping: Building on Lessons Learned from Security Operations* (Palgrave Macmillan, 2015); P. Williams, 'The peace and security council of the African union: evaluating an embryonic international institution', (2009) 47 (4) *The Journal of Modern African Studies* 603; A. Abass (ed.) *Protecting Human Security in Africa* (Oxford University Press, 2010).

2 See, generally, A. Lins de Albuquerque, *The African Peace and Security Architecture (APSA) – Discussing the Remaining Challenges* (FOI, 2016).

of independence by promoting unity of purpose and the complete elimination of colonialism in Africa. This was necessitated by the post-1945 legal order, which 'obligated the OAU to be structured upon the principles of sovereignty, non-interference and territorial integrity'.[3] Understandably, and because of its limited purpose, the OAU adopted the principle of non-interference in the internal affairs of Member States and respecting the sovereignty of each Member State. The OAU, therefore, had severely limited scope to scrutinise or challenge Member States' internal policies or activities that might pose threats to peace, law and order in its early days.[4]

Frequent conflicts since the achievement of independence and, in particular, the genocidal war in Burundi and Rwanda between 1993 and 1994, challenged the OAU's approach to peace and security.[5] Nonetheless, the OAU continued to define its priority as mainly conflict prevention due to its fundamental norm of non-interference and because it saw the United Nations as having the primary responsibility for peace and peacekeeping globally.[6] However, this position became increasingly untenable, as the UN was reluctant to take the lead in resolving major African conflicts. The regional economic communities (RECs) had to take up responsibility for intervening in these conflicts. For instance, in conflict situations in Liberia, Sierra Leone and Guinea-Bissau, the Economic Community of West African States (ECOWAS) had to take responsibility for responding to the conflicts. A similar approach was taken by the Southern African Development Community (SADC) in relation to the conflicts in Lesotho and the Democratic Republic of the Congo (DRC) in 1988.[7]

This is not to say that the OAU had no impact on the evolution of the AU legal order on peace and security. It has been argued that the OAU's main contribution was in setting general and broad norms and standards on peace and security, but it was ineffective in clarifying and enforcing them.[8] However, ironically, the OAU's most fundamental norm was the norm of non-interference in Member States' affairs. As noted earlier, the non-interference norm hindered the OAU's ability to be proactive in activities that may impact Member States. Some of the OAU's significant standard-setting instruments include the Convention

3 *Supra*, Jeng, 180.

4 U. O. Umozurike, 'The Domestic Jurisdiction clause in the OAU Charter', (1979) 78 (311) *African Affairs* 197–202, 205–209 (examining the foundation of the OAU's non-interference policies); P. D. Williams, 'From non-intervention to non-indifference: the origins and development of the African Union's security culture' (2007) 106 (423) *African Affairs* 252, 271 (the author observed that 'the [OAU's] traditional response to *coups d'etats* was official indifference').

5 P. D. Williams, 'The Peace and Security Council of the African Union: evaluating an embryonic international institution' (2009) 47 (4) *The Journal of Modern African Studies* 603–626.

6 United Nations, *Charter of the United Nations*, 24 October 1945, 1 UNTS XVI. Under Chapter VII of the UN Charter, the Security Council has primary responsibility for the maintenance of international peace and security.

7 *Supra*, Williams.

8 B. Moller, 'The African Union as security actor: African solutions to African problems?' *Crisis Working Papers Series No. 2* – Working Paper No. 57 (August 2009) 6.

for the Elimination of Mercenaries (1985), which was put in place in response to the involvement of foreign mercenaries and private companies in wars in Africa;[9] the OAU Declaration on the Political and Socio-economic Situation in Africa and the Fundamental Changes (1990);[10] the African Nuclear Weapon Free Zone Treaty – The Pelinda Treaty (2009);[11] the Bamako Common Africa position on Small Arms (2000);[12] and the Convention on the Prevention and Combating of Terrorism (2002).[13] Apart from standard and norm setting, the OAU also attempted to improve its conflict prevention and management capacity, although with little effect (see the discussion on the OAU Mechanism for Conflict Prevention, Management and Resolution below). In this regard, it engaged in a limited number of military peace-keeping activities with minimal impact.

Arguably, an area where the OAU had some impact is in relation to responding to military coups and violent changes of government. In its later years, the OAU showed a willingness to condemn and challenge unconstitutional changes of government in Member States.[14] For example, although the OAU charter did not contain specific provisions to enable the OAU to promote democracy, at its Thirty-Fifth Ordinary Session it decided to condemn the coup d'état in Sierra Leone in 1997 and encouraged its Member States to refrain from recognising the military regime.[15] Moreover, in 1999, in its 'Algiers Decision', the OAU demonstrated its evolving attitude towards unconstitutional change of government by referring to international standards on democracy and calling for the restoration of constitutional order in all Member States.[16] However, the OAU failed to put in

9 Organisation of African Unity, *OAU Convention for the Elimination of Mercenarism in Africa*, 3 July 1977, CM/817 (XXIX) Annex II Rev. 1, available at: https://au.int/sites/default/files/treaties/7768-treaty-0009_-_oau_convention_for_the_elimination_of_mercenarism_in_africa_e.pdf, accessed 25 November 2017.

10 *Declaration on the Political and Socio-Economic Situation in Africa and the Fundamental Changes Taking Place in the World* (OAU Doc. AHG/Decl.1 (XXVI)), adopted at the 26th Ordinary Session of the Assembly of Heads of State and Government held in Addis Ababa, Ethiopia, 11 July 1990.

11 African Union, *African Nuclear-Weapon-Free Zone Treaty*, 11 April 1996, available at: https://au.int/sites/default/files/treaties/7777-treaty-0018_-_the_african_nuclear-weapon-free_zone_treaty_the_treaty_of_pelindaba_e.pdf, accessed 25 November 2017.

12 Organisation of African Unity, *Bamako Declaration on an African Common Position on the Illicit Proliferation, Circulation and Trafficking of Small Arms and Light Weapons* (2000), available at: https://2001-2009.state.gov/t/ac/csbm/rd/6691.htm, accessed 16 December 2017.

13 Organisation of African Unity, *OAU Convention on the Prevention and Combating of Terrorism*, 1 July 1999, available at: https://au.int/sites/default/files/treaties/7779-treaty-0020_-_oau_convention_on_the_prevention_and_combating_of_terrorism_e.pdf, accessed 25 November 2017.

14 R. Murray, *Human Rights in Africa: From the OAU to the African Union* (Cambridge University Press, 2004) 17–21, 78–79; K. O. Kufuor, 'The OAU and the recognition of governments in Africa: analyzing its practice and proposals for the future', (2011) 17 (2) *American University International Law Review* 369, 375; *supra*, Williams, 273.

15 Decision AHG/Dec.141 (XXXV), adopted during the Thirty-fifth Ordinary Session of the Assembly.

16 Available at: http://archive.au.int/collect/auassemb/import/English/AHG%20Decl%201-2%20XXXV_E.pdf, accessed 13 January 2018.

place any specific policy instrument or enforcement process to follow as standard response to unconstitutional change of government.[17] Apart from this, on many other peace and security challenges the OAU struggled to cope. The failure or lack of capacity of the OAU to respond adequately to these challenges was part of the reason why the AU and its legal order were established.

Ascertaining the legal and normative underpinnings of the AU legal order on peace and security: from the OAU to the AU

The legal underpinnings in the area of peace and security have emerged gradually over the years from the time of the OAU to the AU. The developments have taken various forms but are slowly coalescing into substantial, though not always coherent, standards. These underpinnings are found in a variety of instruments and pronouncements by the AU and its predecessor, the OAU. With regards to the OAU's contribution, a significant instrument is the 1990 OAU Declaration on the Political and Socio-economic Situation in Africa and the Fundamental Changes Taking Place in the World.[18] This declaration represented a significant landmark in the OAU's approach to democracy, peace and security, human rights and development within Africa, hitherto considered to be the exclusive preserve of Member States or the United Nations. The declaration emphasises that peace and security are preconditions for the achievement of other goals, such as development and democratisation. It noted that the continent would be unable to achieve its development objectives without sustained peace and stability in Africa. This declaration paved the way for the creation of the OAU Mechanism for Conflict Prevention, Management and Resolution in 1993 as the central OAU organ for peace and security.[19] The goals of the mechanism were to anticipate and prevent potential conflicts that could lead to war, undertake peace-making and peace-building efforts and to undertake peace-making and peace-building activities post conflict. However, there is a general consensus that the Mechanism achieved very little because of the limitations placed on it by the weak capacity of the OAU itself to address these issues.[20] This Mechanism was initially meant to

17 P. D. Williams, 'The African Union's emerging security culture: options for U.S. policymakers', CSIS Online Africa Policy Forum, July 2007; E. Y. Omorogbe, 'A club of incumbents? The African Union and coups d'état', (2011) 44 (1) *Vanderbilt Journal of Transnational Law* 123, 127.

18 *Declaration on the Political and Socio-Economic Situation in Africa and the Fundamental Changes Taking Place in the World* (OAU Doc. AHG/Decl.1 (XXVI)), adopted at the 26th Ordinary Session of the Assembly of Heads of State and Government held in Addis Ababa, Ethiopia, 11 July 1990.

19 M. Vogt and M. Muyangwa 'An assessment of the Mechanism, which was informed by the now completed OAU/IPA Joint Task Force on Peacemaking and Peacekeeping in Africa', (2000), available at: www.ipinst.org/wp-content/uploads/publications/oau_conflict_1993_2000.pdf, accessed 8 January 2018.

20 Ibid.

be incorporated into the AU framework as its peace and security organ. However, following a review, the decision was made to establish a new Peace and Security Council.[21] The transition from the OAU to the AU transformed the framework for the AU peace and security framework with the introduction of key legal and policy instruments, including the Constitutive Act of the African Union, the AU Protocol on the Establishment of the Peace and Security Council (PSC Protocol)[22] and the Common African Defense and Security Policy (CADSP).[23]

The CADSP, initiated by Nigeria, is one of the three projects, alongside Libya and Gaddafi's quest for pan-African Unity and South Africa's project for an African renaissance, that led to the creation of the AU itself.[24] The CADSP takes a holistic approach to the identification and elaboration of the concept of security in the African context. This approach is taken because of the complexities of the causes of conflict in the continent and the need to take a multi-pronged approach by emphasising 'human security, based not only on political values but also on social and economic imperatives'.[25] The human security dimension is significant because it is now embedded in the AU approach. From that perspective, according to the CADSP, poverty, inequitable distribution of resources and corruption are considered major threats to peace, security and stability in Africa. The principles and values underlying the CADSP therefore include the promotion of social justice to ensure balanced economic development. The social justice underpinning of the policy predates the CADSP. One of the building blocks of the policy is the Conference on Security, Stability, Development and Cooperation in Africa (CSSDCA)[26] security regime. The inspiration for the development of the regime can be traced to lessons learnt from the European experience at the Helsinki Conference on Security and Co-operation in Europe (CSCE).[27] Notably, the CSSDCA's commitment to social justice as part of the security regime is elaborated in the Memorandum of Understanding on Security, Stability, Development and Cooperation.[28] Therefore, although the CSSDCA's main focus is on security issues, it recognises the interdependence between development, peace, security,

21 African Union, *Protocol Relating to the Establishment of the Peace and Security Council of the African Union*, 9 July 2002, available at: www.peaceau.org/uploads/psc-protocol-en.pdf, accessed 16 December 2017.

22 Ibid.

23 Conference on Security, Stability, Development and Cooperation in Africa (CSSDCA) Solemn Declaration (AHG/Decl.4 (XXXVI), 2000.

24 *Supra*, Moller, 7.

25 Supra, African Union, *Protocol Relating to the Establishment of the Peace and Security Council*, 2002; African Union, *Solemn Declaration on the African Common Defence and Security Policy*, 2004; *supra*, Conference on Security, Stability, Development and Cooperation in Africa (CSSDCA).

26 Conference on Security, Stability, Development and Cooperation in Africa (CSSDCA) Solemn Declaration (AHG/Decl.4 (XXXVI), 2000.

27 Conference on Security and Co-operation in Europe (Final Act Helsinki 1975); see also D. J. Galbreath, *The Organization for Security and Co-operation in Europe* (OSCE) (Routledge, 2007).

28 Decision on the Conference on Security, Stability, Development and Cooperation (CSSDCA) AHG/DEC. 175 (xxxviii).

human rights and democracy.[29] The key significance of the CADSP is in setting the tone for the norms and standards on peace and security by anchoring it on the idea of human security.

African Peace and Security Architecture (APSA) and its role in norm creation

The APSA is the umbrella term for the AU's main mechanism for promoting peace and security in Africa.[30] As Berhe correctly observed, the APSA combines the norms and structures that are at the foundation of the AU's approach to peace and security.[31] The APSA has two interconnected layers. The first layer comprises its constituent institutions, which include the Peace and Security Council, the Panel of the Wise, the Continental Early Warning System, the African Standby Force, the African Capacity for Immediate Response to Crises and the Peace Fund. The African Union Commission, through its chairperson, assisted by the AU Commissioner for Peace and Security, also plays a significant role in this regard. The second layer comprises the eight regional economic communities (RECs) recognised by the AU and two regional mechanisms (RMs) that play important roles in the achievement of APSA objectives.[32] In relation to the second layer, the rules governing the relationship between the AU's APSA and the regional bodies is codified in the Constitutive Act, the PSC Protocol and an MOU: Memorandum of Understanding on Cooperation in the Area of Peace and Security between the AU, RECs and the Coordinating Mechanisms of the Regional Standby Brigades of Eastern and North Africa.[33] The Abuja Treaty establishing the African Economic Community also made reference to the relationships.[34]

Article 16 (1) of the PSC Protocol states that the AU has 'the primary responsibility for promoting peace, security and stability in Africa' and also states that the modalities of the partnership between AU institutions and regional mechanisms shall be determined by the comparative advantage of each and the prevailing circumstances. It is further provided in the MOU that the partnership should be exercised in accordance with the principles of subsidiarity, complementarity and comparative advantage.[35] However, these principles were not expatiated upon

29 W. Zartman, 'Security, stability, development and cooperation in Africa: a regional expression of a global policy network in formation', (2002) *The Johns Hopkins University*; African Union, *Solemn Declaration on the Conference on Security, Stability, Development and Co-operation in Africa (CSSDCA)* (Doc. AHG/Decl.4 (XXXVI)), Lomé: African Union, 10–12 July 2000.

30 *Supra*, Lins de Albuquerque, 7.

31 M. G. Berhe, 'The norms and structures for African peace efforts: The African Peace and Security Architecture', (2017) 24 (4) *International Peacekeeping* 661.

32 *Supra*, Lins de Albuquerque, 7–8.

33 *Memorandum of Understanding (MOU) on Cooperation in the Area of Peace and Security between the AU, RECs and the Coordinating Mechanisms of the Regional Standby Brigades of Eastern and North Africa*, available at: www.peaceau.org/uploads/mou-au-rec-eng.pdf, accessed 16 December 2017.

34 Articles 4 and 6.

35 *Supra*, MOU, Article IV.

in the MOU. Nevertheless, the consensus among scholars on the implication of the provision is that conflict should be dealt with at the regional level in the first instance by relevant REC or RMs. If that option is not feasible or possible, then the AU's institutions will have the responsibility to act.[36] The rationale behind this thinking is the fact that REC/RMs are closer in proximity to conflicts and may have a better understanding of the background and context of situations. This possibility thus places them at a better comparative advantage in dealing with the situation than the continental body. However, the problem with the provisions here is in relation to how the process is triggered and administered. There are two pertinent questions that remain ambiguous. In a situation of conflict, do the regional organisations have the independent mandate to act or do they require authorisation or consent from the AU? Furthermore, does the AU have the authority to determine the modus operandi of regional institutions in the deployment of military or other personnel? It has been argued that, based on Article XX of the MOU, AU authorisation is needed before the regional mechanisms can be utilised in peace operations.[37] This, it is argued, would follow a similar pattern to the AU relationship with the UN Security Council, which requires such authorisation by the UN at the international level. Even though Article 16(1) of the PSC Protocol states that the AU has 'the primary responsibility for promoting peace, security and stability in Africa', Article 17(1) of the Protocol acknowledges that the UN Security Council 'has the primacy of authority for international peace and security'.[38] In addition, the PSC 2005 Roadmap states that 'the AU will seek UN Security Council authorisation of its enforcement actions'.[39] However, there is no consensus on this issue, hence the potential for tension between the AU and the regional mechanisms in this area.[40]

The Peace and Security Council (PSC) is central to the AU legal framework for peace and security. The PSC was established by the Protocol Relating to the Peace and Security Council of the African Union (the PSC Protocol).[41] It should be borne in mind that the PSC Protocol itself was adopted under the power conferred on the AU Assembly in Article 5(2) of the Constitutive Act to establish other organs in addition to those mentioned in the Act. The PSC is the highest authority and a standing organ of the AU charged with the prevention, management and resolution of conflicts. The framework was put in place as a direct

36 See *supra*, Lins de Albuquerque, 24; Laurie Nathan *et al.*, *African Peace and Security Architecture (APSA) 2014 Assessment Study Final Report* (FOI, The Total Defense Research Institute (name translated from Swedish) 16 April 2015).

37 *Supra*, Lins de Albuquerque, 25.

38 *Supra*, United Nations, Chapter VII; J. I. Levitt, 'The Peace and Security Council of the African Union: The known unknowns', (2003) 13 (1) *Transnational Law & Contemporary Problems* 110.

39 African Union, *Roadmap for the Operationalization of the African Standby Force*, experts' meeting on the relationship between the AU and the Regional Mechanisms for Conflict Prevention, Management and Resolution, Addis Ababa, AU doc.EXP/AU-RECS/ASF/4(i).

40 *Supra*, Lins de Albuquerque, 26.

41 Available at: https://au.int/en/treaties/protocol-relating-establishment-peace-and-security-council-african-union, accessed 16 December 2017.

response to conflicts and, in particular, the genocide that occurred in parts of the continent in the 1990s. Its structure is modelled loosely on the UN Security Council. As stated previously, the PSC, working with other regional arrangements, has the remit to promote peace, security and stability in the AU.[42] The PSC's core functions include the conduct of early warning and preventive diplomacy, facilitation of peace-making activities, establishment of peace-supporting activities and, in certain situations, recommendation of intervention in Member States' internal affairs in order to promote peace, security and stability. In addition, the PSC also works to support peace-building and post-conflict reconstruction, humanitarian actions and disaster management.[43] However, it is important to emphasise that its main legal power is the ability to recommend intervention in a Member State's internal affairs under Article 4 of the Constitutive Act.

'Non-indifference' norm

From a strictly legal standpoint the Constitutive Act is fundamental to the AU legal order. It has been suggested that the African Union's peace and security framework, as framed under the Constitutive Act, is embedded in three distinct but organically interrelated paradigms.[44] These are, first, the 'non-indifference' concept in Article 4, second, norm formulation and, third, social integration and interdependence. According to Jeng, these principles are derived from the Constitutive Act's transformative and peace-building approaches.[45] The norm formulation paradigm underscores the promotion of common values that are considered important for common identity and for advancing collective interest, as discussed in Chapter 2. The social integration and interdependence paradigm relates to steps put in place to deepen integration and to make recourse to conflicts less attractive, similar to the EU experience. However, from the legal perspective, the non-indifference concept in Article 4 of the Constitutive Act is the most important paradigm. According to Jeng,

> The codification of Article 4 as a template in the 'law' of the African Union is, in this sense, a reflection of past institutional and normative inadequacies and an expressed intention to depart from them. Perhaps nothing less could have been expected from an organisation that envisions an integrated Africa.[46]

The Constitutive Act provides a list of fundamental principles in Article 4 that includes respect for democratic principles, human rights, the rule of law and good

42 A. Abass, *Regional Organisations and the Development of Collective Security: Beyond Chapter VIII of the UN Charter* (Hart Publishing, 2004).
43 See, generally, Article 7 PSC Protocol.
44 *Supra*, Jeng, 182.
45 Ibid.
46 *Supra*, Jeng, 182.

governance, the condemnation and rejection of impunity and political assassination and the rejection of unconstitutional change of government. The scope of Article 4 was widened by a Protocol amending the Act in 2003.[47] Under Article 4(h), the AU has the power to intervene in a Member State's affairs and use force if necessary in 'grave circumstances', such as war crimes, genocide and crimes against humanity. In theory, this provision enables the AU to unilaterally use force to address unconstitutional change of government if the act leading to the change or its consequences involve war crimes, crimes against humanity or genocide. The Protocol mentioned above expanded the scenario to include serious threat to legitimate order in a Member State and the need to restore peace and stability to the Member State upon the recommendation of the AU's Peace and Security Council. This expansion, while generally welcomed, has been criticised by several scholars for its broadness.[48] Nonetheless, Article 4(h) as amended shows that by the adoption and subsequent ratification of the Constitutive Act, Member States have willingly surrendered certain sovereign powers to the AU.[49] The means and methods of implementation appear to be left to the AU under the Act. The ceding of sovereignty in this area is one of the strongest indications of the emerging *aquis* in the continent that underpins the non-indifference approach in the new legal order.

In addition to Article 4(h), Article 4(j) gives AU Member States the ability to request AU intervention 'to restore peace and security'. The implication of this provision is that a Member State's government can, on its own volition, request intervention in its internal affairs in the event of an unconstitutional change of government. These provisions reinforce the objectives of the AU, as stated in Article 3 of the constitution, which include political cooperation, promotion and protection of human rights and commitment to democratic values.

As a side note, the extensive legal powers vested in the AU prima facie may conflict with the powers of the UN Security Council to authorise military action to restore peace and security at the international level. However, as Jeng correctly argued, this is not necessarily so. According to Jeng,

> the legal basis for the Constitutive Act could be situated in Article 52 of the UN Charter. The provision empowers regional organisations to perform functions of a peace enforcement nature. To the extent that the Constitutive Act is a product of a multilateral treaty, with Article 4 intervention seeking the kind of regional peace and stability alluded to in the UN Charter, it falls outside the remit of Article 53(1) of the Charter. This prevails so far so far as the pertinent multilateral treaty was freely negotiated and adopted by state parties.[50]

47 *Protocol on the Amendment to the Constitutive Act of the African Union*, Maputo, Mozambique, 11 July 2003.

48 E. Baimu and K. Sturman, 'Amendment to the African Union's right to intervene: a shift from human security to regime security' (2003) 12 (2) *African Security Review* 37, 42.

49 *Supra*, Jeng, 182.

50 Ibid, 182–184.

Norm on unconstitutional change of government

Closely linked to the above is the norm on unconstitutional change of government. This norm is one of the major normative developments under the AU legal order. The evolution of the norm has a direct link with the AU and its predecessor, the OAU, and their concern for the threat posed by unconstitutional change of government (UCG) to peace and security in the continent. Historically, UCG is perceived as a threat to peace and security and, likewise, a threat to the rule of law across the continent. For instance, there were 88 successful military coups in Africa between 1952 and 2012, which created instabilities in several Member States.[51] As correctly observed by Dersso, the norm on unconstitutional change of government distinguished the AU peace and security order from similar regional and international peace and security arrangements[52] because of the high degree of interventionary power it accorded the AU and its relevant institutions. As Dresso observed, 'the norm on UCG expresses a normative position for defending efforts at establishing and upholding democratic rule from the threat of military coups or other illegal change or seizure of power'.[53] Because of the link between unconstitutional change of government and peace and security, the norm is conceptualised as a peace and security instrument.

The ban on unconstitutional change of government emerged from the collective architecture of the AU peace and security framework. It is predicated on the AU's broad definition of 'peace and security'. The Lomé Declaration is fundamental in this context.[54] Its preamble states that UCG is a threat to peace and security and 'constitutes a very disturbing trend and serious setback to the ongoing process of democratisation in the Continent'.[55] Under the Lomé Declaration, UCG is defined to include military coup d'état against a democratically elected government, intervention by mercenaries to replace a democratically elected government, replacement of democratically elected governments by armed dissident groups and rebel movements, and the refusal by an incumbent government to relinquish power to the winning party after free, fair and regular elections. The definition was expanded by the African Charter on Democracy, Elections and Governance in 2007, in Article 25(5), to include '[a]ny amendment or revision of the constitution or legal instruments, which is an infringement on the principles of democratic change of government'.[56] More recently, unconstitutional change of government has been designated a crime and included as one of the

51 I. K. Souare, 'The African Union as a norm entrepreneur on military coups d'etat in Africa (1952–2012): an empirical assessment', (2014) 52 (1) *Journal of Modern African Studies* 69.

52 S. A. Dersso, 'Defending constitutional rule as a peacemaking enterprise: the case of the AU's ban of unconstitutional changes of government', (2017) 24 (4) *International Peacekeeping* 639.

53 Ibid. 640.

54 Lomé Declaration of July 2000 on the framework for an OAU response to unconstitutional changes of government (AHG/Decl.5 (XXXVI).

55 Ibid.

56 African Union, *African Charter on Democracy, Elections and Governance* (2007), available at: www.achpr.org/instruments/charter-democracy, accessed 16 December 2017.

crimes over which the African Court of Justice and Human Rights has jurisdiction.[57] Article 28E(f) of the Malabo Protocol also added to the definition by providing that unconstitutional change of government includes '[a]ny substantial modification to the electoral laws in the last six (6) months before the elections without the consent of the majority of the political actors'.[58]

The norm not only bans unconstitutional change of government but, significantly, it is also supported by an enforcement regime that has constitutional status because it is contained in the AU Constitutive Act. The norm has played a significant role in the decline of the practice of unconstitutional change of government in the continent in recent years. It is notable that the enforcement of the norm has achieved a level of consistency over the years.[59] As discussed in Chapter 3, the AU Constitutive Act provides for the imposition of sanctions against a Member State whose de facto 'government' has assumed office through unconstitutional means.[60] Furthermore, according to Article 23(2), a Member State's failure to comply with decisions and policies of the AU may lead to imposition of sanctions such as denial of transport and communication links and other political and economic measures. The economic dimension is important because, as discussed in Chapter 5, economic integration, especially at the regional level, has somewhat advanced in recent times. It has been correctly observed that this approach represents a significant move away from the practice of non-interference under the OAU to the non-indifference norm of the AU.[61] The provisions underscore the strengthening of the legal framework of the emergent AU legal order.

It is also worth noting that in 2009 the PSC adopted the Ezulwini Framework for the Enhancement of the Implementation of Measures of the African Union in Situations of Unconstitutional Change of Government in Africa.[62] This framework included the decision to create a sanctions committee for the AU aimed at monitoring implementation of the PSC's sanctions policy.[63] However, despite this, the AU's capacity to monitor compliance of sanctions remains limited, and its record of imposing sanctions is largely restricted to 'medium-sized' States found to have violated the norm.[64]

57 *Protocol on Amendments to the Protocol on the Statute of the African Court of Justice and Human Rights* (Malabo Protocol) available at https://au.int/en/treaties/protocol-amendments-protocol-statute-african-court-justice-and-human-rights, accessed 16 May 2018.

58 Ibid.

59 *Supra*, Dersso, 639.

60 Article 30.

61 *Supra*, Jeng, 183.

62 Peace and Security Council, *Ezulwini Framework for the Enhancement of the Implementation of Measures of the African Union in Situations of Unconstitutional Changes of Government in Africa*, PSC/PR/2(CCXIII)/Assembly/AU3XIV, 17–19 December 2009, available at: www.peaceau.org/en/article/ezulwini-framework-for-the-enhancement-of-the-implementation-of-measures-of-the-african-union-in-situations-of-unconstitutional-changes-of-government-in-africa-ezulwini-kingdom-of-swaziland-17-19-december-2009, accessed 16 December 2017.

63 Ibid.

64 S. Straus, 'Wars do end! Changing patterns of political violence in sub-Saharan Africa', (2012) 443 (111) *African Affairs* 179–201.

The PSC practice has been to impose measures and sanctions against any Member State in which a coup occurs, even if the Member State has not ratified the PSC Protocol. One such example is when the PSC imposed sanctions on Mauritania in 2005, even though it had not yet ratified the Protocol (Mauritania signed the Protocol in May 2003 and ratified it in July 2008). The PSC also imposed sanctions on Guinea in 2009 (Guinea signed the Treaty in July 2002 and ratified it in 2017).[65] It has also worked with RECs and the UN in addressing unconstitutional change of government. For example, following the unexpected coup d'état in Mali in March of 2012, in July of the same year the PSC authorised the regional organisation, the Economic Community of West African States (ECOWAS), to intervene and return governmental control to civilian rule.[66] The mandate of ECOWAS as authorised by the PSC set three main objectives: first, to ensure the security of the transitional institutions; second, the restructuring and reorganising of the Malian security and defence forces; and third, restoring state authority over the northern part of Mali and combating terrorism and criminal networks. These steps were taken in coordination with the United Nations. The United Nations Security Council Resolution (UNSCR) 2071 on Mali validated the presence of international forces in Mali.[67] Following this resolution, ECOWAS leaders agreed to deploy 3,300 soldiers, provided mainly by Nigeria, Niger and Burkina Faso, to Mali to intervene in the Member State.[68] The involvement of ECOWAS, one of the regional economic communities, shows the important role that RECs play in this context. At the moment the commitment of Member States to various RECs within their regions appears stronger than to the AU itself.[69]

Human rights as a norm

The importance of human rights standards and their fundamental significance in the AU legal orders are discussed in Chapters 7 and 8. In addition, the African Charter has an important provision that forms part of the legal underpinnings of AU law on peace and security. Article 23 of the Charter introduced the peoples' right to peace and security into the Africa legal order.[70] The article provides inter alia that '[a]ll peoples shall have the right to national and international peace and security'. The right applies at both the domestic national level and the international level. The African Commission has considered and

65 *Supra*, Omorogbe, 123, 127; *supra*, Williams (2009) 603.

66 African Union, *Strategic Concept for the Resolution of the Crises in Mali*, available at: www.peaceau.org/uploads/psc-strategic-concept-24-10.pdf, accessed 17 December 2017.

67 United Nations Security Council Resolution (UNSCR) 2071 was unanimously adopted on 12 October 2012.

68 A. Vines, 'A decade of African Peace and Security Architecture', (2013) 89 (1) *International Affairs*, 89–109.

69 A.-F. Musah, 'West Africa: governance and security in a changing region', *Africa Program Working Paper* (International Peace Institute, February 2009) 17–18, available at: www.ipinst.org/2009/02/west-africa-governance-and-security-in-a-changing-region, accessed 17 December 2017.

70 See Chapter 8.

applied Article 23 in its jurisprudence. The Commission found violations of the provision in *Malawi African Association and Others* v. *Mauritania*[71] and in *Democratic Republic of Congo* v. *Burundi, Rwanda, Uganda*[72] (these cases are discussed in Chapter 8). The African Commission held in the latter case that Article 23 is a mandated standard that Member States must observe and falls within the remit of the Commission to uphold.[73]

Responsibility to protect as an AU norm

The responsibility to protect norm has its roots in the report of the International Panel of Eminent Personalities (IPEP) set up by the OAU in the aftermath of the Rwanda genocide in 1994.[74] The report was the result of an independent inquiry conducted by an international panel. One of the key recommendations from the panel was stated in the following terms:

> Since Africa recognizes its own primary **responsibility to protect** the lives of its citizens, we call on: a) the OAU to establish appropriate structures to enable it to respond effectively to enforce the peace in conflict situations; and b) the international community to assist such endeavors by the OAU through financial, logistic, and capacity support. (Emphasis added.)

This concept is part of the driving force behind the continent's move from the norm of non-interference to the norm of non-indifference. This responsibility also informed the introduction of the right of the AU to intervene in Member States' affairs under Article 4(h) of the Constitutive Act. Furthermore, the Ezulwini Consensus, adopted in 2005, also acknowledged this responsibility as an integral part of the AU norm.[75] The norm is now globally acknowledged and has been adopted by international organisations such as the United Nations.

Democratic constitutionalism: the rule of law and good governance

Articles 4(m) and (p) of the Constitutive Act underscore the AU approach to the norm of democratic constitutionalism. Article 4(m) affirms the 'respect for democratic principles, human rights, the rule of law and good governance', and Article 4(p) supports the norm on unconstitutional change of government by

71 *Malawi African Association and Others* v. *Mauritania*, African Commission on Human and Peoples' Rights, Comm. Nos. 54/91, 61/91, 98/93, 164/97,196/97 and 210/98 (2000).

72 *Democratic Republic of Congo* v. *Burundi, Rwanda, Uganda*, 33rd Ordinary Session, 15–29 May 2003, Niamey, Niger.

73 Ibid. paragraph 68.

74 African Union, *Rwanda: The Preventable Genocide*, July 2000, available at: www.refworld.org/docid/4d1da8752.html, accessed 17 December 2017.

75 *Supra*, Peace and Security Council, *Ezulwini Framework*.

the ‘condemnation and rejection of unconstitutional changes of governments’. Article 4(p) has been used as the legal basis for the suspension of Member States for violation of the norm on unconstitutional change of government until constitutional order is restored, usually through transparent democratic elections.

Various other instruments, such as the African Charter on Human and Peoples’ Rights[76] and the AU Convention on Preventing and Combating Corruption,[77] also have provisions espousing democratic constitutionalism. Given the importance of the issues connected to the norm, the Member States decided to adopt a comprehensive instrument to govern this area. The African Charter on Democracy, Elections and Governance (ADC)[78] entered into force in 2012 and expands on the AU Constitutive Act. The Charter uniquely establishes democracy and peoples’ participation as fundamental rights of individual citizens. By adopting the Charter, the AU consolidated all past commitments made in relation to democracy and governance in one instrument. The objective of the charter is to change the political culture across the continent to one that allows for democratic, free and fair elections conducted fairly and transparently.

The main goal of the ADC is the encouragement and promotion of democracy, the rule of law and human rights in Africa.[79] The ADC is the first binding instrument adopted by Member States of the AU that attempts to comprehensively address all of the elements necessary for the establishment of liberal democracies in the continent. The ADC contains a number of provisions regarding unconstitutional change of government. As previously mentioned, it widens the scope of ‘unconstitutional change of government’ by providing that it includes any amendments to the constitution or legal instruments of a Member State infringing on the principles of democratic change of government.[80] It is notable that some Member States of the AU are reluctant to ratify the ADC because of the Charter’s expansive provisions regarding the promotion of democracy.[81] Despite this reluctance, the success of democracy in some Member States may serve as a model for uncommitted States going forward.[82] It is noteworthy that the African

76 OAU, *African Charter on Human and Peoples’ Rights*, 27 June 1981, CAB/LEG/67/3 rev. 5, 21 I.L.M. 58 (1982), available at: www.achpr.org/files/instruments/achpr/banjul_charter.pdf, accessed 24 November 2017.

77 African Union, *African Union Convention on Preventing and Combating Corruption*, 11 July 2003, Adopted by the 2nd Ordinary Session of the Assembly of the Union, Maputo, 11 July 2003. Entered into force on 5 August 2006.

78 African Union, *African Charter on Democracy, Elections and Governance* (2007), available at: www.achpr.org/instruments/charter-democracy, accessed 16 December 2017.

79 Ibid.

80 S.-A. Elvy, ‘Towards a new democratic Africa: the African Charter on Democracy, Elections and Governance’, (2013) 27 (1) *Emory International Law Review* 41, 43.

81 Ibid.

82 Ibid. See also M. Hilgers, ‘Evolution of political regime and evolution of popular political representations in Burkina Faso’, (2010) 4 (9) *African Journal of Political Science and International Relations* 350–359.

Court applied the provisions of the instrument in *The matter of Actions Pour la Protection des Droits de l'Homme (APDH)* v. *Republic of Côte D'Ivoire*.[83]

The New Partnership for Africa's Development (NEPAD) initiative is also worth mentioning in this context.[84] The NEPAD is an initiative of African leaders with the support of the European Union. It was established in 2001 by five principal founding member countries: South Africa, Nigeria, Algeria, Egypt and Senegal. The central goals of NEPAD are to promote peace, security and human rights and to foster the creation of democratic institutions throughout the African continent. Though, strictly speaking, it is an initiative outside of the AU legal order, it resonates with some of the core issues on security, rule of law and peacekeeping.[85] However, NEPAD is a non-binding instrument, and therefore Member States are not legally obligated to comply with the provisions of the NEPAD. This has remained a significant flaw in the design of the initiative.[86]

The members of NEPAD introduced a Declaration on Democracy, Political, Economic and Corporate Governance (Democracy Declaration) in 2002.[87] The NEPAD Democracy Declaration acknowledges that in order to achieve socio-economic development in Africa, the AU must promote democracy and good political governance in African states. The Declaration specifically reaffirms the AU's commitment to the promotion of democracy and the protection of human rights associated with democracy including, but not limited to, equality of all citizens before the law, the right to form and join political parties and trade unions, and the inalienable right of the individual to participate in free and fair elections.[88] Another outgrowth of NEPAD is the African Peer Review Mechanism (APRM), a voluntary self-governing instrument introduced by the AU Member States in 2003. The core mandate of the instrument is to drive conformity in governance values, code and standards, including in the spheres of peace, security and rule of law. The mechanism invites Member States to examine and assess each other's political and economic governance, assist each other in problem solving and encourage the adoption of better practices.

83 *The matter of Actions Pour la Protection des droits de l'Homme (APDH)* v. *Republic of Côte D'Ivoire*, Application 001/2014 (2016).

84 African Union, *New Partnership for Africa's Development*, 9–11 July 2001, AHG/Dec. 1–11 (XXXVII), AHG/Decl.1–2 (XXXVII), available at: http://archive.au.int/collect/auassemb/import/English/2001%20AHG%20Dec%20160-170%20(XXXVII)%20_E.pdf, accessed 26 November 2017.

85 *Supra*, Jeng, 191.

86 K. D. Magliveras and G. J. Naldi, *The African Union (AU)* (Wolters Kluwer, 2013) 93–327.

87 *Declaration on Democracy, Political, Economic and Corporate Governance*, Annex 1, O.A.U. Doc. AHG/235 (XXXVIII) (July 8 2002), available at: www.chr.up.ac.za/chr_old/hr_docs/arpm/docs/book2.pdf, accessed 17 December 2017.

88 See R. Ngamau, 'The role of NEPAD in African economic regulation and integration (2004) 10 *Law and Business Review of the Americas* 515, 520–521, 536; S. A. Djoyou Kamga, 'Human rights in Africa: prospects for the realisation of the right to development under the new partnership for Africa's development' 255–256 (June 2011) (LLD thesis, University of Pretoria), available at: https://repository.up.ac.za/handle/2263/25141,accessed 17 December 2017.

Another relevant instrument in this context is the African Convention on Preventing and Combating Corruption (Corruption Convention) of 2003.[89] Recognising that corruption is rampant within Member States and that it has seriously hindered the establishment of democratic institutions and economic development in African countries, Member States of the AU adopted the Corruption Convention.[90] The Convention establishes a number of principles aimed at combating corruption and promoting democracy in Africa. The Corruption Convention provides that Member States must: condemn and reject acts of corruption; respect human rights, as well as democratic principles and institutions; and ensure socio-economic development by promoting social justice.[91] Some of the key provisions of the Convention guarantee access to information and participation of civil society and the media in monitoring the implementation of the Convention. Remarkably, the Convention makes illegal the use of funds acquired through illicit and corrupt practices for political party financing in Member States. Similar to the ADC, as a legal instrument, the provisions of the Convention are mandatory and binding on Member States that have ratified it.

It is noteworthy that the Convention brings the private sector, including foreign companies, within its remit. The AU recognised that corrupt practices in the private sector have socio-economic consequences for society and may, for instance, lead to violations of human rights.[92] The AU has therefore used the opportunity provided by the Convention to address this problem. Article 1 defines the 'Private Sector' as 'the sector of a national economy under private ownership in which the allocation of productive resources is controlled by market forces, rather than public authorities and other sectors of the economy not under the public sector or government'. This definition includes all kinds of private entities such as partnerships, small to medium enterprises and multinational corporations.[93] The provisions in Articles 1, 4(1) (e) and (f) and 11 directly place responsibility on States to regulate the activities of corporations in the areas covered by the Convention. In particular, Article 11 provides that

> State Parties undertake to:
>
> 1 Adopt legislative and other measures to prevent and combat acts of corruption and related offences committed in and by agents of the **private sector**.

89 African Union, *African Union Convention on Preventing and Combating Corruption*, 11 July 2003, adopted by the 2nd Ordinary Session of the Assembly of the Union, Maputo, 11 July 2003. Entered into force on 5 August 2006.

90 Ibid.

91 Ibid. Article 3.

92 O. Amao, *Corporate Social Responsibility, Human Rights and the Law: Multinational Corporations in Developing Countries* (Routledge Taylor & Francis, 2011).

93 I. Carr, 'Corruption in Africa: is the African Union Convention on Combating Corruption the answer?' (2007) 2 *Journal of Business Law* 111.

2 Establish mechanisms to encourage participation by **the private sector** in the fight against unfair competition, respect of the tender procedures and property rights.
3 Adopt such other measures as may be necessary to prevent **companies** from paying bribes to win tenders. (Emphasis added.)

The Convention provides for a follow-up mechanism in Article 22. The Article establishes an Advisory Board of 11 members elected by the AU Executive Council for a term of two years, renewable once. The board has a broad range of responsibilities. For instance, paragraph 5 (1) of the Article provides that the board shall 'collect information and analyse the conduct and behaviour of multi-national corporations operating in Africa and disseminate such information to national authorities designated under Article 18 (1) hereof'.[94] The board is required to submit a report to the Executive Council on a regular basis on the progress made by each State Party in complying with the provisions of the Convention.

Conclusions

The challenges to rule of law and democracy in the continent, as well as the recent increase in mobile insurgency, such as the activities of the Lord's Resistance Army, Al-Qaeda in the Islamic Maghreb, Al-Shabaab and Boko Haram and continuing separatist group activities in Senegal, Libya, Angola and Mali,[95] make it imperative for the AU and its legal order to robustly address the issues of peace and security to effectively respond to the challenges and foster stability in the continent. This chapter has shown that steps taken to date have led to the development of notable norms. Significantly, the AU has moved away from the OAU's non-interference norm to the non-indifference norm. Furthermore, the AU facilitated the emergence of new norms, including the norms on unconstitutional change of government, human rights, the right to protect and democratic constitutionalism. In the future the focus of the AU should be on expatiating on these norms and ensuring their effective implementation and application across the continent.

94 Article 18 (1) of the AU Convention provides as follows:

> In accordance with their domestic laws and applicable treaties, State Parties shall provide each other with the greatest possible technical cooperation and assistance in dealing immediately with requests from authorities that are empowered by virtue of their national laws to prevent, detect, investigate and punish acts of corruption and related offences.

95 I. Salehyan, *Rebels without Borders: Transnational Insurgencies in World Politics* (Cornell University Press, 2009).

7 Human rights in African Union law

Introduction

In its history the African continent has faced enormous challenges in the protection and promotion of human rights. The continent has had to deal with problematic issues on an ongoing basis. These include protracted and catastrophic civil wars, interstate conflicts, ethnic cleansing, coup d'états, corruption of immense proportions, chaotic elections, toxic waste dumping, famine, diseases, child labour and the like. The current situations in Sudan, Somalia, Democratic Republic of Congo, Northern Nigeria and Zimbabwe are glaring examples. The causes of human rights violations are multifarious and are linked to issues relating to peace, security and rule of law discussed in the previous chapter. The causes include: contemporary forms of slavery, neo-colonialism, racism, religious intolerance, poverty, conflicts, mismanagement, bad governance, corruption, monopoly of power, lack of judicial and press autonomy, environmental degradation, terrorism and nepotism. It is therefore not surprising that human rights issues have been very prominent in the development of African Union institutions and its emerging legal order.[1] The African Charter on Human and Peoples' Rights[2] (African Charter) is at the heart of the human rights norms in the African Union legal order. There are other instruments created within Africa before and after the African Charter that have relevance to human rights. These include: the Convention on Specific Aspects of the Refugee Problems in Africa;[3] the African Charter on the Rights and Welfare of the Child;[4] the Protocol on the

1 See generally O. Amao, 'The African regional human rights system', in M. A. Baderin and M. Ssenyonjo (eds), *International Human Rights Law: Six Decades after the UDHR and Beyond* (Ashgate, 2010) 253–251; O. Amao, 'Civil and political rights in the African Charter', in M. Ssenyonjo (ed.), *The African Regional Human Rights System: 30 Years After the African Charter on Human and Peoples' Rights* (Martinus Nijhoff, 2011) 29–53.

2 *African Charter on Human and Peoples' Rights*, adopted 27 June 1981, entered into force on 21 October 1986, OAU Doc. CAB/LEG/67/3 Rev. 5.

3 *Convention on Specific Aspects of the Refugee Problem in Africa*, 1001 U.N.T.S. 45, entered into force 20 June 1974.

4 *African Charter on the Rights and Welfare of the Child*, OAU Doc. CAB/LEG/24.9/49 (1990), entered into force 29 November 1999.

Establishment of an African Court on Human and Peoples' Rights;[5] the Protocol to the African Charter on Human and Peoples' Rights on the Rights of Women in Africa;[6] and the Protocol on the Statute of the African Court of Justice and Human Rights.[7] To complement these are soft law instruments that are usually issued to address specific issues.

This chapter asserts that the human rights framework has led to the development of a unique approach to human rights issues within the African legal order. Furthermore, because of the coverage of the human rights instruments, innovations and application of the instruments, the African Union legal order has advanced significantly compared with other areas in the evolving legal system. As the initial quasi-judicial enforcement body, the African Commission on Human and Peoples' Rights (African Commission) jurisprudence played a significant role in shaping the development of the legal order.[8] However, it is important to point out at the outset that the written decisions of the Commission have been widely criticised for lack of depth. Nonetheless, the Commission has gradually improved on the depth of its analysis over the years. It is also worth noting the limited contribution of the African Court on Human and Peoples' Rights (African Court) to the jurisprudence so far.[9] The Court is relatively new and has delivered decisions in just 32 cases (at the time of writing), however only seven of these cases were decided on the merit. Nonetheless, the Court's establishment was significant because it marked a change from the quasi-judicial approach to the promotion and protection of human rights to a binding judicial process. Unlike the African Commission, the Court has the power to issue binding judgments on Member States.[10] It should also be noted that the Court did not entirely displace the Commission but was designed to complement the work of the Commission in the promotion and protection of human rights.

This chapter focuses on civil and political rights while the next chapter considers economic, social and cultural rights and group rights. In order to understand the minutiae of the developments in this area, this chapter and the next consider the substantive rights guaranteed under the Charter and the evolving jurisprudence on them.

5 *Protocol to the African Charter on Human and Peoples' Rights on the Establishment of an African Court on Human and Peoples' Rights*, 9 June 1998, OAU Doc. OAU/LEG/EXP/AFCHPR/PROT (III).

6 *Protocol to the African Charter on Human and Peoples' Rights on the Rights of Women in Africa*, adopted by the 2nd Ordinary Session of the Assembly of the Union, Maputo, CAB/LEG/66.6 (13 September 2000), entered into force 25 November 2005.

7 *Protocol on the Statute of the African Court of Justice and Human Rights*, adopted by the 11th Ordinary Session of the Assembly, held in Sharm El-Sheikh, Egypt, 1 July 2008.

8 R. Murray and D. Long, *The Implementation of the Findings of the African Commission on Human and Peoples' Rights* (Cambridge University Press, 2015) 112–115.

9 *Supra, Protocol to the African Charter on Human and Peoples' Rights on the Establishment of an African Court on Human and Peoples' Rights*, 1998.

10 Ibid. Preamble, Article 20; Rule 61 (5) *Rules of Court* (2010), available at: http://en.african-court.org/images/Protocol-Host%20Agrtmt/Final_Rules_of_Court_for_Publication_after_Harmonization_-_Final__English_7_sept_1_.pdf, accessed 29 November 2017.

The emergence of human rights in African legal order

The emergence of human rights in the African legal order can be traced back to the establishment of the Organisation of African Unity (OAU) and its approach to human rights. As stated previously, the OAU was established in 1963 with the main aims of fighting colonialism and apartheid.[11] Therefore, the OAU did not have to significantly engage with human right issues except and to a limited extent in the context of self-determination and apartheid in South Africa.[12] The lack of emphasis on human rights under the OAU was also partly due to the strong bias of Member States in favour of non-interference in other States' internal affairs. Nevertheless, the preamble of the OAU Charter makes specific reference to the Universal Declaration of Human Rights (UDHR). It asserts, *inter alia*, that OAU States are:

> [p]ersuaded that the Charter of the United Nations and the Universal Declaration of Human Rights, to the Principles of which we reaffirm our adherence, provide a solid foundation for peaceful and positive cooperation among States.

The OAU Charter further provides in Article 2 that the purpose of the OAU, among others, is to 'promote international cooperation, having due regard to the Charter of the United Nations and the Universal Declaration of Human Rights'. It is therefore not surprising that the UDHR was the main inspiration underlying the creation of the human rights system within the African legal order. Years after the OAU Charter was signed, African leaders started considering the possibility of adopting a specific convention on human rights in line with the Universal Declaration of Human Rights and the United Nations' Charter. This led to the introduction of the African Charter on Human and Peoples' Rights in 1981. The Charter has its independent Commission in Banjul, The Gambia. It is notable that the African Charter has some unique features that set it apart from other regional and international human rights instruments. These include the coverage of economic, social and cultural rights alongside civil and political rights, inclusion of third generation rights, inclusion of peoples' or groups rights and specific duties of individuals and States. These features have significant ramifications for the interpretation and application of the provisions of the Charter.

The AU Constitutive Act further changed the dynamic by bringing human rights firmly into the AU legal order. Under the Constitutive Act, the functions of the AU include securing the continent's democracy, protection of human rights and maintaining a sustainable economy. Furthermore, the objectives of the AU under the Act include the promotion of democratic principles

11 See the *Charter of the Organisation of African Unity*, adopted 25 May 1963, entered into force 13 September 1963, 479 U.N.T.S. 39.

12 A. Lloyd and R. Murray, 'Institutions with responsibility for human rights protection under the African Union', (2004) 48 (2) *Journal of African Law* 165, 166.

and institutions, popular participation and good governance and, most importantly in the context of this chapter, the promotion and protection of human rights.[13] The AU thus appears to have consolidated and advanced the framework for human rights promotion and protection in the continent by giving it constitutional status.

Distinctive features of African human rights law

The drafters of the African Charter were guided by the principle that the Charter 'should reflect the African conception of human rights and should take as a pattern the African philosophy of law and meet the needs of Africa'.[14] Therefore, there was a conscious effort to rationalise African perspectives on the relationship between the individual and society with existing international human rights standards. Udombana observed that the African Charter is as a consequence a fusion of elements of international law and African tradition. He stated that it is:

> more than just a matter of public international law or international customary law; it is a synthesis of universal and African elements. Its organising principle is the balance between tradition and modernity, not only between African tradition and the modernity of international law, but also between African modernity and the tradition of international law.[15]

As noted previously, significantly the Charter recognises not only civil and political rights but also socio-economic rights. It provides for the unconditional realisation of all rights recognised in the Charter unlike similar international human rights instruments. This approach emphasises the indivisibility of human rights and the importance of developmental issues within the African context.[16] The Charter does not allow for derogation or contain a derogation clause.[17] The African Commission has repeatedly held that the rights guaranteed under the Charter cannot be derogated from even in an emergency situation such as a civil war.[18] The only legitimate reasons for any limitations on the rights protected in the Charter are in the general provision in Article 27(2),

13 Article 3, *Constitutive Act of the African Union*, OAU Doc. CAB/LEG/23.15, entered into force 26 May 2001.

14 Meeting of Experts for the Preparation of the Draft African Charter of Human and Peoples' Rights, Dakar 28 November 1979, OAU CAB/LEG/67/3 Rev., 1.

15 J. Udombana, 'Between promise and performance: revisiting States' obligations under the African Human Rights Charter' (2004) 40 (1) *Stanford Journal of International Law* 105, 110.

16 C. Heynes and M. Killander, 'The African regional human rights system' in F. Gomez Isa and K. De Feyter, (eds), *International Protection of Human Rights: Achievements and Challenges* (University of Deusto, Bilbao, 2006) 507–516.

17 Media Rights Agenda, Constitutional Rights Project, *Media Rights Agenda and Constitutional Rights Project* v. *Nigeria*, Communication Nos. 105/93, 128/94, 130/94 & 152/96 (1999) 12th, paragraphs 68 and 69.

18 *Centre on Housing Rights and Evictions* v. *The Sudan*, Communication Nos. 279/03 & 296/05, African Commission on Human and Peoples' Rights (2009), paragraph 167.

which provides that the rights 'shall be exercised with due regard to the rights of others, collective security, morality and common interest'.[19]

A fascinating and progressive development is the creative expansion of the provisions of the charter by the African Commission in its decisions. For example, the Commission has interpreted the provisions of the Charter to include unenumerated rights. In *SERAC* v. *Nigeria*[20] the Commission contended that there are rights that are not explicitly mentioned in the Charter but that should be regarded as being implicitly included. Such rights identified in the *SERAC* case include the right to housing or shelter deduced from the provisions on health, property and family in the Charter.[21] The right to food was also deduced from the right to life, right to dignity, right to health and right to economic, social and cultural development.[22] Furthermore, the Commission affirmed in that case that all rights under the African Charter are enforceable, irrespective of whether the rights are civil and political rights or economic rights or unenumerated rights. Shelton observed in this regard:

> The Commission decision that all rights in the African Charter are enforceable and may be subject to the system's communication procedure advances the African system well ahead of other regional systems – which have moved tentatively toward allowing petitions for economic, social and cultural rights, and which only partially recognize a right to environment.[23]

Another significant feature of the African Charter is its introduction and recognition of 'peoples' rights'. Though the concept is not defined in the Charter it is generally understood to mean collective or group rights. The rights in this category include: equality of people (Article 19); the right of people to existence and self-determination, (Article 20); the right of people to freely dispose of their wealth and national resources (Article 21); the right to development (Article 22); the right to national and international peace and security (Article 32); and the right to 'a generally satisfactory environment' favourable to development (Article 24).

Furthermore, the Charter imposes correlative duties on individuals similar to other international human rights instruments and goes further to impose

19 *Constitutional Rights Project, Civil Liberties Organisation and Media Rights Agenda* v. *Nigeria*, Communications 140/94, 141/94, 145/95 (1999); *Sudan Human Rights Organisation* v. *The Sudan*, Communication No. 279/03 (2009); *supra, Centre on Housing Rights and Evictions* v. *The Sudan*, Communication 296/05 (2009).

20 *Social and Economic Rights Action Centre (SERAC) and The Centre for Economic and Social Rights (CESR)* v. *Nigeria* (2001), Communication No. 155/96 (2001), online: University of Minnesota Human Rights Library, available at: www1.umn.edu/humanrts/africa/comcases/155-96b.html, accessed 27 December 2017.

21 Articles 14, 16 and 18 of the African Charter. See also Paragraph 60 of *SERAC* v. *Nigeria* (*supra*).

22 Articles 4, 5, 16 and 22 of the *African Charter.*

23 D. Shelton, 'Decision regarding Communication 155/96 (*Social and Economic Rights Action Center/Center for Economic and Social Rights* v. *Nigeria*). Case No. ACHPR/Comm. A044/1', (2002) 96 (4) *American Society of International Law* 937, 942.

autonomous duties not connected with rights.[24] Perhaps more distinctive is the imposition of wider and specific duties upon Member States. These duties are contained in Articles 20, 21, 22, 25 and 26 of the African Charter. The duties include: duties to assist in liberation struggle, to eliminate foreign economic exploitation, to ensure the exercise of the right to development, to promote the rights and freedoms contained in the Charter, to guarantee the independence of courts and establish and improve national institutions entrusted with the promotion and protection of human rights.

A major drawback to the scope of the rights guaranteed in the Charter is the wide use of clawback clauses in many of the substantive provisions of the African Charter (Articles 6–14). Many of the clawback clauses subordinate the provisions of the Charter to Member States' laws and to the discretion of individual States in that they qualify the observance of the principles in the Charter under certain circumstances.[25] The use of these clauses has been widely criticised by human rights scholars.[26] It has been contended that even though 'the Charter contains no general derogation clause for suspension of rights during national emergencies, but such a clause might well be redundant, given the limitations that are otherwise permissible' through the inclusion of these clawback clauses.[27] However, the Commission in its jurisprudence has contained the effects of the use of clawback clauses by interpreting the provisions in the light of international human rights standards.[28] In other words, only restrictions on protected rights, which are consistent not only with the Charter but also with Member States' international obligations, would be permissible.[29]

It is also worth acknowledging that some commentators have contended that the African Charter's provisions are lacking in certain respects. These include inadequate or absence of provisions on freedom from slavery, freedom from compulsory or forced labour, the prohibition of the death penalty, marital rights and the right to privacy. While this may be true, it does not detract from the significant and major contribution that the African Charter has made to the evolvement of AU legal order. It is acknowledged that the evolving legal order is incremental but it has the potential to fill any potential gaps going forward.

24 The Preamble and Articles 27 through 29 of the African Charter recognise private duties. See also: *supra*, Udombana, 111.

25 C. M. Shaw, 'The evolution of regional human rights mechanisms. A focus on Africa', (2007) 6 (2) *Journal of Human Rights* 209, 214.

26 K. Hopkins, 'A new human rights era dawns on Africa?', (2003) 18 *South African Public Law* 349.

27 C. Flinterman and C. Henderson, 'The African Charter on Human Rights and Peoples' Rights', in R. Hanski and M. Suksi, (eds), *An Introduction to the International Protection of Human Rights: A Textbook* (Abo Akademi University, 1999) 390.

28 See, for example, *Amnesty International* v. *Zambia*, 12th Annual Activity Report, 1994–2001 compilation, IHRDA, Banjul, 2002, 371–382; *Civil Liberties Organization (in respect of Nigerian Bar Association)* v. *Nigeria*, 8th Annual Activity Report, 1994–2001 compilation, IHRDA, Banjul, 2002, 200–202; *Sir Dawda K Jawara* v. *The Gambia*, 13th Annual Activity Report, 1994–2001 compilation, IHRDA, Banjul, 2002, 108–121.

29 *Article 19* v. *Eritrea*, Communication 275/03 (2007).

The next section shows how complimentary instruments have filled some of the gaps in the Charter over the years.

Expanding the frontiers of rights under the law

Apart from the expansion of rights under the Charter through case law, there has also been a progressive expansion of the substantive provisions on rights protected in the African legal order through complementary instruments. For example, in the Charter, with the exception of Article 18(3), there is no special or specific provision for the rights of children. The African Charter on the Rights and Welfare of the Child (Children's Charter) was introduced to fill this gap. It provisions are very similar to the UN Convention on the Rights of the Child,[30] but in some instances the Children's Charter provides a higher level of protection for children. Similarly, the African Convention on the Ban on the Import into Africa and the Control of Transboundary Movement of Hazardous Waste in Africa (the Bamako Convention)[31] complements the provisions of the African Charter on the right to a generally satisfactory environment (Article 24), right to life (Article 4), right to security of a person (Article 6) and right to health (Article 16). The Convention was introduced to deal with the problem of toxic waste dumping in the continent, which is considered to infringe on the protected rights. The Convention strengthens the framework for the control of the movement of hazardous wastes within the continent.

African States also adopted the Protocol to the African Charter on Human and Peoples' Rights on the Rights of Women in Africa (Maputo Protocol) to expand the rights of women under the African Union legal order.[32] Some of the rights guaranteed under the Protocol can also be found in the African Charter. However, the Maputo Protocol is more comprehensive than the Charter and more specific to women's issues.[33] The rights in the protocol include: respect for dignity (Article 3); freedom from discrimination (Article 2); right to physical and emotional security (Article 4); right to participate in the political process (Article 9); right to peace (Article 10); economic and social welfare rights (Article 13); health and reproductive rights (Article 14); environmental rights (Article 18) and the right to sustainable development (Article 19). In addition, the Protocol introduces some new rights that were not contained in the African Charter. These include: governments' duty to integrate women's perspective in policy

30 *Convention on the Rights of the Child*, G.A. res. 44/25, annex, 44 U.N. GAOR Supp. (No. 49) at 167, U.N. Doc. A/44/49 (1989), entered into force 2 September 1990.

31 OAU, *Bamako Convention on the Ban of the Import into Africa and the Control of Transboundary Movement and Management of Hazardous Wastes within Africa*, 30 January 1991, U.N.T.S, Vol. 2101, 1-36508, available at: https://treaties.un.org/doc/Publication/UNTS/Volume%20 2101/v2101.pdf, accessed 25 November 2017.

32 *Protocol to the African Charter on Human and Peoples' Rights on the Rights of Women in Africa*, adopted by the 2nd Ordinary Session of the Assembly of the Union, Maputo, CAB/LEG/66.6 (13 September 2000), entered into force 25 November 2005.

33 The *African Charter* made specific reference to women only in Article 68.

development (Article 2); the rights of vulnerable groups of women including elderly women, widows, disabled women and women in distress (Articles 20, 21, 22 and 24); rights to food security and housing (Articles 15 and 16); the right to live in a positive cultural environment (Article 17); prohibition of female genital mutilation (Article 5); and the reproductive rights of women (Article 14). This expansion of rights in the AU legal order demonstrates the potential of the African legal order to respond to change and the specific needs of the continent.

The moulding of civil and political rights under the AU legal order

There have been significant developments in the AU legal order in respect of civil and political rights over the years. In its case law, the African Commission has dealt more with cases on civil and political rights compared with other categories of human rights. This is because articles relating to civil and political rights are more frequently invoked before the Commission by complainants. This has enabled the Commission to develop a comparatively reasonable jurisprudence on civil and political rights.[34] Furthermore, it is notable that in practice the human rights law has been invoked more in Sub-Saharan Africa in comparison with North Africa. This may partly be explained by the relatively slow pace of political reforms and the democratic process in North Africa.[35] However, the 'Arab awakening' appears to have changed the dynamics in North Africa to some extent in recent times.[36]

Article 1 of the African Charter is fundamental to all rights protected under the Charter because it not only requires the recognition of all the rights, duties and freedoms in the Charter but it also requires that Member States give effect to them. Consequently, the African Commission has interpreted the Article to the effect that the Charter is not just about what is done by a Member State but also about what it has failed or omitted to do. The implication of this approach is that if a Member State fails or neglects to ensure that the rights guaranteed under the Charter are realised (including under domestic law), the Member State may be held liable for violating the Charter.[37] In *Interights, Institute for Human Rights and Development in Africa, and Association Mauritanienne des Droits de l'Homme* v. *Islamic Republic of Mauritania*,[38] the Commission stated

34 M. Ssenyonjo, 'Economic, social and cultural rights in the African Charter', in M. Ssenyonjo, *The African Regional Human Rights System: 30 Years after the African Charter on Human and Peoples' Rights* (Martinus Nijhoff Publishers, 2012) 57.

35 L. Storm, 'The persistence of authoritarianism in North Africa' (2009) 85 (5) *International Affairs* 997–1013.

36 *In the Matter of African Commission on Human and People's Rights v. Great Socialist People's Libyan Arab Jamahiriya*, Application No. 004/2011.

37 *Commission Nationale des Droits de l'Homme et des Libertés* v. *Chad*, Communication No. 74/92, (1995–1996); *Interights, Institute for Human Rights and Development in Africa, and Association Mauritanienne des Droits de l'Homme* v. *Islamic Republic of Mauritania*, Communication 373/2009 (formerly 242/2001) (2010), paragraph 46.

38 Ibid. (*Interrights*).

that Article 1 imposes a general obligation on Member States to recognise the protected rights under the Charter and requires them to adopt measures to give effect to the rights. Therefore, finding a violation of any of the protected rights is held automatically to be a violation of Article 1.[39] A further legal implication of this approach to the interpretation of Article 1 is that it elevates the status of the Charter above the domestic law. Thus, domestic laws of Member States are required to be brought into conformity with the Charter.[40] Consequently, a Member State is not entitled to revoke measures taken to implement the provisions of the Charter.[41] The Commission has also held that a Member State has the obligation to ensure that the rights, duties and freedoms recognised under the Charter are observed by individuals and entities including private entities within its territory.[42]

Article 2 has been invoked in a number of cases before the commission. The article provides for the

> enjoyment of the rights and freedoms recognized and guaranteed in the . . . Charter without distinction of any kind such as race, ethnic group, color, sex, language, religion, political or any other opinion, national and social origin, fortune, birth or other status.

The Article was considered in *Rencontre Africaine pour la Défense des Droits de l'Homme* v. *Zambia*.[43] In that case the Commission considered whether the expulsion of West African nationals by the Zambian State contravened Article 2 of the African Charter. Zambia had expelled the individuals because they were allegedly living in Zambia illegally. *Prima facie*, the expulsion is contrary to the provision of Article 12 of the Charter, which prohibits mass expulsion of non-nationals. Paragraph 5 of Article 12 defines 'mass expulsion' as 'that which is aimed at national, racial, ethnic or religious groups'. Zambia argued that the African Charter did not remove the regulation of movement across national borders by Member States and the imposition of visa requirements. While the Commission agreed that the African Charter itself does not bar deportation, it ruled that the exercise of the power to deport cannot be exercised in a discriminatory manner. In the case the Commission was of the view that the manner of the expulsion was discriminatory against the expelled individuals because it was based on their nationality. The Commission therefore held that the Zambia State

39 This approach was at the heart of the Commission's decision in *Social and Economic Rights Action Centre (SERAC) and The Centre for Economic and Social Rights (CESR)* v. *Nigeria* (*supra*). In that case, the Nigerian government was found to have neglected its obligation to prevent violations of rights enshrined under the African Charter.

40 *Lawyers for Human Rights* v. *Swaziland*, Communication No. 251/2002 (2005).

41 *Civil Liberty Organization* v. *Nigeria*, Communication No. 129/94, (1995).

42 *Supra*, *Commission Nationale des Droits de l'Homme et des Libertés* v. *Chad*, 9.

43 *Rencontre Africaine pour la Défense des Droits de l'Homme* v. *Zambia*, Communication 71/92, (1995–1996).

violated Article 2 for not securing the rights of the individuals under the African Charter. A similar conclusion was reached in *Organisation Mondiale Contre La Torture* v. *Rwanda*.[44] In *The Nubian Community in Kenya* v. *The Republic of Kenya*[45] it was established that the Nubian ethnic group in Kenya was subjected to a lengthy humiliating and expensive vetting process in order to acquire a Kenyan National Identity document. The National Identity document was necessary for recognition of citizenship and access to public services. The consequence of the vetting process for the Kenyan Nubians was that they were significantly disadvantaged during the process of application and in the event that the identity document was lost. It was alleged that the reason why the Kenyan Nubians were treated differently was because of their ethnic and religious origin. According to the Commission:

> In the present Communication, the Complainants have established and submitted sufficient evidence to the effect that Kenyan Nubians are treated differently from other Kenyans in the acquisition of ID cards. They have outlined significant additional burdens that are imposed on them when they seek to acquire ID cards. In addition to being required to provide supporting documents, such as their grand-parents ID documents, which is not required of other indigenous Kenyan ethnic groups; Nubians must be vetted and approved by a Committee; they must swear an affidavit in support of their claim to an ID card before a Magistrate's Court and they are required to pay a fee to the Court.[46]

The Kenyan State appeared to have admitted to the allegations but argued that the vetting process was necessary to prevent an influx of people from neighbouring countries. The Commission rejected this argument and held that the treatment of the Kenyan Nubians by the State violated Articles 2 and 3 of the Charter.

The commission has also found a violation of Article 2 in the effect of the enactment of law by a Member State in *Purohit and Moore* v. *The Gambia*.[47] The complaint was that the Lunatics Detention Act of 1917 of The Gambia, which was the principal legislation on mental health in the Member State, was discriminatory. The contention was based on the argument that there were no review or appeal procedures for persons affected where a determination is made on their mental state. This, it was argued, made it possible for a person wrongfully assessed to be confined to a mental institution without the ability to request a reassessment. The commission found that the provision of the law 'fails to meet

44 *Organisation Mondiale Contre La Torture* v. *Rwanda*, African Commission on Human and Peoples' Rights, Communication Nos. 27/89, 46/91, 49/91, 99/93, (1996–1997).

45 *The Nubian Community in Kenya* v. *The Republic of Kenya*, Communication 317/2006; see also the African Court's decision in *African Commission on Human and Peoples' Rights* v. *Kenya*, Application No. 006/2012 (2017).

46 Paragraph 127.

47 *Purohit and Moore* v. *The Gambia*, Communication No. 241/2001 (2002–2003).

the antidiscrimination and equal protection of the law as laid down under the provisions of Articles 2 and 3 of the African Charter'.[48] The question whether other 'status' protected in Article 2 includes the right to a sexual orientation was presented in a complaint to the Commission in 1994. However, the complaint was withdrawn before the Commission could deliberate on it.[49]

It is notable that the Commission has linked the interpretation of Article 3, which guarantees the rights of 'every individual' to equality before the law and to equal protection of the law, to the provisions of Article 2 in its jurisprudence. This was demonstrated in *Purohit and Moore* v. *The Gambia*[50] (discussed above).[51] In *Open Society Justice Initiative* v. *Côte d'Ivoire*[52] the Commission confirms this position as follows:

> By adhering to this position, the Commission considers that in reality, the right to non-discrimination which is protected by Article 2 of the Charter constitutes a legal guarantee to ensure the enjoyment of the rights to equality before the law and equal protection of the law under Article 3. In other words, where discrimination occurs, equality and equal protection of the law are automatically undermined. It follows that whenever a violation of Article 2 of the Charter is established, the rights under Article 3 have necessarily been violated. The only exception to this logical position is applicable when the discrimination authorized by law is justifiable and proportionate to the targeted goal. In the Communication under consideration, the Commission has already concluded that an unjustified discrimination has occurred.[53]

The African Commission has had to deal with a number of critical issues under Article 4 that guarantees the right to bodily integrity and the right to life. However, the Charter did not provide guidance on the definition of the right to bodily integrity and the right to life, but this gap has not prevented the application of the provision. For instance, in *Organisation Mondiale Contre La Torture* v. *Rwanda*,[54] the African Commission found a violation of the right to life in the case of extra judicial killings of Rwandan villagers by the State's Armed Forces.[55] It is notable that, in a recent decision, the African Court has delimited the scope of the application of the right to life aspect of the provision. In *African Commission on Human and Peoples' Rights* v. *Kenya*[56] the Court was of the view

48 Ibid. paragraph 54.
49 This case is discussed further in Chapter 9.
50 *Supra*, *Purohit and Moore* v. *The Gambia*.
51 Ibid.
52 *Open Society Justice Initiative* v. *Côte d'Ivoire*, Communication 318/06 (2016).
53 Paragraph 155.
54 *Supra*, *Organisation Mondiale Contre La Torture* v. *Rwanda*.
55 See also *Achutan (on behalf of Banda) and Amnesty International (on behalf of Orton and Vera Chirwa)* v. *Malawi*, Communication Nos. 64/92, 68/92 and 78/92 (1995).
56 Application No. 006/2012 (2017).

that violation of socio-economic rights does not necessarily amount to violation of the right to life. In that case it was argued that the forced eviction of the Applicants threatened their means of livelihood and thus was a violation of their right to life. In rejecting that argument the Court held that the Article relates to the physical rather than the existential understanding of right to life. The Article is thus to be interpreted in the context of physical right to life. A thorny issue in respect of Article 4 is its implication for the death penalty as a form of punishment, which practice is prevalent in the continent.[57] The African Charter, unlike other international and regional human right treaties, does not refer to the death penalty specifically.[58] Furthermore, it is not supplemented by a protocol proscribing the death penalty.[59] Despite this gap, the Commission considered the legality of the death penalty under the Charter in *Interights* et al. v. *Botswana*.[60] In that communication, Mariette Bosch was convicted for murder and sentenced to death. It was argued *inter alia* that the death penalty sentence imposed in the case violated the provision of the African Charter. The Commission noted that the death penalty as a form of punishment is not excluded under the Charter. Nonetheless, the death penalty must only be imposed after careful consideration. While the Commission encouraged African States to put a moratorium on the death penalty, the Commission found that, in the case of Mariette Bosch, there was no violation of the provisions of the Charter.[61] In *International Pen and Others (on behalf of Saro-Wiwa)* v. *Nigeria*[62] the Commission held that the right to life may be violated if there was no proper consideration of the case or if the process leading to the imposition of the death penalty is not fair.[63] Significantly, in *Interights & Ditshwanelo* v. *The Republic of Botswana*,[64] the Commission held that, because of the manner in which death by hanging was carried out, it constituted a violation of Article 4 of the African Charter.

In *Noah Kazingachire, John Chitsenga, Elias Chemvura and Batanai Hadzisi (represented by Zimbabwe Human Rights NGO Forum)* v. *Zimbabwe*,[65] a complaint was brought on behalf of representatives of deceased persons who were

57 L. Chenwi, *Towards the Abolition of Death Penalty in Africa: A Human Rights Perspective* (Pretoria University Law Press, 2007).

58 *Groupe de Travail sur les Dossiers Judiciaires Stratégiques* v. *Democratic Republic of Congo*, Communication 259/2002 (2015).

59 B. Manby, 'Civil and political rights in the African Charter on Human and Peoples' Rights: Articles 1–7', in M. Evans and R. Murray, *The African Charter on Human and Peoples' Rights: The System in Practice, 1986–2006* (Cambridge University Press, 2008), 189.

60 *Interights* et al. v. *Botswana*, African Commission on Human and Peoples' Rights, Communication Nos. 240/2001 (2004).

61 See also *Spilg and Mack & DITSHWANELO (on behalf of Lehlohonolo Bernard Kobedi) v. Botswana*, Communication 277/2003 (2013).

62 *International Pen and Others (on behalf of Saro-Wiwa)* v. *Nigeria*, Communication Nos. 137/94–139/94–154/96–161/97, (1998).

63 See *Egyptian Initiative for Personal Rights and Interights* v. *Arab Republic of Egypt*, 334/06.

64 *Interights and Ditshwanelo v. The Republic of Botswana*, Communication 319/06 (2016).

65 *Noah Kazingachire, John Chitsenga, Elias Chemvura and Batanai Hadzisi (represented by Zimbabwe Human Rights NGO Forum)* v. *Zimbabwe*, Communication no. 295/04 (2013).

killed by state security officers at different times in 2001. One was killed in an attempt by the officers to stop a car, another was beaten to death because he was a member of the opposition to the government, another was killed in the process of arrest, and the last one was killed in the process of quelling a students' protest march. The Commission acknowledged that law enforcement officers are permitted to kill in certain circumstances, such as in self-defence and in defence of others. However, it also observed that the exercise of that licence to kill is a last resort. After considering the facts presented before it, the Commission found that no serious risks to the officers or anyone else were posed in the situations leading to the four deaths. The Commission concluded that there was no justification for the killings. In one of the cases the Commission noted that the law enforcement officers involved were not acting in an official capacity when the killing occurred. The Commission restated its jurisprudence that a human right violation by private actors could lead to international responsibility of a State, where the State failed to exercise due diligence to prevent such violation. The commission found that Zimbabwe had failed to exercise due diligence in its response to the unlawful killings. The Commission concluded that in all of the cases presented there were violations of Article 4.

In 1994, in *Southern African Human Rights NGO Network & Ors* v. *Tanzania*,[66] the High Court of Tanzania gave a decision in a case of murder to the effect that the death penalty under Tanzanian law is unconstitutional. According to the judge, this was because the manner of carrying out the execution by hanging violated the right to the dignity of the human person and constituted inherently cruel, inhuman and degrading treatment under the Constitution of Tanzania. The judge sentenced the accused persons to life imprisonment instead of the mandated capital punishment for the offence committed under Tanzanian law. On appeal by the Tanzanian government to the Court of Appeal the judgment was overturned in 1996. The Court of Appeal held that the death penalty by hanging was constitutional having been saved by clawback clauses under the Constitution. The Court further contended that the death penalty by hanging is permitted under international human rights law, it is an effective deterrent mechanism, it is accepted by the public, it is cheaper to execute and it is widely practised in other Member State parties to the African Charter. In 2006, the Complainant requested that the African Commission declare the decision of the Court of Appeal to be in violation of Article 4 of the Charter. However, the Commission declined to deal with the case on the merit holding that there had been an unreasonable delay of 11 years before the communication was brought and the Complainant did not provide any explanation for the delay. It therefore declared the communication inadmissible. It is discouraging that the Commission chose to dismiss the communication, which required a level of discretion on technical grounds considering the fundamental

66 *Southern African Human Rights NGO Network & Ors* v. *Tanzania*, Communication 333/2006 (2010).

issues involved. However, the Commission has a clearer position when it comes to the application of the death penalty to juveniles and minors. In its decision in *Groupe de Travail sur les Dossiers Judiciaires Stratégiques* v. *Democratic Republic of Congo*[67] the Commission held that the imposition of the death penalty on juveniles aged under 18 years is a violation of the African Charter and the fact that the sentence was subsequently commuted to life sentences did not change the finding that the original sentences constituted a violation of the Charter by the Member State.

A number of cases have also been dealt with by the Commission under Article 5. Article 5 *inter alia* guarantees the right to respect for dignity inherent in a human being and freedom from slavery. In *Media Rights Agenda* v. *Nigeria*,[68] the Commission stated that Article 5 should be interpreted widely in order to extend the protection against a wide range of abuse, which could take various forms.[69] Under Article 5 the Commission has especially been able to address, to some extent, the issue of slavery that is rife in some parts of the continent. In *Bah Ould Rabah* v. *Mauritania*,[70] the Commission applied the provisions of Article 5 in a case of slavery. In that case, the family of the Complainant was expelled from their home after the death of their mother. The person responsible for the expulsion claimed that the mother was his 'slave', which claim entitled him to her property upon her death. The complainant contended that this claim was a violation of Article 5 of the Charter. The Mauritanian State argued that this was a family dispute between members of the same family and not a case of slavery under the Charter. The Commission concluded that this was slavery practice and ordered the Mauritanian State to take appropriate steps to restore the Complainant's rights. Unfortunately, as with most of its decisions, the Commission did not articulate what steps needed to be taken in this regard, which is not very helpful in determining the level of compliance with the order by the Member State. In *S.O.S. Esclaves* v. *Mauritania*,[71] the allegations were that slavery was a common practice in Mauritania[72] and that the State colluded with the perpetrators of the practice. Specific instances of such practices were given. Unfortunately the Commission found the complaint inadmissible because the Complainant did not exhaust available domestic remedies before filing the complaint as required under the Charter.

The Commission has robustly applied Article 5 in cases relating to torture, cruel, inhuman or degrading punishment and treatment. The Commission has

67 *Supra*, *Groupe de Travail sur les Dossiers Judiciaires Stratégiques* v. *Democratic Republic of Congo*.

68 Supra, *Media Rights Agenda and Constitutional Rights Project* v. *Nigeria*.

69 Ibid.

70 *Bah Ould Rabah* v. *Mauritania*, Communication No. 197/97 (2004).

71 Communication No. 198/97 (1999).

72 Mauritania formally abolished slavery in 1980. It was the last country to do so. M. Killander, 'African human rights law in theory and practice' in S. Joseph and A. McBeth, (eds), *Research Handbook on International Human Rights Law* (Edward Elgar Publishing Limited, 2010) 388 at 395.

held that acts of beating, torture, overcrowding in prisons,[73] holding prisoners in handcuffs and chained by foot to the wall while confined to dirty, airless cells[74] and prolonged electrocution by State officers[75] violate the provisions of Article 5. In *Curtis Francis Doebbler* v. *Sudan*,[76] eight university students (who were Muslims) were convicted of committing acts contrary to public morality in a public place in violation of Sudan's criminal law. The students were having a picnic and were alleged to have been kissing, wearing trousers, and engaging in girls dancing, crossing legs, sitting and talking with men. Fines were imposed on the students and they were also ordered to be punished with whip lashes. The lashes were carried out in public supervised by the Sudanese Court. The lashes were inflicted using wire and plastic whips, which caused permanent scars on the victims' backs. The Complainant contended that the punishment by lashing violated Article 5 of the Charter. Sudan argued that it was acting within its criminal laws and that the punishment is more beneficial to the victims when compared with prison confinement. The Commission concluded that the punishment was inconsistent with the Charter because there is no right for individuals, and in particular the government of a country, to apply physical violence as punishment for offences. According to the Commission, such a practice is tantamount to sanctioning State-sponsored torture and it is contrary to the nature of the Charter as a human rights treaty.[77] It would have been useful if the Commission had gone further and given an opinion on the compatibility of physical punishment under the *Sharia* (Islamic law), which permitted such punishment and which also influenced the content of the criminal code in Sudan, with the Charter.[78] The Commission has taken further steps in this area by issuing the Robben Island Guidelines (a non-binding declaration) that is aimed at prohibiting and preventing torture, cruel, inhuman or degrading treatment or punishment and responding to the needs of victims.[79]

In the *Egyptian Initiative for Personal Rights and Interights* v. *Arab Republic of Egypt*,[80] a complaint was filed on behalf of three individuals against the State of Egypt. The complaint alleged that the three individuals were detained, tried and consequently sentenced to death for allegedly participating in two bombings in the Sinai Peninsula. It was further alleged that while in detention the individuals were tortured in various ways to elicit confessions. Evidence of marks

73 *Supra*, *Achutan (on behalf of Banda) and Amnesty International (on behalf of Orton and Vera Chirwa)* v. *Malawi*.

74 Supra, International Pen and Others (on behalf of Saro-Wiwa) v. Nigeria.

75 *Gabriel Shumba* v. *Zimbabwe*, Communication No. 288/04 (2017).

76 Communication No. 236/2000 (2003).

77 Ibid. paragraph 42.

78 *Supra*, Manby, 194–195.

79 *Guidelines and Measures for the Prohibition and Prevention of Torture, Cruel, Inhuman or Degrading Treatment or Punishment in Africa* (The Robben Island Guidelines), African Commission on Human and Peoples' Rights, 32nd Session, 17–23 October 2002, Banjul, The Gambia.

80 Egyptian Initiative for Personal Rights and INTERIGHTS/Egypt, Communication 323/06 (2011).

on the body of the Complainants were presented to the Commission. They were held incommunicado and denied access to a lawyer for a considerable period of time. The Commission noted that the Egyptian State could not provide a satisfactory explanation of how the injuries occurred while the individuals were in custody. Therefore, the Commission concluded that the Egyptian State violated Article 5 of the Charter. Also in *Spilg and Mack & DITSHWANELO (on behalf of Lehlohonolo Bernard Kobedi)* v. *Botswana*,[81] the Commission held that the failure of the authorities to allow a convict to say his last farewell to his family before execution constituted a violation of Article 5.

The application of Article 5 has also been invoked in nationality and citizenship cases. For example, it was held in *The Nubian Community in Kenya* v. *The Republic of Kenya* that adopting a policy that made Kenyan citizenship tenuous for Nubians and with the potential to render Nubians stateless was a violation of their human dignity and also underscored the need to recognise their legal status under Article 5.[82] In *Open Society Justice Initiative* v. *Côte d'Ivoire* the Commission agreed with the Complainant in that case that the lack of clarity of the law on nationality in Côte d'Ivoire had adverse effects on the Dioula community in the Member State. The consequence of this for the Dioula was to deprive them of nationality and the recognition of their legal status. This also put them at the risk of been rendered stateless. They were also alleged to have been treated differently because of their cultural heritage and their religious beliefs. Notably in that case, the Commission considered whether there is a right to a nationality under Article 5 and held:

> In the current circumstance, as suggested copiously by the Complainant in his submissions, it is crucial to solve the issue as to whether there is a 'right to nationality' according to the provisions of Article 5 of the Charter. On this point, the Commission notes that the right guaranteed by Article 5 of the Charter is one of 'recognition of the legal status' as defined above. That said, nationality is a basic component of this right in view of the fact that it is the legal and socio-political manifestation such as the status of a refugee or a resident granted by a State to an individual for the enjoyment of rights and the exercise of obligations. The Commission confirms this position by reaffirming in its Resolution 234 on the right to a nationality that 'the right to a nationality of any human person is a fundamental right derived from the terms of Article 5 of the Charter and essential for the enjoyment of other fundamental rights and freedoms guaranteed by the Charter.[83]

The Commission concluded that a determination of nationality in the African context must proceed from the consideration of the historical, legal and political

81 *Supra, Spilg and Mack & DITSHWANELO* v. *Botswana*.
82 *Supra, The Nubian Community in Kenya v. The Republic of Kenya*.
83 *Supra, Open Society Justice Initiative* v. *Côte d'Ivoire*, paragraph 97.

elements of the case. On that basis, the Dioula had a valid claim to Ivorian nationality and the way and manner by which the right was dealt with under the law by the Member State, Côte d'Ivoire, was inconsistent with Article 5. It therefore held that the Complainant had a right to Ivorian nationality whether by origin, attribution or acquired through a simplified naturalisation process.

The Commission jurisprudence on Article 6 has been rather lacklustre. The Article guarantees liberty and security of the person. It prohibits the deprivation of freedom except for reasons and conditions previously laid down by law. It further prohibits arbitrary unlawful arrest and detention. It is notable that the provision is similar to Article 9 of the International Covenant on Civil and Political Rights (ICCPR) but did not contain the procedural safeguards in the ICCPR such as prompt information of reason of arrest, prompt presentation of the accused before a judge, habeas corpus and compensation for unlawful detention.[84] Another major weakness with this Article, which has been pointed out by several scholars,[85] is the determination of what law the rights under the article are subject to as drafted. If it means domestic law, then the rights may be taken away by the Member State passing a law to exclude the rights. In view of this possibility it would be more desirable to have the rights subject to international law standards.[86] In *Henry Kalenga* v. *Zambia*,[87] the Complainant was detained without trial for about three years. He petitioned the Commission alleging a violation of Article 6 and demanding his release. The Zambian State subsequently informed the Commission that the Complainant had been released. The Commission decided to terminate the proceedings on the grounds that the matter has been amicably resolved without contacting the Complainant or taking into consideration the length of the detention and the need to provide some form of remedy for the victim. A similar approach was taken by the commission in *International PEN* v. *Burkina Faso*.[88] Following criticisms of this approach, the Commission decided to make it part of its procedure to contact the Complainant in situations like the one in *Henry Kalenga* to inquire if they wished to pursue other reliefs apart from the release from detention.[89] In a more recent decision in *Abdel Hadi, Ali Radi & Others* v. *Republic of Sudan*,[90] the Complainants were 88 refugees who fled Dafur (South Sudan) because of war and settled in a refugee camp outside of Khartoum, the Sudanese capital. The Sudanese police arrested them without

84 *Supra*, Killander, 395.

85 See, for example, M. K. Mbondeyi, 'Improving the substance and content of civil and political rights under the African human rights system' (2008) 17 (2) *Lesotho Law Journal* 37.

86 In relation to clawbacks in the African Charter generally, the Commission has stated a general principle that international human rights standards must prevail over contrary national law in order not to defeat the purpose of the rights and freedoms in the Charter. See, *supra*, *Media Rights Agenda and Constitutional Rights Project* v. *Nigeria*.

87 *Henry Kalenga* v. *Zambia*, Communication No. 11/88 (1994).

88 *PEN* v. *Burkina Faso*, Communication No. 22/88 (1994).

89 *Committee for the Defense of Human Rights (in respect of Ms. Jennifer Madike)* v. *Nigeria*, Communication No. 62/91 (1995).

90 Abdel Hadi, Ali Radi & Others v. Republic of Sudan, Communication No. 368/09 (2014).

any explanation and detained them for about 12 months. They had no access to lawyers, family members or medical care. They were also alleged to have been tortured. The Complainant attempted to get the State to investigate these allegations but the State failed to respond to the request. The Commission held that the detention without explanation for 12 months was a violation of Article 6.[91]

The right to fair trial is guaranteed under Article 7 of the charter. The elements of the right under the Charter include the offer of a fair hearing, the right to an appeal, the presumption of innocence, the right to defence and counsel of one's choice, the right to be tried within a reasonable time, the right to be tried before an impartial court or tribunal, the prohibition of *ex post facto* laws and individual criminal responsibility. The Commission has stressed that it does not matter whether a matter is brought before the ordinary civil court or a specialised tribunal such as a military tribunal.[92] The critical factor is whether the process employed is fair, just and impartial. The Commission has found the violation of the right to an appeal in a number of cases. In *Constitutional Rights Project* v. *Nigeria*,[93] Wahab Akamu, Gbolahan Adeaga and others were sentenced to death under the Robbery and Firearms (Special provision) Decree No. 5 of 1984, a law in the Member State of Nigeria. Section 11(4) of the Decree provided that no appeal shall lie from a decision of a tribunal constituted under the law or from any confirmation or dismissal of the decision of the tribunal by the Governor of a State. The effect of the provision was that it prevented appeals by persons convicted under the law. The Commission held that the barring of the right of appeal under the Nigerian law violated Article 7(1)(a) and ordered that the Complainants to be released. The Commission reached a similar conclusion in *Kenneth Good* v. *Republic of Botswana*.[94] The President of Botswana expelled Mr K. Good, an Australian national and a university lecturer, from the country. He was the co-author of an article that was critical of Botswana's political succession process. The president relied on powers conferred on him by section 7(f) of the Botswana Immigration Act to declare Mr Good as an undesirable inhabitant of Botswana. Mr Good's appeals to the domestic courts were dismissed because the courts were of the opinion that the exercise of the power by the President in this case was not subject to judicial oversight. The case was subsequently brought before the Commission. The Commission ruled that the sections of the Immigration Act, which prohibit the review of the President's action, violated Article 7(1)(a) and also threatened the independence of the judiciary guaranteed under Article 2 of the Charter.

The Commission has also found a violation of Article 7(1)(b) on the presumption of innocence in some cases. In *Annette Pagnoulle (on behalf of Abdoulaye Mazou)* v. *Cameroon*,[95] the Commission ruled that the detention of Abdoulaye

91 See also *Jean-Marie Antagana Mebara* v. *Cameroon*, Communication 416/12 (2016).

92 *Civil Liberties Organisation and Others v. Nigeria*, Communication No. 218/98 (2001).

93 *Constitutional Rights Project (in respect of Wahab Akamu, G. Adega and others)* v. *Nigeria*, Communication No. 60/91 (1995).

94 Communication No. 313/05 (2010).

95 Communication No. 39/90 (1997).

Mazou for two years on the speculative ground that he 'may cause problems' was a violation of the presumption of innocence in Article 7(1)(b). Similarly in *Media Rights Agenda* v. *Nigeria*[96] the Commission found a breach of the provision. In that case a Nigerian journalist was subjected to a secret trial after a long detention and subsequently sentenced to life imprisonment. He was not given access to his lawyer, doctors or family members.[97]

Article 7(1)(c) guarantees the right of an accused to a defence and by a counsel of his or her choice. The Commission has found a violation of Article 7(1)(c) where an accused was put on trial without allowing for a defence.[98] Harassing or assaulting a lawyer for the defence has further been held to be a violation of the right.[99] The Commission has also found that imposing a military lawyer on an accused violates the Article 7 rights.[100] Discriminatory application of judicial procedural rules has also been held to be a violation of Article 7. A denial of the ability to make oral submissions while allowing the prosecution to make one has been held by the Commission to be a violation of Article 7.[101]

The right to be tried within a reasonable time by an impartial court or tribunal is provided in Article 7(1)(d). Detention without trial obviously violates this provision. The Commission has held that a detention for seven years without trial is a denial of the right to be tried within a reasonable time.[102] The Commission has also found a violation where the authority or a President exercised a high degree of control over the composition, conduct and outcome of a judicial process.[103] The Commission has ruled that the failure of a State to provide a Court or Tribunal with adequate personnel to ensure fairness and impartiality is contrary to Article 7(1)(d).[104] Furthermore, the Commission has opined that the composition of a tribunal may create 'the appearance of, if not actual, lack of impartiality' which violates Article 7(1)(d).[105] Therefore, it has held that where members of the executives who enacted the applicable law in the first place dominate a judicial panel, the violation of the Article is likely to be found.[106]

96 Communication No. 224/98 (2000).

97 See also *Haregewoin Gabre-Selassie and IHRDA (on behalf of former Dergue Officials) v. Ethiopia*, Communication No. 301/305 (2012).

98 *Supra, Achutan (on behalf of Banda) and Amnesty International (on behalf of Orton and Vera Chirwa)* v. *Malawi*. See also, *supra, Egyptian Initiative for Personal Rights and Interights* v. *Arab Republic of Egypt*.

99 *Media Rights Agenda and Others* v. *Nigeria*, Communication Nos 105/93, 128/94, 130/94 and 152/96 (1999).

100 Ibid.

101 *Avocats Sans Frontières (on behalf of Bwampamye)* v. *Burundi*, Communication No. 231/99 (2000).

102 *Alhassan Abubakar* v. *Ghana*, Communication No. 103/93 (1996).

103 See also, *supra, Egyptian Initiative for Personal Rights and Interights* v. *Arab Republic of Egypt*.

104 Ibid. See also *Amnesty International and Others* v. *Sudan*, Communication Nos 48/90, 50/91, 52/91, 89/93 (1999).

105 *Supra, Constitutional Rights Project (in respect of Wahab Akamu, G. Adega and others)* v. *Nigeria*.

106 Ibid.

Article 7(2) prohibits *ex post facto* laws (creation of offences with retrospective effect) and retroactive punishment and also makes criminal punishment personal (individual criminal responsibility). This is important in the African context because of the prevalence of abuse of power and political scapegoating by governmental authorities in Member States. In *Media Rights Agenda and Others* v. *Nigeria*,[107] a military government in Nigeria introduced a retroactive decree that was subsequently challenged on the basis of inconsistency with the Charter. Nigeria argued that since no one had been convicted under the retroactive decree (law), the law could not be held to be in violation of Article 7(2). The Nigerian State appeared to be suggesting that until the law was enforced it could not be held to be contrary to Article 7(2). In response to this argument, the Commission observed that it (the Commission):

> must take a stand on the issue of justice underlying Article 7(2) and condemn the literal, minimalist interpretation of the Charter offered by the representative of Nigeria. Article 7(2) must be read to prohibit not only condemnation and infliction of punishment for acts which did not constitute crimes at the time they were committed, but retroactivity itself. It is expected that citizens must take the laws seriously. If laws change with retroactive effect, the rule of law is undermined since individuals cannot know at any moment if their actions are legal.

In *African Commission on Human and Peoples' Rights* v. *Libya*, an application was brought before the African Court on Human and Peoples' Rights on behalf of Saif Gaddafi, one of the sons of the deposed and deceased Libyan dictator Muammar Gaddafi. It was alleged that Saif Gaddafi was detained since November 2011 and was held in a secret location following the ousting of the Gaddafi regime. He was not presented before a court and he was not given access to a court. His detention was extended several times without a court involvement and also in his absence. He was eventually arraigned before an extraordinary court that was subsequently found to be unconstitutional. The African Court concluded that the treatment of Saif Gaddafi by the Member State violated Articles 6 and 7 of the African Charter.

A major shortcoming of Article 7 in relation to legal representation is that it contains no explicit provision for legal aid or assistance from the State, which is provided for in equivalent supranational instruments, e.g., Article 6 of the European Convention on Human Rights[108] and in Article 8 of the Inter-American Convention on Human Rights.[109] This may impede access to justice and consequently denies the right to fair hearing before the domestic courts and the African regional institutions. Furthermore, the Article 7 provision on fair trial has been criticised for not making explicit provision for certain aspects of this right. These

107 *Supra*, *Media Rights Agenda and Others* v. *Nigeria*.
108 ETS No. 5.
109 OAS Official Records, OEA/Ser.K/XVI/I/I.

include the right to public (and not secret) hearing, the right to an interpreter where required, the right against self-incrimination, the right against double jeopardy, and the right to compensation in cases of miscarriage of justice.[110] The Commission has tried to address some of these shortcomings through a number of resolutions. In the Resolution on the Right to Recourse and Fair Trial[111] the Commission expatiate on the scope of Article 7 of the African Charter to include, *inter alia*, the presumption of innocence and the right to free assistance of an interpreter where required. The Principles and Guidelines on the Right to a Fair Trial and Legal Assistance in Africa,[112] which were adopted in 2003, amplifies the elements of fair hearing and covers pertinent issues such as public hearing, legal aid and assistance. The Resolution on the Respect and the Strengthening on the Independence of the Judiciary was also adopted by the Commission to strengthen the institutional framework and provide support for the judicial system in Africa.[113] It is commendable that the African Court has taken an approach that interprets Article 7 to accommodate legal assistance and aid, even though it is not explicit in the Charter.

The case of *Wilfred Onyango and Others* v. *Tanzania*[114] also concerns the violation of Article 7, particularly the right to fair hearing and right to legal assistance. The applicants were citizens of Kenya who alleged that they were kidnapped from Mozambique by Tanzania operatives in 2005. They further alleged that they were transported to Tanzania where they were charged with various criminal offences including murder. While in detention they were tortured and subjected to inhuman treatment. Two of them died in custody. Five of them were convicted of armed robbery and conspiracy and sentenced to 30 years in prison. Three of them were eventually released. As at the time the case was brought before the African Court in 2013, some charges were still pending against the applicants in Tanzanian courts. The African Court found that the proceedings were pending for at least six years. The applicants alleged that their prosecution was unduly prolonged and constituted a violation of the Article 7 right to fair hearing. Furthermore, in the course of the proceedings against them, their lawyer left and the applicants had no legal representation thereafter. The Court held that the delay in the prosecution was without justification and constituted a violation of Article 7. In addition, the Court held that the State has an obligation under Article 7 to ensure that the Complainants have legal assistance and aid throughout the judicial process. The failure to provide the Complainants with legal assistance and aid was held to be in violation of the Article.[115]

110 *Supra*, Mbondeyi, 76.

111 The African Commission on Human and Peoples' Rights, meeting in its 11th Ordinary Session, in Tunisia, 2–9 March 1992.

112 *The Principles and Guidelines on the Right to a Fair Trial and Legal Assistance in Africa*, DOC/OS(XXX) 247, reprinted in (2005)12 *International Human Rights Reports* 1180.

113 ACHPR/Res.21(XIX)96, *Resolution on the Respect and the Strengthening on the Independence of the Judiciary* (1996).

114 Application No. 006/2013 (2016).

115 See also *Christopher Jonas* v. *The United Republic of Tanzania*, Application No. 011/2015.

Similarly, in *Mohammed Abubakari* v. *The United Republic of Tanzania*,[116] the Court held that a criminal defendant charged with a serious offence is particularly entitled to legal assistance and aid. However, the Court suggested that if a Member State is able to show that it absolutely had no financial capacity to grant free legal assistance it may be able to justify a failure to provide such assistance. It is noted that this is a high bar that is set for a Member State and one that may be extremely difficult to meet. The Court also found that a number of procedures followed by the Member State in the prosecution of the Complainant violated his right to a fair hearing. These included the failure to give the Complainant access to the indictment and the statements of the witnesses and also the failure to consider an allegation that the prosecutor in the case had a conflict of interest. The Court further held that a failure to provide necessary documentation to the accused in a timely manner also constituted a violation of the Charter. In another case involving Tanzania, *Alex Thomas* v. *Tanzania*,[117] the African Court held that a criminal proceeding that was conducted in the absence of the Complainant while he was in hospital was a violation of Article 7. It further held that an appeal that was delayed for about eight years violated Article 7(1)(d) of the Charter. In that case the Court relied on the approaches of the Inter-American Court of Human Rights and the European Court of Human Rights in deciding what would constitute undue delay. Consequently, it applied the factors established by those courts in its decision, which are the complexity of the case, the procedure involved in the matter and the conduct of judicial authorities. Also in *Beneficiaries of the late Nobert Zongo* et al. v. *Burkina Faso*,[118] the Court found a violation of Article 7. The Complainants in that case were beneficiaries of the estate of four journalists who were assassinated in Burkina Faso. The Complainants alleged that the Member State, Burkina Faso, failed to identify, prosecute and bring to justice those responsible for the assassinations. The Court held that the facts presented to it supported a violation of right to fair hearing under Article 7 and consequently also a violation of Article 1.

There is a link between the provisions of Article 7 and Article 26 of the Charter because the two provisions are connected with the judicial process. Article 26 provides that States have the duty to guarantee the independence of the courts and allow the establishment and improvement of appropriate national institutions entrusted with the promotion and protection of the rights and freedoms guaranteed by the Charter. The Commission had an opportunity to give its opinion on the application of the Article in *Lawyers for Human Rights* v. *Swaziland*.[119] In that case, King Sohbhuza of Swaziland had issued a proclamation, which, among other things, vested the king with the legislature, executive and judicial powers. The Complainant alleged that the action of the king had left the Swazi people without effective judicial remedy contrary to the African Charter arguing that:

116 Application No. 007/2013.
117 Application No. 005/2013.
118 Application No. 013/2011.
119 Communication No. 251/2002 (2005).

> By entrusting all judicial powers to the Head of State with powers to remove judges, the Proclamation of 1973 seriously undermines the independence of the judiciary in Swaziland. The main raison d'être of the principle of separation of powers is to ensure that no organ of government becomes too powerful and abuses its power. The separation of power amongst the three organs of government – executive, legislature and judiciary – ensure checks and balances against excesses from any of them. By concentrating the powers of all three government structures into one person, the doctrine of separation of power undermines [sic] and is subject to abuse.[120]

As the Commission noted in its decision, the Defendant failed to respond to the allegations despite several correspondences from the Commission to the State. The Commission consequently held that the action of the king violated Article 26 of the African Charter.[121]

Article 8 of the African Charter is on the right to freedom of conscience and free practice of religion. However, it is regrettable that under the Charter the Article 8 rights may be restricted if their exercise supposedly threatens law and order. This gives the authorities a ready excuse, should they choose, to infringe the rights protected. Encouragingly, the Commission and the African Court in their jurisprudence only allow restrictions of the rights where there is strong and credible evidence of threat to law and order. In *Free Legal Assistance Group and Others* v. *Zaire*,[122] the Commission found Zaire liable under Article 8 for persecuting members of the Jehovah Witness religious sect on the basis of their religious beliefs. The Commission stated that the government of Zaire did not provide any evidence to show that the practice of the religion threatened law and order to justify its treatment of the sect. In another complaint involving Sudan, the Commission similarly found the violation of Article 8 in the treatment of Christians in Sudan.[123] The African Court has also held that a forceful eviction of an indigenous community leading to a restriction of access to their religious sites is a violation of Article 8.[124] However, in *Gareth Anver Prince* v. *South Africa* the Commission held in favour of a Member State's law.[125] The Complainant had alleged that the refusal of the Law Society of South Africa to register him because he had two previous convictions for possession of cannabis violated *inter alia* Article 8. He stated that the use of cannabis is a requirement

120 Ibid. paragraph 56.

121 See also *Tsatsu Tsikata* v. *Republic of Ghana*, Communication No. 322/06 (2014); *supra*, *Egyptian Initiative for Personal Rights and Interights* v. *Arab Republic of Egypt*.

122 Communication Nos 25/89, 47/90, 56/91, 100/93 (1995) 9th Activity Report.

123 *Amnesty International, Comité Loosli Bachelard, Lawyers' Committee for Human Rights, Association of Members of the Episcopal Conference of East Africa* v. *Sudan*, Communication Nos 48/90–50/91–52/91–89/93 (1999).

124 *Supra*, *African Commission on Human and Peoples' Rights* v. *Kenya*.

125 *Gareth Anver Prince* v. *South Africa*, Communication No. 255/2002 (2004), 18th Activity Report.

of his Rastafarian religion despite being contrary to the domestic law of the country. The Commission rejected the argument holding that there was no violation of Article 8.

In relation to Article 9 provisions on the right to information and freedom of expression, the Commission has declared 'that freedom of expression is a basic human right, vital to an individual's personal development, his political consciousness, and participation in the conduct of public affairs in his country'.[126] In *Amnesty International* v. *Zambia*,[127] the African Commission found a breach of the right to 'receive information'. In that case the Zambian government had failed to provide the Complainants with the reasons for deporting them. In *Kenneth Good* v. *Republic of Botswana*,[128] the African Commission held that the expulsion of a non-national legally resident in Botswana for expressing his views as an academic 'is a flagrant violation of Article 9(2) of the Charter'.[129] The Commission has also held that passing law to proscribe newspapers by a military government in Nigeria is a denial of the right of the public to receive information.[130] Importantly, in that decision, the Commission observed that Article 9 provides no ground for derogation. The African Commission has expanded on the rights under Article 9 over the years. The Commission has relied on the Resolution on the Right to Freedom of Expression (1992)[131] and the Declaration of Principles on Freedom of Expression in Africa (2002)[132] to elaborate on the provisions of the article. Commenting on the implication of the former in *Law Office of Ghazi Suleiman* v. *Sudan (II)*,[133] the Commission stated that:

> In adopting the Resolution on the Right to Freedom of Association, the African Commission noted that governments should be especially careful that:
>
> [. . .]
>
> 2. In regulating the use of this right, the competent authorities should not enact provisions which would limit the exercise of this freedom; 3. The regulation of the exercise of the right to freedom of association should be consistent with states' obligations under the African Charter on Human and Peoples' Rights.[134]

126 *Supra, Media Rights Agenda and Others* v. *Nigeria*, paragraph 54.
127 Communication No. 212/98 (1999).
128 *Supra, Kenneth Good* v. *Republic of Botswana*.
129 Ibid. paragraph 200.
130 *Supra, Constitutional Rights Project, Civil Liberties Organisation and Media Rights Agenda* v. *Nigeria*.
131 Adopted at the 11th Ordinary Session of the African Commission, 2–9 March 1992.
132 Adopted at the 32nd Session, 17–23 October 2002.
133 *Law Office of Ghazi Suleiman* v. *Sudan*, Communication 228/99 (2003).
134 *Supra, Resolution on the Right to Freedom of Expression* (1992) paragraph 46. See also *Monim Elgak, Osman Hummeida and Amir Suliman (represented by FIDH and OMCT)* v. *Sudan*, Communication No. 379/09 (2014), paragraph 112.

Article 9 was also considered by the African Court in the case of *Lohé Issa Konaté* v. *Burkina Faso*.[135] The application alleged the violations of the right to freedom of expression not only under the African Charter (Article 9), but also the International Covenant on Civil and Political Rights (Article 19) and Article 66(2)(c) of the ECOWAS Treaty. The Complainant was an editor of a magazine. The Complainant wrote and published articles alleging that the local prosecutor was involved in certain misconducts. Subsequently the Complainant and another journalist were charged with defamation, public insult and contempt of court. The High Court of the Member State sentenced the Complainant to 12 months in prison and his magazine was suspended for six months. He was also ordered to pay a fine and damages. The complaint contended that the laws under which he was prosecuted were inconsistent with the African Charter, the International Covenant on Civil and Political Rights and the ECOWAS Treaty, especially the criminalisation of defamation. At the preliminary stage, the Complainant sought and was granted provisional measures to be released from custody and provided with adequate health care. In its opinion, the Court noted that the right to freedom of expression is not absolute. According to the Court, restrictions on the right may be provided by domestic law but must be consistent with applicable international norms. Furthermore, such restriction must be to achieve a legitimate aim and, importantly, it must be proportionate to that purpose. In this case the Court acknowledged that the restrictions were provided by law and were sufficiently clear. It further held that the restrictions were put in place to achieve a legitimate aim that was stated to be to protect the honour and reputation of magistrates, jurors and assessors in the performance of their duties. However, the Court held that the restrictions were a disproportionate means to achieve the legitimate aim. According to the Court, proportionality requires a balancing of the interest of the society with the freedom of the individuals and any means of restriction imposed must be the least restrictive possible. Furthermore, in the Court's view, freedom of expression must be subject to a lesser degree of restriction when it relates to public debate relating to public figures. In particular, it stated that any punishment for the damaging of a public figure's reputation must not be more than that for the damaging of the reputation of an ordinary citizen. Criminalising the defamation of certain public figures under the law is therefore disproportionate and unjustifiable. The Court also held that the State failed to show that the suspension of the magazine was necessary and proportionate to protect the reputation of the prosecutor. The Court found a violation of Article 9 of the African Charter, Article 19 of ICCPR and Article 66(2)(c) of the ECOWAS Treaty. The Court ordered that the Member State amend its law to conform with the African Charter.

The individual right to free association is protected under Article 10. The Article also precludes compulsion to join an association except where it is

135 Application No. 004/2013 (2014).

required to strengthen social and national solidarity.[136] The Commission found a violation of Article 10 in *International Pen and Others (on behalf of Saro-Wiwa)* v. *Nigeria*.[137] The case involved the Movement for the Survival of Ogoni People (MOSOP), a campaign organisation. The Complainants alleged the violation of Article 10(1) because they were tried and convicted for murder based on their opinions, as expressed through their work with MOSOP. There was no evidence to directly connect the Complainants to the alleged murder. The domestic tribunal that convicted the Complainants held that by their (the Complainants) membership of MOSOP the convicted persons were responsible for the murder, in other words they were guilty by association. Furthermore, on the facts presented, it appeared that government officials at different times during the trial before the tribunal declared MOSOP and the Complainants guilty of the charges, without waiting for the official judgment from the tribunal. According to the Commission, the facts of the case demonstrated a clear prejudice against the organisation MOSOP and its members, which the government has done nothing to justify. Therefore, the Commission found a violation of Article 10(1).[138] In *Civil Liberties Organization* v. *Nigeria*[139] the Commission observed that,

> Freedom of association is enunciated as an individual right and is first and foremost a duty for the State to abstain from interfering with the free formation of associations. There must always be a general capacity for citizens to join, without State interference, in associations in order to attain various ends. In regulating the use of this right, the competent authorities should not enact provisions which would limit the exercise of this freedom. The competent authorities should not override constitutional provisions or undermine fundamental rights guaranteed by the constitution and international human rights standards.[140]

The Commission has found the breach of the Article 10 right where political parties have been banned,[141] where political gatherings have been prohibited[142] and where political activists have been arrested because of their political views.[143] In finding a violation of the Article in *Malawi African Association and Others* v. *Mauritania*,[144] the Commission stated:

136 *Supra*, Mbondeyi, 87.

137 *Supra, International Pen and Others (on behalf of Saro-Wiwa)* v. *Nigeria*.

138 Ibid. paragraph 108.

139 *Civil Liberties Organization* v. *Nigeria*, Communication No. 101/93 (1995).

140 Ibid. paragraphs 15 and 16.

141 *Dawda Jawara* v. *The Gambia*, Communication Nos 147/95 and 149/96 (2000).

142 *Supra, Amnesty International and Others* v. *Sudan*.

143 *Kazeem Aminu* v. *Nigeria*, Communication No. 205/97 (2000).

144 *Malawi African Association and Others* v. *Mauritania*, Communication Nos 54/91, 61/91, 98/93, 164/97, 196/97 and 210/98 (2000). See also, *supra*, *Monim Elgak, Osman Hummeida and Amir Suliman (represented by FIDH and OMCT)* v. *Sudan*, paragraph 112.

> Some presumed supporters of the Ba'ath Arab Socialist Party were imprisoned for belonging to a criminal association. The accused in the 3rd case relating to the Manifesto . . . were charged for belonging to a secret movement. The government did not provide any argument to establish the criminal nature or character of these groups. The Commission is of the view that any law on associations should include an objective description that makes it possible to determine the criminal nature of a fact or organisation. In the case under consideration, the Commission considers that none of these simply rational requirements was met and that there was violation of article 10(2).[145]

The Commission elaborated on the freedoms protected under the article in its Resolution on the Right to Freedom of Association.[146] The resolution expanded on the freedoms in the following terms:

1. The competent authorities should not override constitutional provisions or undermine fundamental rights guaranteed by the constitution and international standards;
2. In regulating the use of this right, the competent authorities should not enact provisions which would limit the exercise of this freedom;
3. The regulation of the exercise of the right to freedom of association should be consistent with State's obligations under the African Charter on Human and Peoples' Rights.

On its part, the African Court considered Article 10 in the consolidated cases of *Tanganyika Law Society, Legal and Human Rights Centre, and Reverend Christopher R. Mtikila* v. *Tanzania*.[147] The case concerns amendments to the constitution of the Member State Tanzania that were alleged to have the effect of prohibiting independent candidates from contesting elections. The Complainants contended that the amendments constituted the violation of their rights to freedom of association, participation in public affairs, non-discrimination and the 'rule of law'. Tanzania, on the other hand, contended that the arrangement was necessary to foster national unity and solidarity. Similar to its decision on the right to freedom of expression, the Court stated that any restriction on the right to freedom of association must be necessary and proportionate to a legitimate aim pursued by the State. This requires a balancing of the needs of the society against the right of the individual. Having considered the facts of this case, the Court held that the prohibition affecting independent candidates was not proportionate to the need expressed by the State. The Court further found that the facts of the case also resulted in the violation of Article 13(1), right to participate in a

145 Ibid. paragraph 107.
146 *Resolution on the Right to Freedom of Association*, ACHPR /Res.5(XI)92, (1992).
147 Application Nos 009 and 011/2011 (2013).

government. Furthermore, relying on the combination of Article 10(2) – right not to be forced to join an association, Article 27(2) – individual and collective rights, and Article 29(4) – individual obligation in relation to social and national solidarity, the Court held that freedom of association means a right to associate and not to associate. By restricting the participation of independent candidates and, by implication, requiring them to seek sponsorship from a political party, the Member State violated this right. The Court also held that the arrangement is discriminatory against individuals based on their 'political or any other opinion' and therefore violated the prohibition of discrimination under Article 2 and equal protection of law under Article 3. The Court ordered the Member State to take necessary steps to remedy the violations and to keep the Court informed of measures taken in this respect.

The Commission has also considered cases brought under Article 11, which guarantees freedom of assembly 'subject only to necessary restrictions provided for by law in particular those enacted in the interest of national security, the safety, health, ethics and rights and freedoms of others'. The Commission held in *Commission International de Juristes* v. *Togo* that shooting of protesters at a peaceful demonstration by the Togolese military was a violation of the Article.[148] In *Kevin Mgwanga Guneme* et al. v. *Cameroon*,[149] it was alleged *inter alia* that the government in Cameroon arbitrarily arrested, detained, tortured, maimed and killed persons who had advocated for the self-determination of Southern Cameroon. The Commission stated that there was enough evidence before it to find the violation of Article 11. The Commission described its position on Article 11 as follows:

> The Commission does not condone unlawful acts by individuals or organisations to advance political objectives, because such actions or their consequences are likely to violate the African Charter. It encourages individuals and organisations, when exercising their right to freedom of assembly, to operate within the national legal framework. This requirement does not absolve States Parties from their duty to guarantee the rights to freedom of assembly, while maintaining law and order. The Respondent State admits that it detained demonstrators, applied excessive force to enforce law and order, and in some cases lives were lost. The Commission concludes therefore that Article 11 of the African Charter was violated.[150]

Article 12 of the African Charter guarantees the right to freedom of movement and residence. It provides for the right to leave any country and return to one's country of origin or residence. It further provides for the right to seek and obtain asylum when persecuted and prohibits extrajudicial expulsion or mass expulsion.

148 Communication No. 91/91 (1994).
149 Communication No. 266/03 (2009).
150 Ibid. paragraph 138.

The Article is generally subject to national laws. The right to seek and obtain asylum is unique in the African legal order when compared with other international human rights instruments.[151] The provision appears to have incorporated into the African Charter the 1969 Convention Governing the Specific Aspects of Refugee Problems in Africa that prohibits the return of a person to a country where their life, physical integrity or liberty may be threatened.[152] In *Rencontre Africaine pour la Defense des Droits de l'Homme* v. *Zambia*,[153] a complaint was presented by a Senegalese NGO on behalf of 517 West African individuals who were allegedly expelled from Zambia illegally. Before their expulsion, most of the individuals had been subjected to administrative detention for more than two months. In the process the deportees lost all their material possessions they had in Zambia, and many were also separated from their Zambian families. The Commission held that the mass deportation of the individuals concerned, including their arbitrary detention and deprivation of the right to have their cause heard, constituted, *inter alia*, the violation of Article 12(5) of the African Charter. The Commission also found a violation of Article 12 where citizens were denied identity documents and were harassed by public authorities for that reason.[154] Also, creating fears in an individual to the extent that they were unable to return to their home countries was held to be a violation of Article 12.[155]

The right to political participation is guaranteed under Article 13. The article protects the rights of 'every citizen' to 'participate freely in the government of his country, either directly or through freely chosen representatives in accordance with the provisions of the law'. It further provides for the right of 'every individual' to equal access to public property and services. However, by limiting the right to participation in the government to citizens only, Article 13 does not protect the rights of non-citizens, especially from other Member States including permanent residents, to participate in government. In *Constitutional Rights Project and Civil Liberties Organisation* v. *Nigeria*,[156] the military government in Nigeria annulled the democratic elections in Nigeria midway through the voting process and stopped the publication of further results from the election. The actions of the government were held to be a violation of the Article. The Commission has also held that the imposition of a ban on former ministers and members of parliament following a coup d'état is a contravention of their rights to participate

151 *Supra*, Killander, 396.

152 Organisation of African Unity, *Convention Governing the Specific Aspects of Refugee Problems in Africa*, 10 September 1969, U.N.T.S No. 14691. Available at: www.unhcr.org/uk/about-us/background/45dc1a682/oau-convention-governing-specific-aspects-refugee-problems-africa-adopted.html, accessed 24 November 2017.

153 *Supra*, *Rencontre Africaine pour la Défense des Droits de l'Homme* v. *Zambia*.

154 *Supra*, *Open Society Justice Initiative* v. *Côte d'Ivoire*, paragraph 161.

155 *Supra*, *Osman Hummeida and Amir Suliman (represented by FIDH and OMCT)* v. *Sudan*, paragraph 126.

156 Communication No. 102/93 (1998).

freely in the government of their country provided under Article 13(1) of the Charter.[157] In *Open Society Justice Initiative* v. *Côte d'Ivoire* it was held that the provision of the Constitution and judicial decisions that had the consequence of denying Ivorian nationalities to the Dioula community and also restricted their participation in the political process was a violation of the article.[158] The Commission appeared to suggest in *Katangese Peoples' Congress* v. *Zaire*[159] that the violation of this article may be a basis for finding the more contentious right of people to self-determination under Article 21. However, this reasoning was not explored by the Commission in any detail in that case.

Article 14 protects the right to property, which is also considered to be an economic, social and cultural right.[160] The right may only be encroached upon in the interest of public need or in the general interest of the community and in accordance with the provisions of appropriate domestic laws. The Commission has suggested in *Union Inter Africaine des Droits de l'Homme, Federation Internationale des Ligues des Droits de l'Homme and Others* v. *Angola*[161] that the mass deportation of non-nationals without any opportunity to challenge the deportation order with the consequence of separating them from their property is a violation of, *inter alia*, Article 14. The Commission also found a violation of Article 14 in a case where the premises of an NGO was searched without warrant and subsequently seized for no apparent 'public need or community interest'.[162] In *Interights, Institute for Human Rights and Development in Africa, and Association Mauritanienne des Droits de l'Homme* v. *Islamic Republic of Mauritania*[163] the Commission stated that the onus is on the State to demonstrate that the property of the Complainant was confiscated for public interest or in accordance with any established law. Where the State fails to demonstrate such, the conclusion is that the confiscation of property was done arbitrarily in violation of Article 14. The Commission has further held that the failure of the State to protect victims from being evicted from their property or from demolition of their houses by a militia is a violation of Article 14.[164] Also in *Dino Noca* v. *Democratic Republic of the Congo*,[165] where the State authorities took over the property of an Italian national despite compliance with the requirements of domestic law and assigned the property to a third party, the Commission found a violation of Article 14.[166]

157 *Supra*, *Dawda Jawara* v. *The Gambia*.
158 See Chapter 8.
159 Communication No. 75/92 (1995).
160 See Chapter 8.
161 Communication No. 159/96 (1997).
162 *Huri-Laws* v. *Nigeria*, Communication No. 225/98(2000).
163 *Supra*, *Interights, Institute for Human Rights and Development in Africa, and Association Mauritanienne des Droits de l'Homme* v. *Islamic Republic of Mauritania*, paragraph 46.
164 *Sudan Human Rights Organisation* v. *The Sudan*, Communication 296/05 and *Centre on Housing Rights and Evictions* v. *The Sudan*, Communication No. 296/05 (2010), paragraph 205.
165 *Dino Noca* v. *Democratic Republic of the Congo*, Communication No. 286/04 (2012).
166 Ibid.

Conclusion

From the foregoing it is apparent that, compared with other rights guaranteed under the African Charter, civil and political rights appear to have had significant impacts. The African Commission has played a pivotal role in interpreting and applying the provisions of the Charter on civil and political rights to activities that happened in Member States. The Commission's approach has shaped the understanding, practice and implementation of human rights norms across Member States. The jurisprudence of the Commission has also helped shape the harmonisation of standards on civil and political rights within the continent. It is regrettable that sometimes the jurisprudence of the Commission has not been robust enough to provide sufficient clarity as to the ambit of the provisions of the Charter. However, the work of the Commission has laid the foundation for the new African Union legal order in this area. The introduction of the African Court on Human and Peoples' Rights is significant because of the Court's potential to progress AU law in this area. Unlike the Commission, the Court has full judicial powers and its decisions are binding on Member States. The few cases that it has decided on the merit so far indicate that it is consolidating on the jurisprudence of the Commission and is also gradually expanding on that jurisprudence. It is also notable that the decisions from the African Court appear to be more robust when compared with the decisions of the Commission. The introduction of the African Court is a welcome development in the advancement of AU law. Nonetheless, it is worth noting that the AU is in the process of replacing the Court with a broadly similar Court but with a wider jurisdiction.

8 Economic, social and cultural rights and group rights in African Union law

Introduction

As indicated in the previous chapter, this chapter focuses on the economic, social and cultural rights as well as the unique group rights in the African legal order. It is widely acknowledged that the African Charter is the first international human rights treaty to accommodate and protect the three generations of human rights, i.e., civil and political rights, economic, social and cultural rights (ESC), and group and peoples' rights. The consensus within the African Union legal order is that these rights have the same status. Therefore, there is no distinction between the justiciability and implementation of these three generations of rights.[1] The Charter recognises explicitly certain rights that could fall into the category of ESC rights. These include the right to property (Article 14), the right to work under equitable and satisfactory conditions (Article 15), the right to the enjoyment of the best attainable state of physical and mental health (Article 16), the right to education, and the protection of family and cultural rights (Articles 17, 18 and 61). Group rights are protected under Articles 19–24 and could also be regarded, to some extent, as group ESC rights. These include the right to self-determination, freedom in relation to wealth and natural resources, development rights, peace and security and environment-related rights. Similar to the civil and political rights, the ESC rights have been expanded upon in later instruments that target specific and usually vulnerable groups. These instruments include the African Charter on the Rights and Welfare of the Child; the Protocol to the African Charter on Human and Peoples' Rights on the Rights of Women in Africa; the African Youth Charter; the African Union Convention for the Protection and Assistance of Internally Displaced Persons and the Commission's Guidelines and Principles on Economic, Social and Cultural Rights. However, it must be acknowledged that the realisation of these rights has remained poor compared with civil and political rights.[2] This chapter examines the evolving jurisprudence on these rights as a source of AU law and their impact on Member States.

1 See M. Ssenyonjo (ed.), *The African Regional Human Rights System: 30 Years after the African Charter on Human and Peoples' Rights* (Martinus Nihoff Publishers, 2012) 55.

2 M. Ssenyonjo, 'The protection of economic, social and cultural rights under the African Charter' in D. M. Chirwa and L. Chenwi, *The Protection of Economic, Social and Cultural Rights in Africa* (Cambridge University Press, 2016) 91–121.

The moulding of ESC rights under the AU legal order

A significant number of cases alleging infringement of ESC rights have been brought before the Commission. The Commission has therefore had some opportunities to consider and pronounce on these ESC rights. However, compared with civil and political rights provisions, the ESC rights have been employed by parties to proceedings at a much lower rate. There are many different reasons for the relatively low usage of ESC rights provisions. The Commission itself has been partly blamed for this. The Commission has been accused of giving more prominence to civil and political rights in its promotional activities.[3] Furthermore, Member States are generally less interested in implementing ESC rights because of the attendant responsibility and financial implications for national budgeting.[4] Also, for a long time in many Member States, ESC rights were considered non-justiciable. In addition, it is significant and unhelpful that the ESC rights protected under the Charter are drafted in broad, general and vague terms.

A common characteristic of the provisions on ESC rights is that they substantially lack specificity as to their content, the beneficiaries of the rights and the measures required to give effect to them. However, it has been suggested that the broad approach taken in the drafting of the provisions may be deliberate, to allow a degree of flexibility for Member States' actions and discretion in the implementation of these rights.[5] As a consequence of the vagueness, the African Commission has had to approach its tasks in relation to ESC rights creatively and innovatively. Initially, the Commission was less interested in granting remedies to successful complainants, perceiving its role more as a facilitator of constructive dialogue between disputing parties. However, this approach has been described as inadequate because it does not take into consideration the inequality of bargaining power in a dispute between a State and individual complainants.[6] The Commission was more receptive to award of remedies in later cases. It is also worth noting that cases determined before 2001 showed the Commission's initial general reluctance to fully develop the content, scope and application of ESC rights. However, cases decided after 2001 reveal a change in the Commission's approach and a purposeful attempt to develop these rights fully. For example, the Commission increasingly drew inspirations from international human rights jurisprudence to improve the depth of its reasoning and analysis of the provisions.[7]

It is also significant that, with the exception of the right to property, ESC rights are not subject to right-specific limitations. Nevertheless, the rights are subject to the general limitation in Article 27(2) of the Charter. The Commission has stated

3 Ibid. 57.

4 Ibid. 60.

5 Ibid. 59.

6 M. Ssenyonjo, 'The development of economic, social and cultural rights under the African Charter on Human and Peoples' Rights by the African Commission on Human and Peoples' Rights' (2015) 4 (2) *International Human Rights Law Review* 147, 158.

7 Ibid. 157, 159.

that the provision of Article 27(2) is the only legitimate ground for any limitations on the rights protected under the Charter. It has been held that any limitation of the rights in the Charter cannot be justified on the basis of 'popular will'.[8] In addition, the Commission has established in its jurisprudence that any limitation on the rights protected must be 'strictly proportionate' and 'absolutely necessary' for a legitimate need and should also be the least restrictive measure available.[9] It is also notable that the ESC rights are equally not subject to any derogation.[10]

The operationalisation of property rights faces a number of existing challenges across the continent. These challenges include the prevalence of insecurity of title to property in Member States, widespread gender-based discrimination in ownership of property and frequent government interference with property rights. The introduction of Article 14 was meant to address these problems. However, as stated previously, Article 14 like other ESC provisions is couched in broad terms. The broad nature of the property rights was noted in paragraphs 53 and 54 of the Commission's Guidelines and Principles on Economic, Social and Cultural Rights (Commission's Guidelines).[11] In the cases in which the Commission has had the opportunity to consider the right, it has provided minimal clarifications of the normative content of the right. Nonetheless, examples of what constitute the right to property may be gleaned from the Commission's case law. In *Constitutional Rights Project, Civil Liberties Organisation and Media Rights Agenda* v. *Nigeria*[12] the Commission stated that the right to property under Article 14 includes a right to have access to one's own property and not have the property removed, invaded or encroached upon.[13] Also, in *Malawi African Association and Others* v. *Mauritania*,[14] the Commission stated that 'property' includes 'land' under Article 14. A significant point to note is that the Commission has opined that a 'people' or a collective could be a bearer of property if they are an indigenous people in Africa.[15] Consequently, under the Commission's jurisprudence, a collective or communal right exists under Article 14 but it is subject to the same limitation as individual right to property.

8 *Legal Resources Foundation* v. *Zambia*, ACHPR, Communication No. 211/98 (2001).

9 *Centre for Minority Rights Development (Kenya) and Minority Rights Group (on behalf of Endorois Welfare Council)* v. *Kenya*, ACHPR, Communication No. 276/03 (2009).

10 *Supra*, M. Ssenyonjo (2015), 147, 152–153.

11 *Guidelines and Principles on the Implementation of Economic, Social and Cultural Rights in the African Charter on Human and Peoples' Rights*, Adopted 24 October 2011, ACHPR, available at: www.achpr.org/instruments/economic-social-cultural, accessed 11 April 2018.

12 *Constitutional Rights Project, Civil Liberties Organisation and Media Rights Agenda* v. *Nigeria*, ACHPR, Communication Nos 140/94, 141/94 and 145/95 (1999); See also *John K. Modise* v. *Botswana*, ACHPR, Communication No. 97/93 (2000).

13 See *Zimbabwe Lawyers for Human Rights & Associated Newspapers of Zimbabwe v. Zimbabwe*, ACHPR, Communication No. 284/03 (2009); Also see *Association of Victims of Post Electoral Violence & Interights* v. *Cameroon*, ACHPR, Communication No. 272/03 (2009).

14 *Malawi African Association and Others* v. *Mauritania*, ACHPR, Communication Nos 54/91, 61/91, 98/93, 164/97,196/97 and 210/98 (2000).

15 *Front for the Liberation of the State of Cabinda* v. *Republic of Angola*, ACHPR, Communication No. 328/06 (2013).

Furthermore, natural resources on such land could be the subject of ownership by a 'people'. The rationale for this is that the AU legal order recognises the strong traditional attachment that a people could have to their land. Therefore, for such a claim to succeed, the claimant must establish by evidence that they are an indigenous people with strong attachment to the land.[16] For example, in *The Nubian Community in Kenya* v. *The Republic of Kenya*[17] it was shown in evidence that the Kenyan Nubians (who were originally Sudanese soldiers used by the British colonial authorities in their military campaign) were settled by the British in the Kibera settlement in 1904. Each individual settled in Kibera was given a permit to reside and to build a house. No express legal title was conferred but it was understood that Kibera would be home to them. The Kenyan Nubians lived at this location for over a century. However, the fact that they had no express legal title to the land led to encroachment on the land by the government and other influential individuals. The Kenyan government claimed that the Kibera area was government land. Therefore, the Kenyan government routinely evicted individual Nubians from their property with no notice, provision of alternative property or compensation. Also, the Kenyan government did not offer any credible public interest justification for its actions. In its decision in that case the Commission concluded, based on the facts presented, that the Kenyan Nubians had formed an inextricable link to the land that is their only homeland. The Commission therefore held that the action of the Kenyan State was a violation of the Nubian property rights under Article 14.

The African Court took a similar approach in the case of *African Commission on Human and Peoples' Rights* v. *Kenya* where it likewise found a violation of Article 14.[18] This decision is considered a landmark because it was the Court's first decision on the rights of indigenous people. The case was in relation to the Ogiek people, a community of about 20,000 people. The community is based in the Mau Forest in the central rift valley of Kenya. Officials of the Kenyan Forest Service, a government agency, served an eviction notice on the community in 2009 ordering them to leave the Mau Forest within 30 days. The ground for the eviction was that the forest was a reserve water catchment zone and the presence of the community in the forest raised environment concerns. In addition, it was claimed that the forest was State property. The Ogiek people argued that the decision to evict them was taken without consultation with the community. Furthermore, it was contended that the decision did not take into consideration the bond between the community and their land as an indigenous people.

In dealing with the matter, the Court first had to address the question of whether the Ogiek community was an 'indigenous' community deserving of protection as such under the African Charter. Drawing inspiration from the work of the African Commission's Working Group on Indigenous

16 Ibid.

17 *The Nubian Community in Kenya* v. *The Republic of Kenya*, ACHPR, Communication No. 317/06 (2016).

18 Application No. 006/2012 (2017).

Populations/Communities[19] and the United Nations Special Rapporteur on Minorities,[20] and based on the historical evidence provided, the Court concluded that the Ogieks were an indigenous community 'that is part of the Kenyan people having a particular status and deserving special protection deriving from their vulnerability'.[21] On the basis of evidence of long possession and unhindered use of the Mau Forest by the Ogieks the Court was of the opinion that they were entitled to occupy the forest as their ancestral land. Consequently, the Ogieks could not be deprived of the land except for public purpose as provided in Article 14. The Kenyan State had argued that the eviction was necessary to protect the natural ecosystem of the forest. However, the Court held that the Kenyan State did not provide compelling evidence to support this argument. The Court therefore found a violation of Article 14.

The Complainant in *Mbiankeu Geneviève* v. *Cameroon*[22] was a Cameroonian citizen who also had French nationality and was resident in France. The Complainant and her husband purchased a plot of land in Yaounde, Cameroon. The transaction was done on their behalf by a local law firm. Documentation was issued by the Cameroonian authorities to certify the sale. However, when the couple commenced preparation for building on the land, the authorities intervened to stop the work. It was claimed that the land belonged to the government. The Complainants alleged that several acts of intimidation, bullying and destruction of property on the site were subsequently inflicted on them by the government and its agents. They claimed that these acts were designed to force them off the land. An attempt by the claimant's husband to report the matter to the police led to the police assaulting him. The Complainant's husband was subsequently informed that the certificate of ownership issued to the couple has been annulled by the government and that the land had been transferred to another person. The couple's attempts to seek judicial redress in Cameroon were ignored. The Commission noted that from the facts presented by the parties, the Cameroonian authorities did not claim to have denied the Complainant the property in the general interest of the community or for public need, the exceptions permitted in Article 14. Therefore, according to the Commission, what was up for determination was whether the subject matter in the case constituted property under the African Charter and whether the Complainant had necessary legal right in the property. The Commission acknowledged its failure to define with clarity in its previous jurisprudence what constituted 'property' under Article 14. However, the Commission went on to say that, 'property is generally understood as the right to use, enjoy and dispose of something in an exclusive and absolute

19 *Advisory Opinion of the African Commission on Human and Peoples' Rights on the United Nations Declaration on the Rights of Indigenous Peoples*, adopted by The African Commission on Human and Peoples' Rights at its 41st Ordinary Session held in May 2007 in Accra, Ghana.

20 *Report of the Special Rapporteur of the Sub-Commission on Prevention of Discrimination and Protection of Minorities*, E/CNA/Sub.2/1986/7/AddA.

21 Paragraph 122.

22 *Mbiankeu* v. *Cameroon*, ACHPR, Communication No. 389/10 (2015).

manner subject only to the limitations laid down by law'. Relying on its decision in *Malawi African Association and others* v. *Mauritania*[23] the Commission held that a plot of land and any building on it constitute property within the meaning of Article 14. The Commission thereafter observed that, under national and international law, a valid land certificate is regarded as proof of property ownership. The Commission was of the view that the Complainant's land certificate was valid in law and the purported annulment was inconsistent with Article 14 and therefore a violation of the Complainant's property right.

The Complainant also proffered an interesting and ingenious alternative argument. They contended that since the purpose for which they purchased the land was to build a family home, the actions of the authorities constituted a violation of the 'right to housing' under Article 14 read together with Article 16 (right to physical and mental health) and Article 18 (family rights). The Commission noted that in order to determine the existence of such a right, Article 14 has to be understood from three perspectives. In the first place, the right to property has to entail the possibility of including other associated rights. In the second place, the Commission opined that the right is also governed by the saying that 'the accessory follows the principal'. In the third place, the Commission stated that rights under the African Charter are interdependent and so is their realisation. After reviewing its previous jurisprudence, the Commission concluded that the right to housing exists in the AU legal order and that the action of the Cameroonian State was a violation of that right.

The Commission has attempted to address the normative content gap in the interpretation of Article 14 with the introduction of two principles. The first is the principle of ownership and peaceful enjoyment of property. The second is in relation to the conditions required to allow for State interference with the right in the public interest.[24] According to the Commission in *Interights, Institute for Human Rights and Development in Africa, and Association Mauritanienne des Droits de l'Homme* v. *Islamic Republic of Mauritania*,

> The right to property encompasses two main principles as a guide to the analysis of the article. The first one is of a general nature. It provides for the principle of ownership and peaceful enjoyment of property. The second principle provides for the possibility, and conditions of deprivation of the right to property. Article 14 of the Charter recognises that States are in certain circumstances entitled, among other things, to control the use of property in accordance with the public or general interest, by enforcing such laws as they deem necessary for the purpose.[25]

23 *Supra, Malawi African Association and Others* v. *Mauritania*.

24 See *Interights, Institute for Human Rights and Development in Africa, and Association Mauritanienne des Droits de l'Homme* v. *Islamic Republic of Mauritania*, ACHPR, Communication No. 373/2009 (2010); *supra, Malawi African Association and Others v. Mauritania; Centre on Housing Rights and Evictions v. The Sudan*, ACHPR, Communication Nos 279/03 and 296/05 (2009).

25 *Supra, Interights, Institute for Human Rights and Development in Africa, and Association Mauritanienne des Droits de l'Homme* v. *Islamic Republic of Mauritania*, paragraph 46.

Subsequent African human rights instruments have expanded on the right to property. An example is the Protocol to the African Charter on Human and Peoples' Rights on the Rights of Women in Africa, which requires Member States to put in place legal measures that guarantee a married woman's right to acquire property and to administer and manage it freely.[26] It also provides for the right to equitable sharing of joint property in case of separation, divorce or annulment of marriage.[27] Similarly, the right of inheritance for a widow is guaranteed under Article 21 of the protocol.[28]

Article 15 provides that 'every individual shall have the right to work under equitable and satisfactory conditions, and shall receive equal pay for equal work'. In the Commission's Guidelines, the Commission explained that the right to work in Article 15 is not an absolute and unconditional right to obtain employment. The obligation on the State is to 'facilitate employment through the creation of an environment conducive to the full employment of individuals within society under conditions that ensure the realisation of the dignity of the individual'.[29] According to the Commission, broadly, the provision implies the right to enter into employment and not be deprived of employment unfairly. In *Zimbabwe Lawyers for Human Rights and Associated Newspapers of Zimbabwe* v. *Zimbabwe*,[30] the State of Zimbabwe closed the Complainant's business without just cause. The Commission found the action of the State in this case to be a violation of Article 15. Similarly, in *Monim Elgak, Osman Hummeida and Amir Suliman (represented by FIDH and OMCT)* v. *Sudan*,[31] the Commission found that the closing down of the Khartoum Centre for Human Rights and Environmental Development and the freezing of the Centre's account without legitimate reason led to the loss of one of the applicant's sources of income. The Commission held that such unjustifiable interference is a violation of Article 15. Furthermore, the Commission found the violation of the right to work in *Annette Pagnoulle (on behalf of Abdoulaye Mazou)* v. *Cameroon*.[32] In that case the Complainant was previously imprisoned for five years without following due process. He was alleged to have helped his brother who was accused of taking part in a coup attempt against the government of the State. He was subsequently granted amnesty but was not reinstated to his job as a magistrate. The refusal to reinstate him was held to be a violation of Article 15. Similarly, in *Open Society Justice Initiative*

26 African Union, *Protocol to the African Charter on Human and Peoples' Rights on the Rights of Women in Africa*, adopted on 11 July 2003, Article 6 and Article 19.

27 Ibid. Article 7.

28 *Supra*, Ssenyonjo, 2015, 147, 161.

29 *Supra* (note 11), Commission's Guidelines, see paragraph 58; Also see *Monim Elgak, Osman Hummeida and Amir Suliman (represented by FIDH and OMCT)* v. *Sudan*, ACHPR, Communication No. 379/09 (2014).

30 *Zimbabwe Lawyers for Human Rights & Associated Newspapers of Zimbabwe v. Zimbabwe*, ACHPR, Communication No. 284/03 (2009).

31 *Supra, Monim Elgak*, et al. *(represented by FIDH and OMCT)* v. *Sudan*.

32 *Annette Pagnoulle (on behalf of Abdoulaye Mazou)* v. *Cameroon*, ACHPR, Communication No. 39/90 (1997).

v. *Côte d'Ivoire*,[33] the Commission held that where persons of an ethnic group are declared ineligible for certain public offices because of their ethnic origin or have their progression curtailed on that basis, a violation of Article 15 would be found.

The right to health and education are guaranteed under Articles 16 and 17. In a number of cases the Commission found the violation of these rights but with minimal explanation of the articles' normative content. In the Commission's Guidelines it is stated that the right to health includes the right to control one's health and body. Furthermore, it encompasses the right to be free from interference that affects health.[34] It has been held that where an individual is in the detention of a State, the observance of the right is greater and it is the responsibility of the State to ensure compliance.[35] Where the medication offered, in the case of ill health of a detainee, is inadequate and leaves the complainant vulnerable, a violation of the right will be found.[36] In *Free Legal Assistance Group and Others* v. *Zaire*,[37] the Commission found a violation in a case that alleged mismanagement of public finances, government failure to provide basic services, medicine supply shortages and closure of education institutions, among other complaints.[38]

It is noteworthy that the Commission took a more robust approach to the interpretation of Article 16 (and Article 24) in *SERAC* v. *Nigeria*.[39] The communication was filed by two NGOs: the Social and Economic Rights Action Centre and the Centre for Economic and Social Rights. The communication was against the Nigerian government and Shell Petroleum Development Corporation (SPDC), a subsidiary of Shell International, which was in a consortium with the Nigerian National Petroleum Corporation (NNPC).[40] The communication stated

33 *Open Society Justice Initiative* v. *Côte d'Ivoire*, ACHPR, Communication No. 318/06 (2015).

34 Ibid. paragraphs 64 and 65.

35 *Media Rights Agenda, Constitutional Rights Project, Media Rights Agenda and Constitutional Rights Project* v. *Nigeria*, Communication Nos 105/93, 128/94, 130/94 and 152/96 (1999), paragraphs 68 and 69.

36 *Supra*, *Monim Elgak*, et al. *(represented by FIDH and OMCT)* v. *Sudan*, paragraph 137.

37 *Free Legal Assistance Group and Others* v. *Zaire*, ACHPR, Communication Nos 25/89, 47/90, 56/91, 100/93 (1995).

38 Also see *International Pen and Others (on behalf of Saro-Wiwa)* v. *Nigeria*, ACHPR, Communication Nos 137/94, 139/94, 154/96 and 161/97 (1998); *Union Inter Africaine des Droits de l'Homme, Federation Internationale des Ligues des Droits de l'Homme and Others* v. *Angola*, ACHPR, Communication No. 159/96 (1997); *International PEN, Constitutional Rights Project, Civil Liberties Organisation and Interights (on behalf of Ken Saro-Wiwa Jnr.)* v. *Nigeria*, ACHPR, Communication Nos 137/94, 139/94, 154/96 and 161/97 (1998).

39 D. Shelton, 'Decision regarding Communication 155/96 (Social and Economic Rights Action/ Center for Economic and Social Rights v Nigeria). Case No. ACHPR/ Comm. A044/1' (2002) 96 (4) *The American Journal of International Law* 937; F. Coomans, 'Case comment: the Ogoni case before the African Commission on Human and Peoples' Rights' (2003) 52 (3) *International and Comparative Law Quarterly* 749; J. C. Nwobike, 'The African Commission on Human and Peoples' Rights and demystification of second and third generation rights under the African Charter: Social and Economic Rights Action Center (SERAC) and the Centre for Economic and Social Rights (CESR) v Nigeria' (2004–2005) 1 (2) *African Journal of Legal Studies* 129.

40 The NNPC is a Nigerian State-owned corporation created under the Nigerian National Petroleum Decree No. 33 of 1977.

that the government of Nigeria was involved in oil production through the NNPC. The communication alleged that the operations of SPDC caused health problems in Ogoni land among other allegations. The communication further alleged that the oil consortium exploited oil reserves with no regard for the health or environment of the local communities and disposed of toxic wastes into the environment and local waterways in violation of international standards. The activities of SPDC, according to the communication, led to the contamination of water, soil and air, which had serious short- and long-term health impacts. The communication alleged that the Nigerian government condoned and facilitated the violations by placing legal and military powers at the disposal of the oil companies. The communication accused the government of failing to monitor the activities of the oil companies, failing to conduct environmental impact studies, preventing independent scientists carrying out the environmental impact studies and keeping information on oil production from local communities.

The Nigerian government did not contest the substance of the claim. The government conceded that 'there is no denying the fact that a lot of atrocities were and are still being committed by the oil companies in Ogoni Land and indeed in the Niger Delta area'.[41] The government asserted, however, that it was taking remedial measures to correct the situation. In its decision, the Commission underscored the first line responsibility of States in the protection of human rights by holding that African governments have a duty to monitor and control the activities of domestic and multinational corporations.[42] Furthermore, the Commission held emphatically that African States should ensure respect for economic, social and cultural rights. Relying on its earlier decision in *Union des Jeunes Avocats* v. *Chad*,[43] and the decision of the Inter-American Court of Human Rights in *Velasquez Rodriguez* v. *Honduras*[44] as well as that of the European Court of Human Rights in *X and Y* v. *Netherlands*,[45] the Commission held that governments have the duty to protect their citizens through appropriate legislation and effective enforcement and also to protect them from damaging acts that may be perpetrated by private parties.[46]

The Commission criticised the way in which the Nigerian government related to the corporations, finding that the government had failed to exercise

41 *Social and Economic Rights Action Centre (SERAC) and The Centre for Economic and Social Rights (CESR)* v. *Nigeria*, ACHPR, Communication No. 155/96 (2001), paragraph 42.

42 See also, *supra*, Shelton (2002) at 941.

43 *Union des Jeunes Avocats* v. *Chad*, ACHPR, Communication No. 74/92 (1995); *Ninth Annual Activity Report of The African Commission on Human and Peoples' Rights* 1995–1996, 32nd Ordinary Session, 7–10 July 1996, ACHPR/AHG/207(XXXII).

44 Inter-American Court of Human Rights, *Velasquez Rodriguez* v. *Honduras*, judgment of July 19, 1988, Series C, No. 4.

45 European Court of Human Rights, *X and Y* v. *Netherlands*, judgment of March 26, 1985, Series A, No. 91, at 32.

46 *Supra*, *Social and Economic Rights Action Centre (SERAC) and The Centre for Economic and Social Rights* (CESR) v. *Nigeria*, paragraph 57.

the necessary degree of care required in the circumstances.[47] The Nigerian government was found to have facilitated the destruction of communities and also to have given the 'green light' to private actors, especially the oil companies, to devastatingly affect the well-being of the Ogonis.[48] According to the Commission:

> the Government of Nigeria facilitated the destruction of the Ogoniland. Contrary to its obligations and despite such internationally established principles, the Nigerian Government has given green light to private actors, and the oil companies in particular, to devastatingly affect the well-being of the Ogonis. By any measure of standards, its practice falls short of the minimum conduct expected of governments, and therefore, is in violation of the African Charter.[49]

The Commission expanded on its interpretation of the normative content of Article 16 in *Centre on Housing Rights and Evictions* v. *The Sudan*.[50] The Commission relied on a similar interpretation of the right in international law to achieve this. The Commission noted with approval the considerable developments in international law with respect to the normative definition of the right to health, which it observed 'includes both health care and healthy conditions'. The Commission made reference to the UN Committee on Economic, Social and Cultural Rights General Comment No. 14 on the right to health adopted in 2000, which states, *inter alia*, 'the right to health extends not only to timely and appropriate health care but also to the underlying determinants of health, such as access to safe and portable water, an adequate supply of safe food, nutrition, and housing'. Based on the General Comment, the Commission identified the four elements of the right to health that include availability, accessibility, acceptability and quality. Furthermore, it identified States' obligations in this regard to include the duty to respect, fulfill and protect the right to health. It also emphasised the duty on States to ensure that non-state actors do not infringe on the right to health. It noted that '[v]iolations of the right to health can occur through the direct action of States or other entities insufficiently regulated by States'. Referencing its previous decision in *Free Legal Assistance Group and Others* v. *Zaire*,[51] it affirmed that the failure of a State to provide basic services such as safe drinking water and electricity and the shortage of medicine constitutes a violation of Article 16. It finally held in that case that the destruction of homes, livestock and farms as well as the poisoning of water sources such as wells exposed the victims to serious health risks and therefore amounted to a violation of Article 16 of the Charter.

47 Ibid. paragraph 59.
48 Ibid. paragraph 58.
49 Ibid.
50 *Supra, Centre on Housing Rights and Evictions* v. *The Sudan*.
51 *Supra, Free Legal Assistance Group and Others* v. *Zaire*.

In its Guidelines, the Commission laid down the minimum core obligations of Member States in relation to the right to education under Article 17(1) as follows:

> a To ensure that all children enjoy their right to free and compulsory primary education. No children should be denied this right because of school fees or related costs of education. Special measures may be required to ensure that children belonging to disadvantaged or vulnerable groups receive free primary education. To achieve this objective states are bound to progressively increase the amount of national resources allocated to education.
>
> b To implement policies to eliminate or reduce the costs of attending primary school which include the provision of stipends, providing free or subsidised uniforms (or lifting of uniform requirements), provision of free textbooks, provision of free or subsidised transportation or free school meals to encourage the attendance of poor children at school.[52]

The Commission considered the violation of Article 17(1) on the right to education in *Kevin Mgwanga Gunme* et al. v. *Cameroon*[53] but found that the facts of the case did not support the finding of a violation. It is notable that a sub-regional court, the ECOWAS Court, had held that the right to education in Article 17 is justiciable and enforceable by the ECOWAS court itself.[54] In relation to Article 17(2) on cultural rights the Commission has defined 'culture' to include 'cultural diversity'. The Commission stated in *Centre for Minority Rights Development (Kenya) and Minority Rights Group (on behalf of Endorois Welfare Council)* v. *Kenya*[55]

> that Article 17 of the Charter is of a dual dimension in both its individual and collective nature, protecting, on the one hand, individuals' participation in the cultural life of their community and, on the other hand, obliging the state to promote and protect traditional values recognised by a community. It thus understands culture to mean that complex whole which includes a spiritual and physical association with one's ancestral land, knowledge, belief, art, law, morals, customs, and any other capabilities and habits acquired by humankind as a member of society – the sum total of the material and spiritual activities and products of a given social group that distinguish it from other similar groups. It has also understood cultural identity to encompass a group's religion, language, and other defining characteristics.

52 Ibid. paragraph 71; *Supra*, Commission's Guidelines.

53 *Kevin Mgwanga Gunme* et al. v. *Cameroon*, ACHPR, Communication No. 266/03 (2009).

54 *Socio-Economic Rights and Accountability Project (SERAP)* v. *Federal Republic of Nigeria and Universal Basic Education*, ECW/CCJ/APP/0808 (2008).

55 *Supra*, *Centre for Minority Rights Development (Kenya) and Minority Rights Group (on behalf of Endorois Welfare Council)* v. *Kenya*.

In its practice, in order to expatiate on the normative content of the right, the Commission has interpreted the concept of 'culture' with the aid of the United Nation's International Covenant on Economic, Social and Cultural Rights.[56]

In *African Commission on Human and Peoples' Rights* v. *Kenya*[57] the African Court made an important finding in relation to the right to culture in Article17(2) and (3) of the Charter. In that case it was contended that the cultural rights of the Ogieks were violated by Kenya through its restrictions of access to the Mau Forest that hosts the Ogieks' cultural sites. In response the Kenyan State argued that the Ogieks no longer led their original lifestyles because of modernity and had therefore lost any claim to a distinctive cultural identity. The Court rejected this argument, holding that 'stagnation or the existence of a static way of life is not a defining element of culture or cultural distinctiveness'.[58] The Court recognised that certain changes are bound to happen to culture overtime and these changes do not necessarily defeat the claim to cultural rights.

Article 18 provides protection for the family unit, which it recognises as the custodian of morals and traditional values in the society. In subparagraph 3 of that Article a specific duty is imposed on States to eliminate discrimination against women and to ensure the protection of women and children's rights under international law. The Article also provides for the provision of special measures for the aged and the disabled. In *Egyptian Initiative for Personal Rights and INTERIGHTS* v. *Egypt*[59] a complaint was brought on behalf of four women who were part of a protest by the European Movement for Change. It was alleged that, during the protest, the protesters were cornered by the riot police in such a way that allowed supporters of the government to attack the protesters. In the circumstances the women (the Complainants) were intimidated, insulted and sexually harassed. The women made an official complaint but this move led to further threats from the State Security Intelligence officers and certain unidentified individuals. The Commission *inter alia* found a violation of Article 18(3) because the acts targeted the Complainants as women and were aimed at silencing or discouraging their participation in the political affairs of the country. In *Amnesty International* v. *Zambia*, African Commission on Human and Peoples' Rights,[60] the Commission concluded that forced expulsion leading to the dispersal of families of the complainants is a violation of Article 18. Similarly, it concluded in *Open Society Justice Initiative* v. *Côte d'Ivoire*[61] that the restriction of the movement of the Complainant that made family visits difficult was a violation of Article 18. Also, in *Union Inter Africaine des*

56 UN General Assembly, *International Covenant on Economic, Social and Cultural Rights*, 16 December 1966, G.A. Res. 2200A (XXI), 21 U.N. GAOR Supp. (No. 16) at 49, U.N. Doc. A/6316 (1966), 993 U.N.T.S. 3, entered into force 3 January 1976.

57 *Supra, African Commission on Human and Peoples' Rights* v. *Kenya*.

58 Ibid, paragraph 185.

59 *Egyptian Initiative for Personal Rights and INTERIGHTS v. Egypt*, ACHPR, Communication No. 323/06 (2011).

60 *Amnesty International* v. *Zambia*, ACHPR, Communication No. 212/98 (1999).

61 *Supra, Open Society Justice Initiative* v. *Côte d'Ivoire*.

Droits de l'Homme, Federation Internationale des Ligues des Droits de l'Homme and Others v. *Angola*[62] a case alleging unlawful expulsion of West African Nationals in 1996, the Commission found violations of Article 18.

Group rights

Generally speaking, these are rights that could be collectively held. These rights are also known as peoples' rights, collectivities rights, communities' rights or solidarity rights.[63] Group rights are important in the African context because they embody a core principle of African philosophy – the preservation of community and group – as discussed in Chapter 2. This informs the pre-eminence that the African Charter accorded to these rights. Group rights are part of the foundation principles of the Charter and the AU legal order.[64]

Group rights are a controversial subject in the human rights and international law discourse. The source of the controversy is in the nature of the rights themselves. Critics of group rights have argued that a 'collective' or 'group' could not be a 'human' so as to have human rights. It has also been argued that the human rights concept protects people in their individual capacity. Furthermore, it is also contended that the idea of group rights may lead to a conflict between the interests of an individual and that of a community. This may unwittingly enable the State (acting for the collective) to undermine individual rights. It has also been argued that it is difficult to ascertain group rights and the nature of the rights.[65] As will be shown presently, the conceptualisation of group rights in the African legal order addresses these issues to a reasonable extent.

Certain group rights are generally accepted as well-established concepts. These include minority rights, rights of indigenous people and the right to self-determination narrowly defined. However, other types of group rights, such as the right to development and the right to a clean environment, remain controversial. As stated previously and in order to give a level of precision to the concept, group rights are provided for in Articles 19–24 of the African Charter. These include peoples' equality rights and freedom from domination (Article 19), right to existence and self-determination (Article 20), right to freely dispose of wealth and natural resources (Article 21), right to development (Article 22) peace and security (Article 23) and environment and development rights (Article 24). However, the concept of group right is not defined anywhere in the Charter itself.[66]

62 *Supra, Union Inter Africaine des Droits de l'Homme, Federation Internationale des Ligues des Droits de l'Homme and Others* v. *Angola*.

63 M. Ssenyonjo (ed.), *The African Regional Human Rights System: 30 Years After the African Charter on Human and Peoples' Rights* (Martinus Nijhoff, 2011) 102.

64 D. M. Chirwa, 'Group rights and the protection of economic, social and cultural rights in Africa' in D. M. Chirwa and L. Chenwi, *The Protection of Economic, Social and Cultural Rights in Africa* (Cambridge University Press, 2016) 212.

65 Ibid. 214.

66 *Antonie Bissangou* v. *Congo*, ACHPR, Communication No. 253/02 (2006).

The failure to define the concept may have been deliberate in an attempt to avoid controversies in the negotiation of the provisions of the Charter given its controversial nature. This is more so because of the concept's potential to conflict with the concept of sovereignty and territorial integrity that are also fundamental to the political order in Africa. Furthermore, as noted previously, there is the potential for this category of rights to conflict with individual rights, thereby raising the question of whether or not group rights could trump individual rights. It has been suggested that one way of avoiding the controversies around this concept and the potential conflict is to treat group rights as *sui generis*.[67] This suggestion is consistent with the *sui generis* nature of the evolving African legal order.

Another problem with the concept as expressed in the Charter is its failure to identify with clarity the beneficiaries of the rights, i.e., 'people'. However, the African Commission has attempted to elucidate on the concept in its practice. The Commission has put forward three main meanings that could be ascribed to the word 'people' as beneficiaries under the Charter. According to the Commission, 'people' may mean the entire people of a country or a specific group of people within a Member State who perceive themselves as distinct or as an indigenous people.[68] In *Legal Resources Foundation* v. *Zambia*,[69] it was alleged by the Complainant that a Member State, Zambia, had put in place a constitution that infringed on the right of 35% of the population including the State's first president Kenneth Kaunda. The constitution required potential candidates for the office of the president in Zambia to positively prove that both of their parents are or were Zambians by descent. This requirement effectively barred the 35% from aspiring to the office of president. Therefore, the Complainant alleged that the law violated Article 2 of the Charter (on freedom from discrimination) and Article 19. This argument is significant because it called for a consideration of the distinction between Article 2 on the prohibition of discrimination against individuals and Article 19, which is similar but in the context of a 'people' as a collective. In its ruling the Commission readily found a violation of Article 2. However, in relation to Article 19, the Commission was of the opinion that the provision did not apply for the following reasons:

> The Commission believes that recourse to Article 19 of the Charter was mistaken. The section dealing with "peoples" cannot apply in this instance. To do so would require evidence that the effect of the measure was to affect adversely an identifiable group of Zambian citizens by reason of their common ancestry, ethnic origin, language or cultural habits. The allegedly offensive provisions in the Zambia Constitution (Amendment) Act, 1996 do not seek to do that.[70]

67 *Supra*, Ssenyonjo, (2011) 107.
68 Ibid. 108.
69 *Supra, Legal Resources Foundation* v. *Zambia*.
70 Ibid. paragraph 73.

Also, in *Malawi African Association and Others* v. *Mauritania*,[71] the Commission could not find a violation of Article 19 because of the gap in the information presented to it, but instead relied on Article 2 in its finding against the Member State. Again, the rationale for this decision was that, for an action to succeed based on Article 19, sufficient evidence of the violation of peoples' rights as opposed to individual rights must be provided by the complainant. This was successfully done in *Kevin Mgwanga Guneme* et al. v. *Cameroon*.[72] In that case it was alleged that the decision to relocate certain business activities and economic projects from the Complainants' territory in Limbe, Southern Cameroon, to the Francophone part of the Member State generated negative effect on the economic life of Southern Cameroon and therefore was a violation of Article 19. The Member State did not respond directly to the allegation but contended that it relocated the activities and projects because of the need to monitor movements of persons, ensure security and efficient customs control. The Commission was not persuaded by this contention and held that:

> Every State has an obligation under international law to preserve the integrity of its entire territory. The maintenance of security and movements of persons and goods on the territory is part of that obligation. The argument by the Respondent State that it could not guarantee the security of persons and goods at Limbe, unless it moved the port, is tantamount to acknowledging that it had no control of Limbe. The Commission believes that the security and customs authorities could have effectively monitored the movement of persons and goods, even if the seaport had continued to be at Limbe. The Commission states that the relocation of business enterprises and location of economic projects to Francophone Cameroon, which generated negative effects on the economic life of Southern Cameroon, constituted violation of Article 19 of the Charter.[73]

Article 20 on existence and self-determination has been invoked in only a handful of cases. The issue of self-determination is not only controversial because of its sensitive nature but also because of its potential to conflict with territorial integrity and sovereignty. The Commission has thus been very cautious in its approach to the interpretation and application of Article 20. The Commission tends to be less likely to find a violation if the complaint is brought by a specific group within a Member State.[74] In *Kevin Mgwanga Guneme* et al. v. *Cameroon*[75] the Complainant argued that Southern Cameroonians are a 'separate and distinct people' under Article 20. The claim was based on the contention that during the colonial period Southern

71 *Supra, Malawi African Association and Others* v. *Mauritania*.
72 *Supra, Kevin Mgwanga Gunme* et al. v. *Cameroon*.
73 Ibid. paragraphs 161–162.
74 See, for example, *Katangese Peoples' Congress* v. *Congo*, ACHPR, Communication No. 75/92 (1995).
75 *Supra, Kevin Mgwanga Gunme* et al. v. *Cameroon*.

Cameroon was colonised and administered as part of the British Empire, in contrast to most of the rest of the country that was under French colonial rule. The experience made the people distinct to the rest of the country. For example, the people of Southern Cameroon speak English and also follow the English common law tradition. The rest of the country mostly speak French and follow the French civil law tradition. The Commission acknowledged the controversial nature of the concept of peoples' rights and the fact that the drafters of the Charter intentionally refrained from defining the concept to avoid controversy. The Commission therefore relied on a UNESCO group of experts' characterisation in determining the nature of the rights. The characteristics were stated to include a common historical tradition, a racial or ethnic identity, cultural homogeneity, linguistic unity, religious and ideological affinities, territorial connection and a common economic life. In addition, 'a group may also identify itself as a people, by virtue of their consciousness that they are a people'.[76] Based on the above, the Commission stated that the peoples' rights provisions under the Charter could 'be exercised by a people, bound together by their historical, traditional, racial, ethnic, cultural, linguistic, religious, ideological, geographical, economic identities and affinities, or other bonds'.[77] The Commission was of the view that the Southern Cameroonians presented sufficient evidence to establish their distinct right as a 'people' and thus could claim group rights. According to the Commission, 'they manifest numerous characteristics and affinities, which include a common history, linguistic tradition, territorial connection and political outlook. More importantly they identify themselves as a people with a separate and distinct identity'.[78]

The Commission briefly considered the relationship between peoples' rights and individual rights under the Charter. The Commission emphasised that the two categories are important and should be accorded equal status. According to the Commission, each member of a group carried their individual rights into a group to create collective rights. It is noted that the attempt to explain the relationship does not comprehensively address the criticisms highlighted previously in this chapter. Despite the fact that the Commission accepted the argument that Southern Cameroonians were a people for the purpose of Article 20, it rejected the argument put forward to support the violation of Article 20. The reason for this was that the claim is secessionist in nature and will therefore jeopardise the territorial integrity of a Member State. According to the Commission, a complainant cannot invoke the article to threaten the territorial integrity of a Member State. The Commission stated:

> The Commission states that secession is not the sole avenue open to Southern Cameroonians to exercise the right to self-determination. The African Charter cannot be invoked by a Complainant to threaten the sovereignty and

76 Ibid. paragraph 170.
77 Ibid. paragraph 171.
78 Ibid. paragraph 179.

> territorial integrity of a State party. The Commission has however accepted that autonomy within a sovereign state, in the context of self-government, confederacy, or federation, while preserving territorial integrity of a State party, can be exercised under the Charter.[79]

However, in *Dawda Jawara* v. *The Gambia*,[80] the Commission found a violation of the article because the violation established in the case affected the entire people in the Member State. Also, in *Democratic Republic of Congo* v. *Burundi, Rwanda, Uganda*,[81] the Commission was of the opinion that unlawful occupation of the territory of another Member State is a violation of Article 20. The Commission has also found a violation of the right to self-determination where a government unlawfully annulled a democratic election. This is because such action interferes with the right of people to make political choices freely.[82] Similarly, the Commission has held that a military coup against an elected government is a violation of Article 20.[83] From the foregoing it is therefore reasonable to conclude that the Commission is willing to enforce the right to self-determination within a very narrow scope.

Article 21 protects the right of all people to freely dispose of their wealth and natural resources. The right is required to be exercised to the exclusive interest of the people and it is specifically stated that 'people' must not be deprived of this right. The right extends to Member States in their individual capacity and as a collective in the pursuit of African unity and solidarity. Interestingly, the provision also addresses 'foreign exploitation', which may impact on the enjoyment of the right in subparagraph 5 as follows:

> State Parties to the present Charter shall undertake to eliminate all forms of foreign exploitation particularly that practised by international monopolies so as to enable their peoples to fully benefit from the advantages derived from their national resources.

According to the Commission in *The Social and Economic Rights Action Centre and the Centre for Economic and Social Rights* v. *Nigeria*,[84] the origin of this provision dates back to the exploitation of human and material resources from Africa during the colonial period. In *Antonie Bissangou* v. *Congo*,[85] the Commission stated that, in view of origin of the article and its wordings, the article could only

79 Ibid. paragraphs 191–192.

80 *Dawda Jawara* v. *The Gambia*, ACHPR, Communication Nos 147/95 and 149/96 (2000).

81 *Democratic Republic of Congo* v. *Burundi, Rwanda, Uganda*, ACHPR, Communication No. 227/99 (2003), paragraph 77.

82 *Constitutional Rights Project and Civil Liberties Organisation* v. *Nigeria*, ACHPR, Communication No. 102/93 (1998).

83 *Supra, Dawda Jawara* v. *The Gambia*.

84 *Supra, The Social and Economic Rights Action Centre and the Centre for Economic and Social Rights* v. *Nigeria*.

85 *Supra, Antonie Bissangou v. Congo*.

be invoked where the rights of a 'people' to dispose of their wealth and natural resources have been infringed. Therefore, the provision will not apply where assets belonging to an individual or property were in dispute.[86] In *Democratic Republic of Congo* v. *Burundi, Rwanda, Uganda,*[87] the Democratic Republic of Congo *inter alia* accused the armed forces of the respondent countries of systematic looting during their occupation of the Complainant's territory. The Commission emphatically disapproved of the occupation and held that the evidence of looting presented sufficiently supported a finding of the violation of Article 21. In *African Commission on Human and Peoples' Rights* v. *Kenya,*[88] the African Court held that ethnic groups and communities could claim Article 21 rights as long as the group or community do not use such a claim as a guise for calling into question the sovereignty and integrity of the Member State.

With respect to Article 22, the Commission stated in *Open Society Justice Initiative* v. *Côte d'Ivoire* that Article 22 of the Charter is a pioneer international instrument that proclaims and guarantees the right to development.[89] The Commission has adopted a definition of this right by application rather than conceptualisation.[90] Drawing on its case law, the Commission was of the view that:

> there is indeed a fundamental convergence to comprehend the right to development as an inalienable, individual or collective right, to participate in all forms of development, through the full realization of all fundamental rights, and to enjoy them without unjustifiable restrictions.

The Commission emphasised the need for a gradual implementation of the right and, at the minimum, States' obligations to create opportunities and an environment conducive to the enjoyment of the Article 22 right. In its decision in *Open Society Justice Initiative* v. *Côte d'Ivoire*, the Commission concluded that the restrictions placed on the recognition of the nationality of the Dioula ethnic group by the Member State (Côte d'Ivoire) violated the Dioula's right to development under Article 22 because it inhibited their participation in and enjoyment of the right.

In *Sudan Human Rights Organisation & Centre on Housing Rights and Evictions (COHRE)* v. *Sudan,*[91] it was alleged that Sudanese government forces and an Arab militia (the Janjaweed) attacked the black African tribes in the Darfur region and thereby violated their rights under the African Charter. The attacks led to forced displacement, which denied the people the opportunity to engage in economic, social and cultural activities. Furthermore, it was alleged that the displacement interfered with the right to education for the tribes' children and

86 Ibid. paragraphs 81–82.

87 *Supra, Democratic Republic of Congo* v. *Burundi, Rwanda, Uganda.*

88 *Supra, African Commission on Human and Peoples' Rights* v. *Kenya.*

89 *Supra, Open Society Justice Initiative* v. *Côte d'Ivoire*, paragraph 181.

90 Ibid. paragraph 182.

91 *Sudan Human Rights Organisation & Centre on Housing Rights and Evictions (COHRE)* v. *Sudan*, ACHPR, Communication Nos 279/03–296/05 (2009).

pursuit of other activities. The Commission held that these allegations were sufficiently proven and had led to marginalisation and underdevelopment of the Complainants. Therefore the Commission concluded that the Sudanese Member State violated Article 22.[92]

Article 23 introduced the peoples' right to peace and security into the African legal order.[93] According to Article 23(1) the right applies at both the domestic national level and the international level. The Article provides that all peoples shall have the right to national and international peace and security. The Commission has had the opportunity to consider this unique right in a couple of cases. In *Malawi African Association and Others* v. *Mauritania*,[94] the Commission was of the view that an unprovoked attack by the Mauritanian State forces on villages in another Member State was a violation of the right of the people in the village to live in peace and security under Article 23. It further extended the right to cover the State's responsibility for non-State actors in the territory of a Member State such as rebel forces. According to the Commission it is part of a Member State's responsibility to ensure that non-State actors do not violate the Article 23 right. It is worth noting that the Commission did not address the question of what constituted a 'people' in the context of Article 23. But it is safe to conclude that the villagers under attack in that case were regarded as 'a people' by the Commission. It is also notable that the Commission rejected a part of the communication that alleged that black Mauritanians were discriminated against as 'a people', but instead considered the discrimination as violations of individual rights under the Charter.[95]

Also in *Democratic Republic of Congo* v. *Burundi, Rwanda, Uganda*[96] the Commission considered the cross-border implication of Article 23. In that case the Democratic Republic of Congo had alleged that the respondent Member States occupied its territory without justification and perpetrated a range of illegal acts on the territory and its people. In deciding in favour of the Complainant, the Commission held that there is an obligation on Member States not to violate the territorial integrity of other Member States by force, threat or other act of aggression. Furthermore, in this case the Commission stated that Article 23 places an obligation on Member States to seek amicable solutions to disputes rather than resorting to use of force.

As mentioned in the previous discussion on Article 16, the Commission considered the peoples' right to a general satisfactory environment under Article 24 in *SERAC* v. *Nigeria*.[97] This is the only communication in which the right has

92 See also the African Court's decision in *African Commission on Human and Peoples' Rights* v. *Kenya*, Application No. 006/2012 (2017).

93 See Chapter 6 on the wider peace and security architecture of the AU legal order.

94 *Supra, Malawi African Association and Others* v. *Mauritania*.

95 *Supra, Sudan Human Rights Organisation & Centre on Housing Rights and Evictions (COHRE)* v. *Sudan*.

96 *Supra, Democratic Republic of Congo* v. *Burundi, Rwanda, Uganda*.

97 *Supra, Social and Economic Rights Action Centre (SERAC) and The Centre for Economic and Social Rights (CESR)* v. *Nigeria*.

been considered so far. In that case the Commission was of the view that the article places an obligation on Member States to take reasonable measures to prevent pollution and economic ecological degradation, promote conservation and to secure an ecologically sustainable development and use of natural resources.

Conclusions

The African Commission has played a pivotal role in the development and harmonisation process of human rights standards within the AU legal order. It has not only advanced the rights guaranteed under the Charter but has incrementally maintained its uniqueness. The provisions on economic, social and cultural rights and group rights are substantially unique and distinguish AU legal order on human rights from comparable supranational and international instruments. Furthermore, the Commission has expanded upon these rights as discussed in Chapter 7. The expansion was achieved through the use of the concept of unenumerated rights and recourse to international law and international human rights laws in its decisions. The African Commission's approach to its interpretation has enabled the emergence of a *sui generis* human rights system within the African legal order. It is envisaged that the work of the Commission has provided a solid foundation for AU law in this area and will be carried forward by the new African Court going forward.

9 Custom, morality and African Union law

The case of sexual orientation in Africa

Introduction

One of the challenges that the evolvement of a continental-wide legal order faces in Africa is how to reconcile the African diversity of customs and concepts of morality with the emerging legal order. This is significant because, as previously discussed in Chapter 2, customary law historically plays a significant role as a source of law in Africa. Customary law largely reflects communities' notion of morality. An issue that has given rise to major controversy in recent times is the issue of sexual orientation/homosexuality and its compatibility with custom, morality and law in the continent. In this chapter the tension between custom/morality and law is examined through the lens of sexual orientation. This is important because many Member States' approach to the issue and recent national legislation in some Member States appear to contradict the AU legal order. The chapter will consider how the emerging AU legal order can deal with these tensions and be a positive force for the harmonisation of the Member States' position that is also consistent with international standards.

Background

According to Chitando and Mateveke, 'homosexuality has occupied a site that is problematic and heavily contested' in the continent.[1] There was and perhaps still is a wide perception across the continent that homosexuality is alien to Africa or 'un-African', or a Western import. However, from the scant available evidence, there is support for the notion that experimentation with sexuality existed in Africa prior to colonisation. For example, the historical paintings of Nyankh-Khnum and Khnum-hotep, two high officials in Ancient Egypt, suggest that they might have been in a same-sex relationship. However, Egyptologists and historians disagree on the interpretation of the paintings. Furthermore, from extensive studies carried out on the subject of sexuality it appears that European missionaries, colonial officials and explorers have recorded instances

1 E. Chitando and P. Mateveke, 'Africanizing the discourse on homosexuality: challenges and prospects' (2017) 9 (1) *Critical African Studies*, 124, 126.

of homosexuality in the continent.[2] It thus seems that, traditionally, in most communities in pre-colonial Africa, there was, at the least, ambivalence towards the issue of homosexuality or other sexual orientations. Significantly, the introduction of the Abrahamic and monotheistic religions of Christianity and Islam have emphatically reshaped the African perception on other sexual orientations to a largely negative one over time. As the influence of the Abrahamic religions increased across the continent, so did the hardened stance against other sexual orientations. Most worryingly, the issue has been politicised, with some Member States introducing laws to criminalise and restrict homosexuality and other sexual orientations.

The prevailing attitude has its origin in colonialism. Part of the colonial legacy in Africa is the introduction of laws that criminalise and punish same-sex relationships. In recent times these laws have been extended, made more draconian or widened to cover other areas such as same-sex marriage, social life and advocacy.[3] For example, Nigeria introduced the Same-Sex Marriage (Prohibition) Act 2013, which bans same-sex marriage and imposes ten years' imprisonment for anyone participating, formalising or witnessing a same-sex marriage. It went further to place a ban on gay clubs and organisations in Nigeria. It is also notable that, under the Sharia law that is applicable in some of the states in the northern part of Nigeria, the punishment for homosexuality is death by stoning.

Similarly, Uganda attempted to extend its inherited laws on homosexuality by introducing the Uganda Anti-Homosexuality Act of 2014. It introduced a sentence of life imprisonment for what it called 'aggravated homosexuality'. However, the law was struck down by the Ugandan Constitutional Court on procedural grounds. Nevertheless, through its actions and policies, the Ugandan government continues to curtail the expression of same-sex orientation. Another example is the legal framework in The Gambia. Under s.144 of The Gambia Criminal Code (as amended) by the Criminal Code Amendment Act 2005, homosexuality is described as 'unnatural' and punishable by 14 years' imprisonment. In addition, The Gambia Penal Code was amended in 2005 to introduce the crime of 'aggravated homosexuality' with the punishment of lifetime imprisonment. Similar laws that explicitly criminalise homosexuality could be found in 36 of the 54 Member States of the African Union. Only 16 countries have laws that directly or indirectly (by silence) permit sexual relationships other than heterosexuality[4] and currently South Africa has the most advanced law on sexual orientation in the continent.

2 M. Epprecht, *Heterosexual Africa? The History of an Idea from the Age of Exploration to the Age of AIDS* (Ohio University Press, 2008); S. O. Murray, *Boy-Wives and Female-Husbands: Studies in African Homosexualities: Studies of African Homosexualities* (Palgrave Macmillan, 2001).

3 A. Rudman, 'The protection against discrimination based on sexual orientation under the African human rights system' (2015) 15 (1) *African Human Rights Law Journal* 1, 3.

4 K. Esom, B. Nibogora and R. Armstrong (eds), *African Reflections on Sexuality and Equality*, Vol. 12 (African Men for Sexual Health and Rights [AMSHeR] Johannesburg: South Africa, 2015).

The African Charter and sexual orientation

The status of sexual orientation under the African Charter itself appears unsettled.[5] The right to sexual orientation is not explicitly and directly protected under the African Charter. However, this is not peculiar to the African Charter because some of the major human rights instruments such as the European Convention on Human Rights (ECHR), Universal Declaration of Human Rights (UDHR) and its two Covenants[6] do not contain explicit protection for sexual orientation. Nonetheless, under the UDHR framework, sexual orientation has been accommodated under existing protected rights. According to the UN Human Rights Committee, a UN body that examines reports and rules on individual complaints in relation to the International Covenant on Civil and Political Rights (ICCPR), sexual orientation is a prohibited ground as part of the wider prohibition against discrimination in Article 2(1) and 26 of the ICCPR. Even though the Articles specifically reference 'sex' as the prohibited ground, the Committee has held that 'sex' also includes sexual orientation. This was the approach taken by the Human Rights Committee in *Toonen* v. *Australia*[7] and *Joslin* v. *New Zealand*.[8] However, in subsequent cases, *Edward Young* v. *Australia*[9] and *X* v. *Colombia*,[10] the Committee simply stated that under Article 26 discrimination on the ground of sexual orientation is prohibited. In *Toonen* v. *Australia*[11] the UN Committee further held that the criminalisation of homosexuality in a State (Tasmania) was unreasonable and was an arbitrary interference with the individual's right to privacy under Article 17(1) of the ICCPR.

Also, the United Nations Committee on Economic, Social and Cultural Rights has stated in its General Comment 20 that 'any other status' used in Article 2(2) of the International Covenant on Economic, Social and Cultural Rights (ICESCR) covers the prohibition of discrimination on the ground of sexual orientation.[12] Similar opinion has been expressed by the United Nations Committee on the Rights of the Child, the Committee against Torture and the Committee on the Elimination of Discrimination against Women.

5 *Supra*, Rudman, 8.

6 *European Convention for the Protection of Human Rights and Fundamental Freedoms* (213 U.N.T.S. 222 as amended); *Universal Declaration of Human Rights*, G.A. Res. 217A (III), U.N. Doc A/810 at 71 (1948); *International Covenant on Economic, Social and Cultural Rights*, 16 December 1966, G.A. Res. 2200A (XXI), 21 U.N. GAOR Supp. (No. 16) at 49, U.N. Doc. A/6316 (1966), 993 U.N.T.S. 3, entered into force 3 January 1976; *International Covenant on Civil and Political Rights*, G.A. Res. 2200A (XXI), 21 U.N. GAOR Supp. (No. 16).

7 *Toonen* v. *Australia*, Communication No. 488/1992, U.N. Doc CCPR/C/50/D/488/1992 (1994).

8 *Ms. Juliet Joslin* et al. v. *New Zealand*, Communication No. 902/1999, U.N. Doc. A/57/40 at 214 (2002).

9 *Mr. Edward Young* v. *Australia*, Communication No. 941/2000, U.N. Doc. CCPR/C/78/D/941/2000 (2003).

10 *X* v. *Colombia, Merits*, Communication No. 1361/2005, U.N. Doc CCPR/C/89/D/ 1361/2005

11 *Supra, Toonen* v. *Australia*.

12 Available at: www.refworld.org/docid/4a60961f2.html, accessed 3 January 2018.

The phrase 'other status' is also used in Article 2 of the African Charter. Article 2 provides for the

> enjoyment of the rights and freedoms recognized and guaranteed in the . . . Charter without distinction of any kind such as race, ethnic group, color, sex, language, religion, political or any other opinion, national and social origin, fortune, birth or other status.

On the face of it, the rights in the African Charter are granted to everyone in the continent without distinction. This position runs through key provisions of the Charter including Articles 2, 3, 5–13, 15–17 and 28. However, since sexual orientation is not explicitly mentioned in the Charter, the question then is whether the articles could be interpreted to cover sexual orientation or whether 'other status' in Article 2 includes sexual orientation, similar to the UN Committees' approach.

It has been suggested that in view of Articles 60 and 61 of the African Charter, which made international human rights instruments relevant in the interpretation of the Charter, Articles 2 and 3 should be construed as covering prohibition of discrimination on the ground of sexual orientation.[13] This is because, as mentioned previously, the approach of the UN Committees is to interpret similar provisions in the UN Covenants in that manner.

This question of whether 'other status' in Article 2 of the Charter includes sexual orientation was presented in a complaint to the Commission in 1994. To date, this remains the only case that came for adjudication at the continental level that directly addressed the issue of sexual orientation. The complaint was in respect of the legal status of homosexuals in a Member State, Zimbabwe. Under domestic law in Zimbabwe sexual contacts between consenting adult homosexuals is prohibited and criminalised. Apart from the legal restrictions, the Complainants also referred to statements against homosexuals made by the President and by the Minister for Home Affairs in Zimbabwe. The Complainant alleged violations of the African Charter on Human and Peoples' Rights including Article 1. The Complainant also relied on the decision of the UN Human Rights Committee in the case of *Toonen* v. *Australia* based on Article 60 of the African Charter. However, the complaint was withdrawn before the Commission could deliberate on it. Nonetheless, the commissioner acting as the rapporteur in the case stated that homosexuality is against the African sense of morality and dignity. According to the rapporteur,

> 'because of the deleterious nature of homosexuality, the Commission seizes the opportunity to make a pronouncement on it. Although homosexuality and lesbianism are gaining recognition in certain parts of the world, this is not the case in Africa. Homosexuality offends the African sense of dignity and morality and is inconsistent with positive African values.[14]

13 R. Murray and F. Viljoen, 'Towards non-discrimination on the basis of sexual orientation: the normative basis and procedural possibilities before the African Commission on Human and Peoples' Rights and the African Union' (2007) 29 (1) *Human Rights Quarterly* 86.

14 African Commission, 16th Ordinary Session 1994.

However, in 2006 in *Zimbabwe Human Rights NGO Forum* v. *Zimbabwe*[15] the Commission appears to have affirmed that, under Article 2 of the Charter, sexual orientation should be protected. In that case the Commission observed that:

> Together, with equality before the law and equal protection of the law, the principle of nondiscrimination provided under Article 2 of the Charter provides the foundation for the enjoyment of all human rights (. . .) The aim of this principle is to ensure equality of treatment for individuals, irrespective of nationality, sex, racial or ethnic origin, political opinion, religion or belief, disability, age or **sexual orientation**. (Emphasis added.)

Nonetheless, it is conceded that this was an observation that was made *obiter* without directly addressing the subject of sexual orientation because that was not the subject matter of the case. In the absence of an authoritative position on this subject from the AU and its institutions, Murray and Viljoen have suggested that 'other status' should be interpreted to include sexual orientation.[16] Alternatively, the ban on discrimination based on sex in Article 2 should be interpreted to include 'sexual orientation'.[17] Notably, the African Court have recently observed that, '[t]he expression "any other status" under Article 2 encompasses those cases of discrimination, which could not have been foreseen during the adoption of the Charter'.[18]

Apart from the ambiguity around Article 2, there are other provisions in the African Charter that appear to limit or could be interpreted to limit the protections afforded other sexual orientations under the Charter. For instance, Article 27(2) of the Charter provides that, '[t]he rights and freedoms of each individual shall be exercised with due regard to the rights of others, collective security, morality and common interest'. This provision suggests, for example, that individual rights and freedoms could be limited on the ground of what a Member State considered to be morally acceptable or to be in the common interest in its jurisdiction. Such a ground could thus include other sexual orientations. However, to its credit, the Commission has held that any limitation by a Member State on the rights under the Charter must be 'strictly proportionate with and absolutely necessary for the advantages that are to be obtained'.[19] Furthermore, such 'a limitation may not erode a right to such an extent that the right itself becomes illusory'.[20] Significantly, the African Commission has further stated that the argument that the majority of people supported a particular moral viewpoint

15 *Zimbabwe Human Rights NGO Forum* v. *Zimbabwe*, Communication No. 245/02 (2006).

16 *Supra*, Murray and Viljoen.

17 Ibid.

18 *African Commission on Human and Peoples' Rights* v. *Kenya*, Application No. 006/2012 (2017).

19 *Interights, Institute for Human Rights and Development in Africa, and Association Mauritanienne des Droits de l'Homme v. Islamic Republic of Mauritania*, Communication No. 373/2009 (formerly 242/2001) (2010), 28th Activity Report.

20 *Media Rights Agenda and Others* v. *Nigeria*, Communication Nos 105/93, 128/94, 130/94 and 152/96 (1998); *Civil Liberties Org* v. *Nigeria*, Communication No. 129/94 (1995).

is not a conclusive basis for imposing a limitation. In *Legal Resources Foundation* v. *Zambia*,[21] the Commission stated that '[j]ustification . . . cannot be derived solely from popular will, as this cannot be used to limit the responsibilities of state parties in terms of the Charter'.

Perhaps an apposite comparator with the situation in the African Union and its framework is the experience within the Inter-American Human Rights system. This is because the cultural and moral backdrop, especially in Latin America and the Caribbean, is somewhat similar to the African context in relation to sexual orientation.[22] Furthermore, the African Commission and the African Court have in the past used decisions from the Inter-American Human Rights system in their reasoning.[23] The *Karen Atala Riffo and Children* v. *Chile* case is a landmark decision from the Inter-American Court of Human Rights that demonstrates the evolvement of the system on the subject of sexual orientation.[24] The decision was handed down in 2012. This was the first time that the Court had been required to make a pronouncement on the issue of discrimination based on sexual orientation and gender identity under the protection against discrimination enshrined in the American Convention. In this case the Court, for the first time, recognised unlawful discrimination on the basis of sexual orientation and gender identity.

Ms Atala Riffo (the petitioner) was a lawyer and judge in Chile. She was the mother of three girls and was previously married to the father of the girls. The couple separated in 2002 and agreed that the girls would be in the care of the petitioner. Sometime later the petitioner started a live-in relationship with a lesbian partner. Her ex-husband initiated a custody process for the girls on the grounds that Ms Atala Riffo's sexual orientation and cohabitation with a lesbian partner was inflicting serious psychological and social harm on the children thereby endangering their health. He argued that it was in the best interests of the children to protect them from the negative consequences of the petitioner's lifestyle. He further argued that he and his new heterosexual partner could provide a better and safer environment for the children.

In 2003 the Villarrica Juvenile Court in Chile initially gave provisional custody to the petitioner's ex-husband. However, a second decision was issued later in the year that reversed the provisional order and rejected the custody suit.

21 *Legal Resources Foundation* v. *Zambia*, ACHPR, Communication No. 211/98 (2001).

22 Ibid.

23 See, for example, *Yogogombaye* v. *The Republic of Senegal*, Application No. 001/2008, separate opinion of judge Fatsah Ouguergouz, available at: www1.chr.up.ac.za/images/files/documents/africancases/institution/africancourt/yogogombaye_v_senegal_separate_opinion_2008.pdf , accessed 3 January 2018; *Majuru* v. *Zimbabwe* (2008) AHRLR 146 (ACHPR 2008), paragraph 59; *Mouvement Ivoirien des Droits Humains (MIDH)* v. *Côte d'Ivoire* (2008) AHRLR 75 (ACHPR 2008), paragraph 48; *Zimbabwe Lawyers for Human Rights & Another* v. *Zimbabwe* (2008) AHRLR 120 (ACHPR 2008), paragraphs 64–65, 67, 69 and 79–80; *Article 19* v. *Eritrea* (2007) AHRLR 73 (ACHPR 2007), paragraphs 51 and 75; *Social and Economic Rights Action Centre (SERAC) & Another* v. *Nigeria* (2001) AHRLR 60 (ACHPR 2001), paragraph 57.

24 IACHR, Report No. 139/09 (merits), Case 12.502, *Karen Atala and daughters* v. *Chile*, 18 December 2009.

In March 2004 the Temuco Court of Appeal affirmed that decision. The ex-husband appealed to the Fourth Chamber of the Supreme Court of Justice of Chile. In May 2004 the Supreme Court panel voted 3–2 to award custody to the ex-husband. In granting custody the Supreme Court said *inter alia* that:

> a) dispensing with the oral testimony, [. . .] with respect to the deterioration felt in the social, family and educational environment inhabited by the minors, after the mother began to co-habit in the home with her homosexual partner and that the children could be the objects of social discrimination based on this fact; b) the house [sic], they make reference to games and attitudes of the girls that demonstrate confusion about their mother's sexuality that must have been perceived due to living in the home with their mother's new partner; c) [Ms. Atala] has placed her own interests above those of her daughters, especially by co-habiting with her homosexual partner in the same home in which she raised and cared for her daughters without their father; d) the eventual confusion of sexual roles which can be produced by the lack of a father of the male sex and his replacement by another person of the female gender, creates a situation of risk for the integral development of the minors from which they should be protected, [and] e) it is evident that the girls' exceptional family environment was significantly different from that of their friends from school and from the neighbourhood, thereby exposing them to be the objects of isolation and discrimination that will equally affect their personal development.[25]

Ms Atala Riffo subsequently sought relief before the Inter-American Commission on Human Rights. In 2009 the Commission found that the Chilean State violated her right to live free from discrimination and in 2010 the Commission referred the case to the Inter-American Court.

The Court correctly noted that its jurisdiction was not to determine whether the mother or father would have offered a better home to the children or determine the issue of custody. Rather, the core issue was whether or not the Chilean State violated the American Convention on Human Rights when the Supreme Court removed custody of the petitioner's three daughters from her because she entered into a relationship with another woman. The Court held that Chile had violated the petitioner's rights to equality, non-discrimination and privacy because parental sexual orientation is not a factor in child custody cases. Significantly, the Court affirmed that sexual orientation is a protected ground under Article 1 of the American Convention on Human Rights. Article 1 prohibits discrimination 'for reasons of race, color, sex, language, religion, political or other opinion, national or social origin, economic status, birth, or any other social condition' in similar terms as Article 2 of the African Charter. According to the Court, the

25 Official summary issued by the Inter-American Court of the Decision, 24 February 2012, available at: http://williamsinstitute.law.ucla.edu/wp-content/uploads/Summary-AtalaDecision-English-Mar-2012.pdf, accessed 3 January 2018.

term 'other social condition' in Article 1 includes sexual orientation and gender identity. The Court held that all persons regardless of their sexual orientation enjoy the right to family life.

In addition, the Court affirmed the legitimacy of the best interest of the child doctrine in custody cases, which, according to it, is embedded in Article 19 of the American Convention and the preamble to the 1989 Convention on the Rights of the Child. However, the Court was of the view that the doctrine could not be used to justify discrimination on the basis of sexual orientation in custody cases. Notably, the Court disapproved of the reliance on speculation, presumptions, stereotypes and generalisations made by the Supreme Court of Chile in its determination of the traditional concept of the family and the impact of non-traditional family structure on the children. According to the Court, the American Convention did not protect any specific form of traditional family. States must therefore recognise and protect diverse family structures. The Court held that failure to protect diverse family structure was a violation of the State's obligation to protect.

The Court further held that by discriminating in contravention of Article 1, Chile also violated Article 24, which contains the right to equality before the law and equal protection under the law. Similar positions were taken in relation to rights of respect for private and family life (Article 11), the rights of the family (Article 17), the right to a fair trial (Article 8) and the rights of the child in Article 19. These rights are to a large extent also protected under the African Human Rights framework.

In addition to the findings, the Court ordered that the State should provide free, immediate, adequate and effective medical, psychological or psychiatric treatment to the affected parties if requested. Second, the decision should be publicised as directed by the Court and the State should organise public events acknowledging international responsibility in cases of this nature. Third, the State should implement wide-ranging educational programmes and courses on State responsibility on these issues for civil servants and especially judicial personnel. Fourth, the State should pay indemnification and compensation as necessary.

This is a significant decision because of the creative way in which the Court interpreted Article 1 and thereby facilitated the recognition of new grounds that may constitute discrimination. This was a bold move on the part of the Court and shows that it was developing a proactive approach in its decision-making on gender issues.

The Court took the same approach in the 2016 case, *Angel Duque* v. *Colombia*.[26] In that case a private pension fund denied Mr Duque the pension of his deceased partner of ten years on the basis that, under relevant Colombian legislation on social security, the union of two persons of the same sex was not legally recognised. The consequence of this is that such a relationship could not

26 IACHR, Report No. 5/14, Case 12.841, *Ángel Alberto Duque (Colombia)*, 2 April 2014, available at: www.oas.org/en/iachr/decisions/court/12841FondoEn.pdf, accessed 3 January 2018.

be a basis for provision of beneficiary status to the surviving spouse under the law. When the case was taken to a domestic court it was dismissed and the court said:

> No violation of fundamental constitutional rights was committed. . . since the survivor's pension is intended to protect the family. . . formed by the union of a man and a woman, the only beings capable of preserving the species through procreation. . . a homosexual union does not, in itself, constitute a family.[27]

The Inter-American Court reversed this decision stating that domestic law making it possible to obtain the survivor's pension by heterosexual couples but denying the same to same-sex relationships without objective and reasonable justification was discriminatory and inconsistent with the right to equality. While the Court recognised the Colombian government's claim of pursuing a legitimate aim of protecting the family as a fundamental basis of society, it observed that Colombia's definition of family is too limiting and stereotypical with the consequence of arbitrarily excluding other types of families such as those of same-sex couples. The Court noted that an absence of consensus among Member States on the rights of same-sex relationships was not a relevant factor in deciding the issue.

The approach of the Inter-American Court is instructive and could provide guidance for the AU and its institutions in their approach to the interpretation and application of Article 2 of the AU Charter. This is especially because the provisions are broadly similar to Article 1 of the Inter-American Charter. The creativity of the Inter-American Court gives credibility to interpreting Article 2 to cover the ground of sexual orientation.

It is instructive that in 2012 Mexico's Supreme Court of Justice (the highest court in the country), unanimously struck down a Member State law (Oaxaca) that prohibited same-sex marriage.[28] The decision was partly influenced by the Inter-American Court decision in the *Atala Riffo* case, which prohibits any rule, act, or discriminatory practice based on sexual orientation. Potentially, clarity from the African Commission and the African Court on Human and Peoples' Rights could influence the approach of Member States' courts to sexual orientation. At present, the lack of clarity from the continental level is not helping litigants at the domestic level in Member States. For example, after the introduction of the Same-Sex Marriage (Prohibition) Act 2013, a Nigerian citizen resident abroad challenged the validity of the law at the Federal High Court in the Member State. The law prohibits same-sex marriages in the country, bans gay organisations and clubs, and also imposes imprisonment terms for violations of the law. The Claimant contended that the law violated the provisions of the African Charter and also the Nigerian Constitution. However, the Court

27 Ibid. paragraph 49.

28 Human Rights Watch, *World Report – 2014. Events of 2013*, available at: www.hrw.org/sites/default/files/wr2014_web_0.pdf, accessed 20 November 2017.

did not allow the case to go to trial on the tenuous basis that the Claimant had not suffered from the law himself and he could not bring the action on behalf of other Nigerians.

It is relevant to observe that the legal framework for the protection of people of other sexual orientations in the EU is more advanced than other regional arrangements. This is because the framework is underpinned by a long jurisprudence and robust legal framework. Articles 10 and 19 of the Treaty on the Functioning of the European Union (TFEU) gives the EU extensive powers to enact legislation against discrimination on the grounds of sex and sexual orientation. Therefore, there are extensive primary and secondary EU laws on the subject. Significantly, since 2009, when the Charter of Fundamental Rights[29] came into force, its Article 21 prohibits discrimination on grounds including sexual orientation. This has led to significant changes in Member States and at the minimum same-sex activity is legal in all Member States of the EU. The framework offers protections in most areas except social protection and advantages, education and supply of goods. There are ongoing efforts to cover these areas under EU law. The European Court of Justice and the European Court of Human Rights (ECtHR) have also, through case law, extended the protection afforded under the EU framework.

The ECtHR jurisprudence is relevant and important because it has a direct connection with EU law under Article 6 of the Treaty of European Union. The original approach of the ECtHR was to employ the right to privacy under Article 8 to protect people of other sexual orientation. It struck down laws that criminalise homosexual activities as an infringement on the right to privacy.[30] It is notable that the African Charter does not have an explicit provision protecting the right to privacy, which makes it unlikely for this approach to be crucial in the African context. However, the ECtHR subsequently shifted its approach to the protection of people of other sexual orientation on the ground of discrimination under Article 14. Notably, Article 14 of the European Convention on Human Rights (ECHR) provides that,

> The enjoyment of the rights and freedoms set forth in this Convention shall be secured without discrimination on any ground such as sex, race, colour, language, religion, political or other opinion, national or social origin, association with a national minority, property, birth or other status.

The guarantee under Article 14 does not constitute a separate or independent ground of protection from discrimination. Article 14 must be pleaded alongside

29 European Union, *Charter of Fundamental Rights of the European Union*, 26 October 2012, 2012/C 326/02, available at: www.refworld.org/docid/3ae6b3b70.html, accessed 3 January 2018.

30 See *Dudgeon* v. *United Kingdom*, Application No. 7525/76, Council of Europe: European Court of Human Rights, 22 October 1981; *Norris* v. *Ireland*, Application No. 10581/83, Council of Europe: European Court of Human Rights, 26 October 1988; *Lustig-Prean and Beckett* v. *United Kingdom* (2000) 29 ECHR 548.

other substantive rights guaranteed under the ECHR. Strikingly, and similar to Article 2 of the African Charter, the ECHR did not make reference to 'sexual orientation' directly. Indeed the defunct European Commission of Human Rights stated that there was ambiguity as to whether 'sexual orientation' is included in 'sex' or 'other status' under Article 14.[31] However, this ambiguity was removed by the European Court of Human Rights in *Salgueira da Silva Mouta* v. *Portugal*.[32] In that case the court held in the affirmative that sexual orientation is covered by Article 14 because Article 14 is non-exhaustive as shown by its use of the words 'any ground such as'. Therefore, it is neither part of 'sex' nor 'other status' but a separate ground in Article 14.

The case of the Coalition of African Lesbians (CAL)

A non-judicial case relevant to this chapter is the case relating to the Coalition of African Lesbians (CAL), an organisation that described itself as 'a feminist, activist and pan Africanist network of 14 organisations in 11 countries in sub-Saharan Africa committed to advancing freedom, justice and bodily autonomy for all women on the African continent and beyond'.[33] The African Commission has the power to grant observer status to NGOs, which allows a level of participation in the Commission's activities.[34] In 2008 CAL applied for observer status with the African Commission. At a public hearing of the application in 2009 many of the delegates from the Member States opposed the application. It was reported that Uganda threatened to leave the body if the application was ever granted.[35] Because of the disagreements, the application was deferred until the Commission's 2010 session. The application was eventually rejected on the spurious and dubious ground that the activities of the applicant did not promote and protect any of the rights guaranteed under the African Charter. However, following a fresh application by CAL in 2014, the Commission voted in favour of granting observer status to CAL in 2015. The AU political organ, the Executive Council, led at the time by the openly prejudiced ex-president of Zimbabwe Robert Mugabe, was not favourable to the granting of observer status to CAL. In its decision of July 2015 the Executive Council urge the Commission to withdraw the observer status granted to CAL and to review its criteria for granting observer status to reflect 'fundamental African values'.[36] This was a direct interference with the process and procedure

31 *Sutherland* v. *The United Kingdom*, 25186/94, Council of Europe: European Court of Human Rights, 27 March 2001.

32 *Salgueiro da Silva Mouta* v. *Portugal*, 33290/96, Council of Europe: European Court of Human Rights, 21 December 1999.

33 www.cal.org.za/about-us/why-we-exist, accessed on 28 November 2017.

34 Rule 68, *Rules of Procedure of the African Commission on Human and Peoples' Rights*, 2010.

35 S. Ndashe, 'Seeking the protection of LGBTI rights at the African Commission on Human and Peoples' Rights' (2011) 15 *Feminist Africa* 28.

36 *Decision on the 38th Activity Report of the African Commission on Human and Peoples' Rights*, EX.CL/Dec.887(XXVII).

of the Commission, which undermines the independence of the Commission.[37] In response, the African Commission decided to undertake a detailed legal analysis on the matter. This decision was included in the Commission's 39th Activity Report.[38] In paragraphs 50 and 51, the Commission stated that,

> In response, following extensive deliberations, the Commission decided to undertake a detailed legal analysis on this matter, including considering issues relating to the Commission's relationships with its various stakeholders, the notion of African values, the legal basis for the grant of Observer Status by the Commission, and the implications of withdrawing or retaining the observer status of NGOs.
>
> In that regard, it was also made known to the Commission that the request to withdraw the registration of CAL is now the subject matter of a request for an Advisory Opinion before the African Court on Human and Peoples' Rights.

The matter referred to in the quotation above was brought before the African Court by the Centre for Human Rights of the University of Pretoria and CAL. The applicants requested an advisory opinion on the competence of the Executive Council in its consideration of the Commission's report under Article 59(3) of the African Charter to override the Commission's decision the way it did in the CAL case.[39] However, disappointingly, the African Court did not rule on the merit of the case, holding that the applicants had no standing to request advisory opinion because they were not an 'African organisation recognised by the AU' for the purpose of Article 4(1) of the African Court's Protocol. The Court had previously ruled in *Advisory Opinion on the Request for Advisory Opinion by the Socio-Economic Rights and Accountability Project (SERAP)*[40] that only NGOs with a memorandum of understanding with the AU or organisations with observer status with the AU itself (not the African Commission) can request advisory opinion before the Court.

Conclusion

The difficulty that the AU and its institutions have faced in relation to addressing the issue of sexual orientations exemplifies the ongoing challenges facing the emergent AU legal order. A mix of historical factors, colonial legacies and religious

37 M. Killander, 'Human rights developments in the African Union during 2015' (2015) 15 (2) *African Human Rights Law Journal* 532.

38 *39th Activity Report of the African Commission on Human and Peoples' Rights*, available at: www.achpr.org/files/activity-reports/39/actrep39_2015_eng.pdf, accessed 3 January 2018.

39 Application No. 002/2015, *Request for Advisory Opinion by the Centre for Human Rights (CHR) University of Pretoria, and the Coalition of African Lesbians (CAL)*.

40 Application No. 001/2013, *Advisory Opinion on the Request for Advisory Opinion by the Socio-Economic Rights and Accountability Project.*

traditions has made the task of making progress on the subject of sexual orientation more daunting. However, experience from the Inter-American system shows that these challenges are not insurmountable. At the AU level itself, there are positive signals coming from the African Union institutions that show potential for the future. For example, the decision of the African Commission to reverse its previous decision and grant observer status to CAL is a welcome development. It is disappointing that the AU Executive continues to oppose this decision and is actively undermining the independence of the African Commission on this issue. In addition, in its Resolution 275, the African Commission specifically called on Member States to put in place

> appropriate laws prohibiting and punishing all forms of violence including those targeting persons on the basis of their imputed or real sexual orientation or gender identities, ensuring proper investigation and diligent prosecution of perpetrators, and establishing judicial procedures responsive to the needs of victims.[41]

The resolution made references to the African Charter including its Article 2. These developments demonstrate some willingness at the continental level to take steps to address the issue of sexual orientation.

41 African Commission on Human and Peoples' Rights, Resolution 275: *Resolution on Protection against Violence and Other Human Rights Violations against Persons on the Basis of Their real or Imputed Sexual Orientation or Gender Identity*. The African Commission on Human and Peoples' Rights (the African Commission), meeting at its 55th Ordinary Session held in Luanda, Angola, from 28 April to 12 May 2014.

10 Enforcement of African Union law

Introduction

The mechanism for the enforcement of the emergent AU law is a work in progress. Indeed enforcement of its laws is one of the biggest challenges that undermines the legitimacy of AU legal order. The OAU and its successors recognised this problem and that is why, for example, steps were taken to introduce a Court system at the continental level. Before the introduction of the Court, the African Commission as a quasi-judicial body played a significant role in the human rights sphere. The developments in relation to the evolving continental Court show that the enforcement process is expanding and becoming more robust compared with that of the African Commission. Significant issues related to the enforcement process included in this chapter include a discussion of access to the Court, the requirement of exhaustion of local remedies, confidentiality, the granting of provisional measures, legal aid and assistance, compensation/reparation and Member States' reporting system. It notable that AU law, especially in the human rights sphere, is having some impact on Member States with the potential to aid smooth harmonisation of standards in the future.

The African Court on Human and Peoples' Rights (African Court)

Before the introduction of the African Court on Human and Peoples' Rights (African Court), the African Commission under its protective duties exclusively had the responsibility to receive communications (cases) on violations of rights protected under the African Charter, communicating them to States and investigating the cases with a view to reconciling the parties. Where reconciliation is not possible, the Commission exercises its quasi-judicial function to adjudicate on such cases. The decisions arising from proceedings are included in the Commission's annual activity report. Although the African Charter directly refers only to communications from States, the Commission also accepted communications from non-State actors under the provision for 'Other Communications'.[1] This made it

1 Articles 55–59 *African Charter.*

possible for individuals and NGOs to bring complaints before the Commission. This laid the foundation for the vertical direct effect of AU human rights law. However, a communication can only be brought against a Member State Party to the Charter and not against private persons or individuals, thereby preventing horizontal direct effect.[2] Therefore, a private person or individual can only be implicated when a State is held liable for the violation of human rights. As mentioned previously, the African Commission was a quasi-judicial body, which brought into question the bindingness of its decisions. Furthermore, the Commission had no independent mechanism for the purposes of enforcing its decisions. It has also been argued that the Commission, in most of its decisions, failed to enunciate clear and specific remedies, which may have affected compliance.[3] It has been opined that the Commission was 'more inclined to order for remedies couched in broad formulations lacking generally in specificity, for instance requiring that the respondent state adopt relevant legislation, or bordering on the vague or "futuristic", requiring that the state undertakes "measures to see the full respect of the Charter"'.[4] Consequently there is a question mark over the Commission's competence as a quasi-judicial body.[5] The Commission has also been criticised for its lack of independence. This is because of its close links with African Heads of State and Government.[6] Under Article 33 of the African Charter, the 11 members of the Commission are elected by secret ballot by the Assembly of Heads of States and Government, from a list of persons nominated by the Member States. This ensures that Member States have significant control over the Commission and its activities. This is exemplified by the AU Executive Council's decision in 2015 that, *inter alia*, requested the Commission to withdraw observer status granted to the Coalition of African Lesbians and to also review the Commission's provisions relating to the granting of provisional measures against Member States.[7]

The African Court was established to strengthen the mechanism for the protection of human rights and to address the limitations of the African Commission's enforcement procedure. The Court complements the protective mandate of the Commission. In addition, the Commission has the responsibility to prepare cases for submission to the African Court under the current arrangement.[8] Under the Protocol establishing the Court (African Court Protocol), the

2 Ibid. Article 47.

3 R. Murray, *The African Commission on Human and Peoples' Rights and International Law* (Hart Publishing, 2000) 32.

4 G. M. Musila, 'The right to an effective remedy under the African Charter on Human and Peoples' Rights' (2006) 6 (2) *African Human Rights Law Journal* 441–464.

5 R. Wright, 'Finding an impetus for institutional change at the African Court on Human and Peoples' Rights' (2006) 24 (2) *Berkeley Journal of International Law* 463, 471.

6 Ibid. 472.

7 *Decision on the 38th Activity Report of the African Commission on Human and Peoples' Rights*, EX.CL/Dec.887(XXVII). See also Chapter 9.

8 Article 5 of the *Protocol to the African Charter on Human and Peoples' Rights on the Establishment of an African Court on Human and Peoples' Rights*, 1998, OAU Doc. OAU/LEG/EXP/AFCHPR/PROT (III); *African Commission on Human and Peoples' Rights* v. *Kenya*, Application No. 006/2012.

Court is empowered to exercise jurisdiction over all human rights instruments 'ratified by the States concerned'.[9] It has been suggested that this may include regional, sub-regional, bilateral and multilateral international treaties.[10] Indeed, this was the approach taken by the African Court in its decision in *The Matter of Actions Pour la Protection des Droits de l'Homme (APDH)* v. *Republic of Côte D'Ivoire*, where the Court held *inter alia* that it had jurisdiction over sub-regional human rights instruments ratified by Member States.[11] This means that a person whose rights are not adequately protected under the African Charter can invoke other treaties that Member State parties have signed up to.[12] This is in contrast to the jurisdiction of the Commission, which is limited to the interpretation and application of the African Charter. The jurisdiction of the Court covers wide ranging human rights areas including violations of civil and political rights, socio-economic rights and collective rights of people.

The Court has both advisory and contentious jurisdiction. The Court is generally empowered to receive complaints alleging violations of human rights submitted by Member States, the African Commission on Human and Peoples' Rights, African Intergovernmental Organisations and (subject to certain restrictions) NGOs and individuals.[13] It has jurisdiction to entertain requests for advisory opinion on any legal matter relating to the Charter or any other relevant human rights instrument from Member States, the AU and its organs or any other organisation recognised by the regional body.[14] The Court has held in the matter of the *Advisory Opinion on the Request for Advisory Opinion by the Socio-Economic Rights and Accountability Project (SERAP)*[15] that only NGOs with a memorandum of understanding with the AU or organisations with observer status with the AU itself (not the African Commission) can request advisory opinion before the Court. As discussed in Chapter 9, this was a very narrow interpretation of Article 4(1) of the African Court's Protocol, which further limits access to the Court by NGOs.[16] It is notable that, following an advisory opinion of the Court stating that the African Committee of Experts on the Rights and Welfare of the Child could not refer cases to the Court under the Court's Protocol,[17] the AU

9 Ibid. Article 3(1).

10 R. W. Eno 'The Jurisdiction of the African Court on Human and Peoples' Rights' (2002) 2 (2) *African Human Rights Law Journal* 223, 226; N. J. Udombana, 'Towards the African Court on Human and Peoples' Rights: better late than never' (2000) 3 (1) *Yale Human Rights & Development Law Journal* 45.

11 Application 001/2014 (2016).

12 *Supra*, Eno (n. 46) at 226.

13 Article 5, *African Court Protocol.*

14 Ibid. Article 4.

15 Application No. 001/2013, *Advisory Opinion on the Request for Advisory Opinion by the Socio-Economic Rights and Accountability Project (SERAP).*

16 Application No. 002/2015, *Request for Advisory Opinion by the Centre for Human Rights (CHR) University of Pretoria, and the Coalition of African Lesbians (CAL).*

17 Application No. 002/2013, *In the matter of request for advisory opinion by the African Committee of Experts on the Rights and Welfare of the Child on the standing of the African Committee of Experts on the Rights and Welfare of the Child before the African Court on Human and Peoples' Rights.*

Executive Council in July 2016 recommended that Article 5(1) of the Court's Protocol be amended to allow the Committee to refer cases to the Court.[18] The Court also has the jurisdiction to interpret its own judgment, if requested to do so.[19] The temporal jurisdiction of the Court extends to the time the Court Protocol entered into force in respect of a particular state, except in cases that emanate from what is considered 'continuing violation' under the principle of continuing violation established by the African Commission in *Lawyers for Human Rights* v. *Swaziland*.[20] Remarkably, the Court in its nascent jurisdiction appears to expand its jurisdiction to assessing the constitutionality of Member States' laws in the light of the African Charter.[21]

Access of individuals and NGOs to the Court

For the purpose of exercising its contentious jurisdiction, the Court can exercise compulsory (automatic) or optional jurisdiction. Under its compulsory jurisdiction, Article 5(1) provides that the following are entitled to submit cases to the Court:

a the African Commission;
b the State that has lodged a complaint to the African Commission;
c the State Party against which the complaint has been lodged at the Commission;
d the State Party whose citizen is a victim of a human rights violation;
e African Intergovernmental Organisations.

Furthermore, under Article 5(2) matters may be referred to the Court by a State Party that has an interest in a case in which it was not originally involved.[22]

The Court's optional jurisdiction is for other claimants such as individuals and NGOs that have observer status with the AU Commission. The access of such non-State actors is severely restricted in comparison with access to the

18 M. G. Nyarko and A. O. Jegede, 'Human rights developments in the African Union during 2016' (2017) 17 (1) *African Human Rights Law Journal* 294, 297.

19 Application No. 001/2017, Interpretation of Judgment of 20 November 2015 – *Alex Thomas* v. *United Republic of Tanzania*; Application No. 003/2017, Interpretation of the Judgment of 18 November 2016 – *Actions pour la Protection des Droits de l'Homme* v. *Republic of Côte D'Ivoire*.

20 *Lawyers for Human Rights* v. *Swaziland*, Communication No. 251/2002; Application No. 002/2017, Interpretation of Judgment of 3 June 2016 – *Mohamed Abubakari* v. *United Republic of Tanzania* 5, 18th Activity Report.

21 Application Nos 009 & 011/2011, *Tanganyika Law Society and The Legal and Human Rights Centre* v. *The United Republic of Tanzania* and *Reverend Christopher Mtikila* v. *The United Republic of Tanzania*; Application No. 003/2012, *Peter Joseph Chacha* v. *The United Republic of Tanzania*, Application, 114.

22 *Protocol to the African Charter on Human and Peoples' Rights on the Establishment of the African Court on Human and Peoples' Rights.*

Commission's procedure. The Court may only allow cases brought by other claimants, first, where a Member State has made an express declaration accepting the Court's jurisdiction to hear such a case.[23] Even though 30 Member States have accepted the Court's jurisdiction to date, only eight States have made the necessary declaration allowing direct access by individuals and NGOs. These include Benin, Burkina Faso, Côte d'Ivoire, Ghana, Malawi, Mali, Tanzania and Tunisia. The effect of not making the declaration is that the Court would have no jurisdiction over cases brought by individuals and NGOs against Member States that have not made the declaration.[24] It is notable that Member States have the ability to withdraw their declarations. Indeed, Rwanda withdrew its declaration in 2016. This possibility is seen as a weakness and a challenge to the Court's legitimacy going forward.[25] Second, the Court reserves a discretionary power to grant or deny access as it deems fit in particular cases.[26] Juma has described these hurdles placed on the access to the Court as an 'assault on the African human rights system'.[27]

The approach of the African system in requiring State declaration is in line with the procedural law of other international human rights systems.[28] However, it has been posited that the lack of direct access under the Inter-American Court system has been one of its greatest weaknesses because it limits the role of the victim and requires the intervention of the Inter-American Commission of Human Rights to refer individual cases to the Court.[29] The position is different under the European system. Under Protocol 11 of the European Convention,

23 Ibid. Article 34(6).

24 See Application No. 002/2012, *Delta International Investments* v. *Republic of South Africa;* Application No. 004/2012, *Emmanuel Joseph Uko and Others* v. *Republic of South Africa;* Application No. 005/2012, *Amir Adam Timan* v. *Republic of the Sudan*; Application No. 007/2012, *Baghdadi Ali Mahmoudi* v. *Republic of Tunisia*; Application No. 001/2008, *Michelot Yogogombaye* v. *The Republic of Senegal*; Application No. 002/2011, *Soufiane Ababou* v. *People's Democratic Republic of Algeria;* Application No. 005/201, Daniel *Amare & Mulugeta Amare* v. *Mozambique Airlines & Mozambique* (ACtHPR, 16); Application No. 006/2011, *Association Juristes d'Afrique pour la Bonne Gouvernance* v. *La Côte d'Ivoire;* Application No. 008/2011, *Ekollo Moundi Alexandre* v. *Republic of Cameroon and the Federal Republic of Nigeria*; Application No. 012/2011, *National Convention of Teachers Trade Union* v. *The Republic of Gabon*.

25 *Supra*, Nyarko and Jegede (2017).

26 *Supra* (note 22), Article 5(3).

27 D. Juma, 'Access to the African Court on Human and Peoples' Rights: a case of the poacher turned gamekeeper' (2007) 4 (2) *Essex Human Rights Review* 1 at 3.

28 See Article 41 *ICCPR* (*International Covenant on Civil and Political Rights*, G.A. res. 2200A (XXI), 21 U.N. GAOR Supp. (No. 16) at 52, U.N. Doc. A/6316 (1966), 999 U.N.T.S. 171); Article 21(1) *Convention Against Torture* (G.A. res. 39/46, [annex, 39 U.N. GAOR Supp. (No. 51) at 197, U.N. Doc. A/39/51 (1984)]); Articles 25(1) and 46(1) *European Convention for the Protection of Human Rights and Fundamental Freedoms* (213 U.N.T.S. 222 as amended); Article 44(1) of the *American Convention on Human Rights* (O.A.S. Treaty Series No. 36, 1144 U.N.T.S. 123).

29 *Supra*, Wright, 478.

> the Court may receive applications from any person, non-governmental organisation or group of individuals claiming to be the victim of a violation by one of the High Contracting Parties of the rights set forth in the Convention or the protocols thereto.[30]

The provision in the African Court's Protocol may have been included to encourage countries to sign up to it without fear that the platform would be used against them by non-State entities. According to Eno:

> While the limitation under article 5(3) of the Protocol on the African Court may be necessary to bring states on board to ratify the Protocol, it is nevertheless disappointing and a terrible blow to the standing and reputation of the African Court. After all, it is individuals and NGOs, and not the African Commission, regional intergovernmental organisations or state parties who would be the primary beneficiaries and users of the African Court. The Court is not an institution for the protection of rights of states. A human rights court exists primarily for protecting citizens against the state and other government agencies.[31]

Another area where access to the Court is unduly restrictive is the provision that only 'relevant Non Governmental Organisations with observer status before the Commission' have access to the Court.[32] As Eno correctly notes, this is a unique and potentially dangerous restriction.[33] There is no guide to determine what is meant by a relevant NGO. Eno therefore argues that the determination may be left within the competence of the Commission, which may consider those NGOs that have been submitting their periodic reports to it. The implication of this is that NGOs that do not have observer status with the Commission would be excluded completely.[34] This is significantly different to the position under the Inter-American system. The Inter-American system permits any NGO legally recognised in one or more Member States to lodge a petition with the American Commission, which may transmit the case to the Inter-American Court for consideration where necessary.[35] However, if the African Court adopts a liberal attitude to the interpretation of these provisions in its jurisprudence, then the provisions may not necessarily constitute impediments going forward.

30 Protocol No. 11 to the *Convention for the Protection of Human Rights and Fundamental Freedoms*, Article 34, which replaced Article 44 of the European Convention.

31 *Supra*, Eno, 231.

32 Article 5(3), *African Court Protocol.*

33 *Supra*, Eno, 231.

34 Ibid.

35 Ibid; Article 44 *American Convention on Human Rights.*

Exhaustion of local remedies

The requirement for the exhaustion of local remedies is a key issue in the enforcement process in the AU legal order. Under Article 6 of the African Court's Protocol the Court is required to take into consideration the provisions of Article 56 of the African Charter when ruling on the admissibility of cases. Article 56 of the African Charter laid out the criteria for consideration and admissibility of communications before the African Commission and the African Court. Two of the admissibility criteria are critical and are frequently invoked in the proceedings of the African Commission and the Court. These are set out in Article 56(5) and (6). They are, first, that communications or cases must be brought only after exhausting domestic remedies, if any, unless it is obvious that the domestic procedure is unduly prolonged and, second, that they must be submitted within a reasonable period from the time local remedies are exhausted or from the date the Commission is seized with the matter. The determination of what is considered a reasonable period in relation to the second criterion is based on facts and done on a case-by-case analysis. For instance, in *Dr. Farouk Mohamed Ibrahim (represented by REDRESS)* v. *Sudan*,[36] the Commission held that the communication presented was inadmissible under Article 56(5), on the ground that the 15-month period between the exhaustion of local remedies and the filing of the communication at the Commission was not a reasonable length of time based on the evidence provided. A delay of two years has also been held to be unreasonable.[37] Also in J. *E. Zitha & P. J. L. Zitha (represented by Prof. Dr. Liesbeth Zegveld)* v. *Mozambique*, a 13-year delay was considered unreasonable delay.[38]

It must be observed that many of the cases that come to the African Commission and the African Court failed because of the failure to exhaust local remedies. The jurisprudence of the African Commission and, to a limited extent, of the African Court have developed and shaped the application of this provision substantially over time. Usually, domestic remedies are considered exhausted if a complaint has effectively gone through all levels of adjudication at the domestic level. Failure to comply with the requirement to exhaust local remedies would render a complaint inadmissible.[39] The Commission has held that proceedings before a national human rights commission did not satisfy the exhaustion of local remedies requirement, thereby suggesting that the acceptable procedure is an action by a judicial court. According to the African Commission in *Cudjoe* v. *Ghana*, the internal remedy to which Article 56(5) refers entails remedy sought from courts of a judicial nature and, as such, the Ghanaian Human Rights Commission is not such a forum in the context of that case.[40] Therefore a complainant must take

36 *Dr. Farouk Mohamed Ibrahim (represented by REDRESS)* v. *Sudan*, February 2013, ACHPR, 386/2010, 13th Extra-ordinary Session.

37 *Article 19 and Others* v. *Zimbabwe*, Communication No. 305/05 (2010).

38 Communication 361/08, paragraphs 95–116 (2011).

39 *Diakite Couple* v. *Republic of Mali*, Application No. 009/2016.

40 *Alfred B. Cudjoe* v. *Ghana*, Communication No. 221/98 (2000).

their complaints through the judicial forum of a Member State and the forum must be independent. The forum must also have mandatory and enforceable powers to provide remedies. Quasi-judicial bodies are not recognised as such under the Charter.[41] The Commission has also held that acts such as writing letters to the President of a Member State, the UN Special Rapporteur and Amnesty International would not satisfy the requirement to exhaust domestic remedies.[42]

Furthermore, the African Commission has established that a complainant must only exhaust domestic remedies that are 'available, effective, and sufficient'. According to the African Commission in *Dawda Jawara* v. *The Gambia*, first, a remedy is 'available' if the petitioner can pursue it without impediment. Second, a remedy is 'effective' if it offers a reasonable prospect of success to provide relief and, third, a remedy is 'sufficient' if it is capable of producing the redress sought.[43] However, the African Commission has held that merely casting doubts about the effectiveness of the domestic remedies is not sufficient to displace the requirement of Article 56. In *Anuak Justice Council* v. *Ethiopia*[44] the Commission stated:

> the complainant is simply casting doubts about the effectiveness of the domestic remedies. This Commission is of the view that it is incumbent on every complainant to take all necessary steps to exhaust, or at least attempt the exhaustion of, local remedies. It is not enough for the complainant to cast aspersion on the ability of the domestic remedies of the State due to isolated or past incidences. In this regard, the African Commission would like to refer to the decision of the Human Rights Committee in *A v Australia* in which the Committee held that 'mere doubts about the effectiveness of local remedies . . . did not absolve the author from pursuing such remedies'. The African Commission can therefore not declare the communication admissible based on this argument. If a remedy has the slightest likelihood to be effective, the applicant must pursue it. Arguing that local remedies are not likely to be successful, without trying to avail oneself of them, will simply not sway this Commission.

Exhaustion of domestic remedies would not apply if the remedies are not readily accessible and if they cannot be invoked without detriment to the complainant.[45] Similarly the requirement will not apply where it is established that remedies could not be obtained within a reasonable time. The African

41 *Priscilla Njeri Echaria (represented by Federation of Women Lawyers, Kenya and International Center for the Protection of Human Rights)* v. *Kenya*, Communication No. 375/09 (2011).

42 *Supra*, *J.E. Zitha & P.J.L. Zitha (represented by Prof. Dr. Liesbeth Zegveld)* v. *Mozambique*.

43 *Dawda Jawara* v. *The Gambia*, Communication Nos 147/95 & 149/96 (2000).

44 *Anuak Justice Council* v. *Ethiopia*, Communication No. 299/05 (2006). See also *David Mendes (represented by Centre for Human Rights)* v. *Angola*, Communication No. 413/12 (2013).

45 *The Attorney General of the United Republic of Tanzania* v. *African Network for Animal Welfare*, Appeal No. 3 of 2014, 61–62.

Commission explained the rationale behind its approach in *Nixon Nyikadzino* v. *Zimbabwe*.[46] According to the Commission,

> The African Commission through its jurisprudence made it clear that the whole purpose of asking Complainants to exhaust local remedies before approaching the Commission is to give the Respondent State a chance to redress the alleged human rights violations through its structures and organs. This is derived from the principle of complementarity which dictates that international or regional mechanisms do not and cannot substitute national courts; it is only when national courts or tribunals fail to deliver justice that international or regional organs will have jurisdiction to receive cases. This is why the African Commission has been stringently applying the exhaustion of local remedies rule and only in few justified circumstances has it waived such condition.

According to Article 56 the requirement under the Article may be waived if the process of exhausting local remedies is 'unduly prolonged'. While what is considered to be 'unduly prolonged' is not defined in the Article, the African Commission has held that an appeal proceeding that is left pending for 18 months before a domestic appellate court is unduly prolonged and therefore a communication arising from such proceedings is admissible.[47] A similar determination was made in relation to a case pending for 12 years.[48] It has also been held that threat to the complainant's life or that of his relatives in the Member State could be a relevant consideration in determining the accessibility to domestic remedy.[49] The African Commission held in *Dr. Farouk Mohamed Ibrahim (represented by REDRESS)* v. *Sudan*[50] that the fear of persecution is an exception to the requirement to exhaust local remedies. This decision is in contrast to the decision of the Commission in *Givemore Chari (represented by Gabriel Shumba)* v. *Republic of Zimbabwe*.[51] In that case the Commission was not persuaded by the Complainant's argument that he was unable to exhaust local remedies because he feared for his life if he returned to Zimbabwe. In addition, the Commission also held that the applicant need not be physically present in the Member State in order to access the domestic courts and exhaust local remedies. The Commission

46 *Nixon Nyikadzino (represented by Zimbabwe Human Rights. NGO Forum)* v. *Zimbabwe*, Communication No. 340/07 (2012).

47 *Odjouoriby Cossi Paul* v. *Benin*, Communication No. 199/97 (2004).

48 African Commission, *Enga Mekongo* v. *Cameroon*, Communication No. 59/91 (1995).

49 *Gabriel Shumba* v. *Zimbabwe*, Communication No. 288/2004 (2012), 63, 74; *Rights International* v. *Nigeria*, Communication No. 215/98 (1999), 24; *Alhassan Abubakar* v. *Ghana*, Communication No. 103/1993 (1996), 31; *John D. Ouko* v. *Kenya*, Communication No. 232/99 (2000), 19, 39; *supra*, *Dawda Jawara* v. *The Gambia*, 35; *Institute for Human Rights and Development in Africa (on behalf of Jean Simbarkiye)* v. *Democratic Republic of Congo*, Communication No. 247/02 (2006).

50 *Supra*, *Dr. Farouk Mohamed Ibrahim (represented by REDRESS)* v. *Sudan*.

51 *Givemore Chari (represented by Gabriel Shumba)* v. *Zimbabwe*, Communication No. 351/07 (2012).

has also held that where the normal process of law is hampered by a state of turmoil in a Member State, leading to a declaration of a state of emergency, the requirement to exhaust domestic remedies would not apply.[52] The requirement will also not apply where the government of a Member State has made a law or decree to oust the jurisdiction of domestic courts thereby making domestic remedy non-existent or where a Member State passed an amnesty law to prevent the seeking of remedy against alleged violators of protected rights.[53]

On its part, the African Court has held that the exhaustion of local remedy requirement is not applicable to 'extraordinary' remedies. In *Onyachi and Njoka* v. *Tanzania*[54] it was argued by the Respondent that the Applicant who was convicted by a Member State judicial system should have filed a constitutional petition for a review in the Member State before approaching the Court. The Court, relying on its previous decision in *Mohammed Abubakari* v. *The United Republic of Tanzania*,[55] held that such a constitutional petition for review is not a common procedure, it is only granted exceptionally and available as an extraordinary remedy. As such, failure to pursue the remedy does not render the Applicants case inadmissible.[56]

Going forward, the approach of the African Court will be significant for access of litigants to the Court. If the provision of Article 56 is applied restrictively by the Court, it may discourage access by individuals and NGOs. It has been suggested that the Rules of Procedure for the Court should contain explicit reference to the fact that domestic remedies must be both effective and adequate or exhaustion will not be required.[57] Such provisions could follow the example of the Inter-American Commission of Human Rights' Rules of Procedure, which provide as follows:

1 In order to decide on the admissibility of a matter, the Commission shall verify whether the remedies of the domestic legal system have been pursued and exhausted in accordance with the generally recognized principles of international law.

2 The provisions of the preceding paragraph shall not apply when:

   a the domestic legislation of the State concerned does not afford due process of law for protection of the right or rights that have allegedly been violated;

52 *Law Office of Ghazi Suleiman* v. *Sudan*, Communication No. 220/98 (2003); *Civil Liberties Organisation* v. *Nigeria*, Communication No. 129/94 (2000).

53 *Media Rights Agenda and Others* v. *Nigeria*, Communication Nos 105/93, 128/94, 130/94 and 152/96 (1998); *Civil Liberties Org* v. *Nigeria*, Communication No. 129/94 (1995); *Law Society of Zimbabwe* et al. v. *Zimbabwe*, Communication No. 321/06 (2013); *Zimbabwe Human Rights NGO Forum* v. *Zimbabwe*, Communication No. 245/02 (2006); *Monim Elgak, Osman Hummeida and Amir Suliman (represented by International Federation for Human Rights (FIDH) and World Organization Against Torture (OMCT))* v. *Sudan*, Communication No. 379/09 (2014).

54 Application No. 003/2015.

55 *Mohammed Abubakari* v. *The United Republic of Tanzania*, Application No. 007/2013.

56 See also *Christopher Jonas* v. *The United Republic of Tanzania*, Application No. 011/2015.

57 *Supra*, Wright, 479.

- b the party alleging violation of his or her rights has been denied access to the remedies under domestic law or has been prevented from exhausting them; or,
- c there has
- d been unwarranted delay in rendering a final judgment under the aforementioned remedies.

3 When the petitioner contends that he or she is unable to prove compliance with the requirement indicated in this article, it shall be up to the State concerned to demonstrate to the Commission that the remedies under domestic law have not been previously exhausted, unless that is clearly evident from the record.[58]

The Commission has also rejected cases on the ground of Article 56(2). Article 56(2) requires that complaints or cases must be compatible with the African Charter. In *Mohammed Abdullah Saleh Al-Asad* v. *The Republic of Djibouti*, the Commission declared the communication inadmissible because the complainant did not provide conclusive evidence that the alleged violations took place in the territory of the Member State. The Complainant's case was that he was kidnapped and taken to an undisclosed location that he 'believed' was the respondent Member State.[59]

Confidentiality requirement

There is an emphasis on confidentiality under the African Charter. Article 59 of the Charter provides that all measures taken within the provisions of the Charter in respect of matters including communications shall remain confidential until the Assembly of Heads of State and Government shall otherwise decide. This provision gives leverage to Heads of State and Government to exert improper influence over proceedings. However, with respect to the Court, Article 10(1) of the African Court Protocol provides that the Court shall conduct its proceedings in public. Nonetheless, it may conduct proceedings in camera as may be provided for in the Rules of Procedure.[60] The rules of Court currently give wide latitude to the Court in relation to holding a proceeding in camera. Rule 43 provides that, 'the Court may, of its own accord or at the request of a party, hold its hearings in camera if, in its opinion, it is in the interest of public morality, safety or public order to

58 *Rules of Procedure of the Inter-American Court of Human Rights, Annual Report of the Inter-American Court of Human Rights*, 1991, O.A.S. Doc. OEA/Ser.L/V/III.25 doc.7 at 18 (1992), reprinted in *Basic Documents Pertaining to Human Rights in the Inter-American System*, OEA/Ser.L.V/II.82 doc.6 rev.1 at 145 (1992).

59 *Mohammed Abdullah Saleh Al-Asad* v. *The Republic of Djibouti*, Communication No. 383/10 (2014).

60 Ibid.

do so'.[61] The Court has been exercising the discretion not to hold hearings in public since its inception.[62] It has been suggested that the rule should stipulate that confidentiality would apply only in very limited cases such as the necessity to protect the privacy of individuals.[63] Considering that publicity is a major way by which Member States can be compelled to comply with decisions of human rights bodies, these provisions somewhat reduce the threat of adverse publicity from the Court's decisions for States.

Provisional measures/orders

Perhaps the most potent enforcement mechanism employed by the African Commission in its quasi-judicial capacity was the granting of interim or provisional measures such as injunctions. The Commission occasionally grants interim or provisional measures to prevent irredeemable or irreparable harm.[64] The Commission has been proactive in making orders for provisional measures when requested by a complainant.[65] Significantly, in *International Pen and Others (on behalf of Saro-Wiwa)* v. *Nigeria*, the Commission held that such provisional measures are binding and where a Member State ignores or refused to obey such a measure it would be held to be in violation of Article 1 of the African Charter.[66] The exercise of the power to grant provisional measures was further strengthened with the introduction of the African Court. The Court is empowered either on its own motion or on an application by the parties to grant provisional measures to preserve the respective rights of the parties. Under Rule 51 of the Rules of Court the Court has the power to grant provisional measures in cases of extreme gravity, urgency, and when necessary to avoid irreparable harm. A case on this point is *African Commission on Human and People's Rights* v. *Great Socialist People's Libyan Arab Jamahiriya*[67] where the court made a provisional order *suo motu*. In that case, as a consequence of the heavy handed and repressive Gaddafi government response to the protests in Libya, the African Commission brought a complaint against Libya before the African Court on Human and Peoples'

61 Rules of Court (2010), available at: http://en.african-court.org/images/Protocol-Host%20Agrtmt/Final_Rules_of_Court_for_Publication_after_Harmonization_-_Final__English_7_sept_1_.pdf, accessed 29 November 2017.

62 *Supra*, *Diakite Couple* v. *Republic of Mali*.

63 *Supra*, Wright, 482.

64 Rule 111 of the *Rules of Procedures of the African Commission on Human and Peoples' Rights*, adopted on the 6 October 1995, allows the Commission to grant interim provisional orders. See U. O. Umozorike, 'The African Charter on Human and Peoples' Rights: suggestions for more effectiveness' (2007) 13 *Annual Survey of International & Comparative Law* 179, 186.

65 *Supra*, Musila.

66 See *International Pen and Others (on behalf of Saro-Wiwa)* v. *Nigeria*, Communication Nos 137/94, 139/94, 154/96 and 161/97 (1998). See also, *supra*, Wright, 463, 471.

67 In the Matter of *African Commission on Human and People's Rights v. Great Socialist People's Libyan Arab Jamahiriya*, Application No. 004/2011.

Rights in March 2011.[68] The application alleged that, following peaceful demonstrations in Benghazi, Al Baida, Ajdabiya, Zayiwa and Derna in Libya, security forces violently suppressed the demonstrations and opened fire at random, consequently killing and injuring many people. The application suggested that the force employed by the security forces was excessive and disproportionate. The application further alleged that the actions of the security forces amounted to serious violations of the right to life and to the integrity of persons, freedom of expression, demonstration and assembly in contravention of the rights enshrined in Articles 1, 2, 5, 9, 11, 12, 13 and 23 of the African Charter.[69] The African Commission, in its application to the Court, did not expressly request the Court to order provisional measures. However, the Court, relying on its powers under Article 27(2) of the Protocol to the African Charter and Rule 51(1) of the Rules of Court, proceeded to consider whether such an order should be made in this case. The Court decided that a provisional order was required in view of the *prima facie* evidence that irreparable harm may be done to people in Libya. It therefore ordered the Libyan State to 'immediately refrain from any action that would result in loss of life or violation of physical integrity of persons'.[70] It also ordered the Libyan State to report to the Court within 15 days from the date of the order on steps taken to implement the order.[71] On face value, this is a laudable move on the part of the Court. However, the fact that the Libyan government at the time chose to ignore the order and carried on with its clamp down on protesters after the order was issued showed the weakness in the enforcement process. To date the African Court has granted provisional measures in about 25 different cases.[72]

68 Ibid.

69 Ibid. paragraph 2.

70 Ibid. paragraph 25.

71 Ibid.

72 Application No. 004/2011 – *African Commission on Human and Peoples' Rights* v. *Great Socialist People's Libyan Arab Jamahiriya*; Application No. 006/2012 – *African Commission on Human and Peoples' Rights* v. *Republic of Kenya*; Application No. 002/2013 – *The African Commission on Human and Peoples' Rights* v. *Libya*; Application No. 004/2013 – *Lohe Issa Konate* v. *Burkina Faso*; Application No. 001/2015 – *Armand Guehi* v. *United Republic of Tanzania*; Application No. 007/2015 – *Ally Rajabu and Others* v. *United Republic of Tanzania*; Application No. 003/2016 – *John Lazaro* v. *United Republic of Tanzania*; Application No. 004/2016 – *Evodius Rutechura and Theobard Nestory* v. *United Republic of Tanzania*; Application No. 015/2016 – *Habiyalimana Augustino and Another v. United Republic of Tanzania*; Application No. 017/2016 – *Deogratius Nicolaus Jeshi* v. *United Republic of Tanzania*; Application No. 018/2016 – *Cosma Faustine* v. *United Republic of Tanzania*; Application No. 021/2016 – *Joseph Mukwano* v. *United Republic of Tanzania*; Application No. 024/2016 – *Amini Juma* v. *United Republic of Tanzania*; Application No. 048/2016 – *Dominick Damian* v. *United Republic of Tanzania*; Application No. 049/2016 – *Chrizant John* v. *United Republic of Tanzania*; Application No. 050/2016 – *Crospery Gabriel & Another* v. *United Republic of Tanzania*; Application No. 051/2016 – *Nzigiyimana Zabron* v. *United Republic of Tanzania*; Application No. 052/2016 – *Marthine C. Msuguri* v. *United Republic of Tanzania*; Application No. 053/2016 – *Oscar Josiah* v. *United Republic of Tanzania*; Application No. 056/2016 – *Gozbert Henerico* v. *United Republic of Tanzania*; Application No. 057/2016 – *Mulokozi Anatori* v. *United Republic of Tanzania*; Application No. 012/2017 – *Prof. Lèon Mugesera* v. *Republic of Rwanda*.

Compensation (reparation)

The African Charter itself does not have express provisions on compensations for complainants who successfully establish that their rights under the Charter have been violated. In its practice, it is evident that the African Commission itself does not encourage complainants to request specific compensation or to submit evidence to support a claim for compensation.[73] A look at the cases that were brought before the Commission shows that most of them did not include specific claims for compensation.[74] However, the general approach of the Commission to the award of compensation or other specific individual remedies where this is requested is similar to the approach of the Inter-American Human Rights system.[75] The Commission in its practice left it to Member States to make the final decision on the amount of damages under domestic law to remedy a finding of violation of the Charter. However, to its credit, the Commission has on a few occasions directly made specific orders concerning individual specific claims.[76] *Egyptian Initiative for Personal Rights and INTERIGHTS* v. *Egypt*[77] was the first case in which the African Commission made such an order.

In that case a complaint was brought on behalf of four women who were part of a protest in Egypt. It was alleged that, during the protest, the protesters were cornered by the riot police in such a way that allowed supporters of the government to attack them. In the circumstances the women (Complainants) were intimidated, insulted and sexually harassed. The Complainants include in their prayers the payment of 57,000 Egyptian pounds to each Complainant. The Commission found the violation of several rights of the Complainants as protected by the African Charter. However, significantly, the Commission went further to request that the Member State, Egypt, compensate each of the Complainants by paying each of them 57,000 Egyptian pounds for the physical and emotional damages and trauma they suffered.

In contrast to the Commission, the African Court has a direct mandate to award compensation where there has been a violation of the rights protected under the African Charter. Article 27 of the African Court Protocol provides that 'if the Court finds that there has been violation of a human or peoples' rights, it shall make *appropriate* orders to remedy the violation, including the payment of fair compensation or reparation'. In the exercise of this function, the

73 REDRESS, *Reaching for Justice: The Right to Reparation in the African Human Rights System*, October 2013, available at: www.refworld.org/docid/528343bf4.html, accessed 4 January 2018.

74 Ibid.

75 Article 25, *American Convention of Human Rights* 1144 UNTS 123, *Velasquez Rodriquez* v. *Honduras* (Preliminary Exceptions) (1987) 1 Inter-Am Ct HR (ser C), paragraph 91, *Genie Lacayo* v. *Nicaragua* (1998) 30 Inter-Am Ct HR (ser C).

76 *Malawi African Association & Others* v. *Mauritania* (2000) AHRLR 149 (ACHPR 2000); *Pagnoulle (on behalf of Mazou)* v. *Cameroon* (2000) AHRLR 55 (ACHPR 1995); *Mouvement Burkinabé des Droits de l'Homme et des Peuples* v. *Burkina Faso* (2001) AHRLR 51 (ACHPR 2001).

77 *Egyptian Initiative for Personal Rights and INTERIGHTS* v. *Egypt*, ACHPR, Communication No. 323/06 (2011).

African Court appears to be performing functions usually reserved for courts at the domestic level.[78] The provision in relation to compensation has been further widened in respect to the African Court under the Malabo Protocol as follows:

> the Court shall establish in the Rules of Court principles relating to reparations to, or in respect of, victims, including restitution, compensation and rehabilitation. On this basis, in its decision the Court may, either upon request or on its own motion in exceptional circumstances, determine the scope and extent of any damage, loss or injury to, or in respect of, victims and will state the principles on which it is acting. [79]

It is notable that the Court could make orders including those that would have direct impact on the legal order of Member States. For instance, in *Lohé Issa Konaté* v. *Burkina Faso* the Court made an order for an amendment to a national legislation and how it should be done. According to the Court, the Member State of Burkina Faso was required

> to amend its legislation on defamation by repealing custodial sentences for acts of defamation, and by adapting its legislation to ensure that other sanctions for defamation meet the test of necessity and proportionality.[80]

Legal aid and assistance

As discussed in Chapter 7, a major shortcoming in the enforcement process is the provision in Article 7 in relation to legal representation. Article 7 contains no explicit provision for legal aid or assistance from the State, which is provided for both in Article 6 of the European Convention on Human Rights[81] and in Article 8 of the Inter-American Convention on Human Rights.[82] This may impede access to justice and consequently denies the right to a fair hearing before the African Court and also at the domestic courts of Member States. Article 7 has also been criticised for not *inter alia* guaranteeing the right to an interpreter where required.[83] The Commission has tried to address these shortcomings through a number of resolutions. In the Resolution on the Right to Recourse and Fair Trial[84] the Commission amplifies on the scope of Article 7 of the African Charter

78 G. Pecorella, 'The African Court on Human and Peoples' rights and its case law: towards a Supreme Court for Africa?', available at: https://aninternationallawblog.wordpress.com/2015/06/22/the-african-court-on-human-and-peoples-rights-and-its-case-law-towards-a-supreme-court-for-africa/#_ftn5, accessed 4 January 2018.

79 Article 45, Malabo Protocol.

80 *Lohé Issa Konaté* v. *Burkina Faso*, Application No. 004/2013 (2014).

81 ETS No. 5.

82 OAS Official Records, OEA/Ser.K/XVI/I/I.

83 M. K. Mbondeyi, 'Improving the substance and content of civil and political rights under the African Human Rights System' (2008) 17 (2) *Lesotho Law Journal* 37, 76.

84 The African Commission on Human and Peoples' Rights, meeting in its 11th Ordinary Session, in Tunisia, 2–9 March 1992.

to include, *inter alia*, the right to free assistance of an interpreter where required. In addition, the Principles and Guidelines on the Right to a Fair Trial and Legal Assistance in Africa,[85] which were adopted in 2003, provide for legal aid and assistance.

The future: The African Court of Justice and Human and Peoples' Rights

As discussed in Chapter 3, at the African Union Summit in July 2008 a protocol was adopted for the purpose of merging the Court of Justice of the African Union with the African Court on Human and Peoples' Rights and renaming the merged entity as the 'African Court of Justice and Human Rights'.[86] The reason behind the decision was the need to save costs and to reduce the proliferation of human rights institutions within the continent. The Malabo Protocol has made further fundamental changes to the court including changing the name of the court to 'The African Court of Justice and Human and Peoples' Rights'.[87]

Under the Malabo Protocol, the Court is divided into three sections, a General Affairs Section, a Human Rights and Peoples' Rights Section and an International Criminal Law Section. As mentioned in Chapter 3, one of the major changes made to the court was the widening of its jurisdiction to cover international crimes as defined under the protocol. The General Affairs Section deals with matters such as breaches of treaty obligations by State parties and the exercise of the powers of the AU and all cases submitted under Article 28, as amended by the Malabo Protocol except those assigned to the other sections of the Court. The Human and Peoples' Rights Section is devoted exclusively to human and peoples' rights matters while the International Law Section has the competence to hear cases relating to crimes specified in the Malabo Protocol.[88]

Under Article 29 of the Statute of the African Court (as amended) Member States, the Assembly, the Parliament, other organs of the AU, staff of the African Union, the Peace and Security Council and the Office of the Prosecutor are entitled to bring cases to the Court. The Statute of the African Court expressly excludes non-Member States of the African Union and Member States that have not ratified the Protocol from its jurisdiction.[89]

Under Article 30 (as amended) Member States, the African Commission, the African Committee of Experts on the Rights and Welfare of the Child,

85 *The Principles and Guidelines on the Right to a Fair Trial and Legal Assistance in Africa*, DOC/OS(XXX) 247, reprinted in (2005)12 *International Human Rights Reports* 1180.

86 *Protocol on the Statute of the African Court of Justice and Human Rights* adopted by the 11th Ordinary Session of the Assembly of the African Union, held in Sharm El-Sheikh, Egypt, 1 July 2008 (Statute of the African Court).

87 *Protocol on Amendments to the Protocol on the Statute of the African Court of Justice and Human Rights* (Malabo Protocol).

88 Ibid. Article 7.

89 Article 29 of the Statute of the African Court as amended by the Malabo Protocol.

accredited African Intergovernmental Organisations, African National Human Rights Institutions and individuals can submit cases relating to human rights legal instruments.[90] However, it must be noted that the access for NGOs and individuals to the Court is restricted. The Court would only accept such cases where the State party against which a complaint is made has made special declaration to accept the Court's competence to hear cases brought by NGOs and individuals.[91] The provision is more restrictive when compared with the restriction placed by Article 55 of the African Charter in respect of access of non-State entities to the Commission. It is unlikely that Member States would be eager to make such a voluntary declaration that will potentially expose them to more litigation. The original provision in the original African Court protocol has received very little patronage. In fact, only two States (Burkina Faso and Mali) have made the necessary declaration to allow access. Furthermore, NGOs are required to be accredited to the AU or its organs before they can be allowed access to the Court.

There are provisions in the Statute of the African Court that may potentially make it more effective than the African Court and the African Commission. The jurisdiction of the Court is very wide when compared with the African Commission or the African Court, or even the European Court of Human Rights and the Inter-American Court of Human Rights that enforce one treaty each. In addition, as mentioned previously, the Court is empowered either on its own motion or on an application by the parties to grant provisional measures (such as injunctions) to preserve the respective rights of the parties.[92] The enforcement of the judgment of the Court is also more robust than that of the African Court and the African Commission. Member State Parties are obliged to comply with the decisions of the Court.[93] However, where a Member State fails to comply, the Court may upon application by either party to a dispute refer the matter to the AU Assembly, which may decide upon measures to be taken to give effect to the judgment.[94] Under Article 46(5) such measures may include sanctions.

Other mechanisms

Under Article 62 of the African Charter, each Member State undertakes to submit every two years, from the date the Charter came into force, a report on the legislative or other measures introduced with a view to giving effect to the rights and freedoms recognised and guaranteed under the Charter. Member State reporting under the Charter is designed to monitor State compliance with the provisions of the Charter and establish on-going dialogue with Member States on the promotion and protection of human rights. The reporting

90 Ibid. Article 30.
91 Ibid. Articles 8(3) and 30(f).
92 Ibid. Article 35.
93 3 Ibid. Article 46(1).
94 4. Article 46(3).

mechanism is also designed to encourage Member States to learn from each other's experiences in the implementation of the provisions of the Charter. In practice, the reporting mechanism has had very limited success. There is a high default record by Member State parties. Even where parties have submitted reports, the reports have generally been lacking in depth, quality and consistency. As at 2016, fewer than half of the Member States were reporting regularly. Nineteen Member States have up-to-date reports, two Member States have one report overdue, seven have two reports overdue, five have three reports overdue, fourteen have more than three reports overdue, while six have never submitted a report.[95] At its 4th Ordinary Session in 1998 the African Commission adopted a general guideline on the form and content of the report in order to encourage compliance.[96] The guideline was not helpful because of its complexity, repetitiveness, length and lack of coherent organisation.[97] The Commission's attempt to address the problem with the guideline by adopting an 11-point amendment to the guideline went to the other extreme.[98] The amendment was too brief to be meaningful and has not improved compliance with Article 62.

There are other control systems established for specific instruments. These include the African Committee of Experts on the Rights and Welfare of the Child (ACERWC), which receives and examines State reports on the measures adopted to implement the Children's Charter and the progress achieved. The body also has the power to investigate issues covered by the Children's Charter. Based on Article 46 of the African Charter, the Commission has also appointed Special Rapporteurs to investigate and report on specific issues. These include: the right to life and protection from extrajudicial killings, the rights of women, the rights of prisoners, press freedom and the right to information, refugees and internally displaced persons and the matter of human rights defenders.

The AU legal order on human rights and its impact on Member States' legal order

A notable development in Africa is that domestic courts are increasingly applying the provisions of the African Charter on Human and Peoples' Rights directly in the domestic context and also employing the Charter as an interpretative aid. It must be noted that the extent of the use of the Charter in particular domestic jurisdictions depend on the status that the Charter enjoys in the forum.[99] Where the Charter has not been incorporated into domestic

95 *Supra*, Nyarko and Jegede, 298.

96 T. S. Bulto, 'Beyond the promises: resuscitating the state reporting procedure under the African Charter on Human and Peoples' Rights' (2006) 12 *Buffalo Human Rights Law Review* 57 at 77.

97 Ibid.

98 *Guidelines to Periodic Reporting under Article 62 of the African Charter on Human and Peoples' Rights* by U. O. Umozurike, adopted at the Commission's 23rd session in 1998.

99 F. Viljoen, 'Application of the African Charter on Human and Peoples' Rights by domestic courts in Nigeria' (1999) 43 (1) *Journal of African Law* 1.

law (if required under domestic legislation), domestic courts generally have minimal recourse to the Charter.[100] Nonetheless, the examples of such usage at the domestic level are increasing.

In the Ghanaian case of *New Patriotic Party* v. *Inspector General of Police*,[101] the plaintiffs challenged the provisions of the Public Order Decree 1972, which conferred power on the police to issue permits for all processions, meetings and public celebrations. The decree made it an offence to hold such activities without a permit. The decree also empowered a senior police officer to stop or disperse such activities even where a permit had been obtained. The plaintiffs argued that these provisions are contrary to the provisions on freedom of association under the Ghanaian constitution and should be declared void and unenforceable. In interpreting the relevant domestic laws the Supreme Court made reference to the African Charter. According to the court:

> Ghana is a signatory to this African Charter and member states of the OAU and parties to the Charter are expected to recognise the rights, duties and freedoms enshrined in the Charter and to undertake to adopt legislative and other measures to give effects to the rights and duties. *I do not think the fact that Ghana has not passed specific legislation to give effect to the Charter means that the Charter cannot be relied upon.*[102] (Emphasis added.)

The Court suggested that even where the African Charter has not been expressly incorporated into domestic law, Member States have to respect the rights guaranteed under the Charter. The Court subsequently declared some of the provisions of the Decree to be inconsistent with the constitution. Similarly, in the Tanzanian case of *Director of Public Prosecutions* v. *Daudi Pete*,[103] the Tanzanian Court of Appeal was tasked with interpreting the constitutional right to bail under the Tanzanian Bill of Rights. The Court held that, because Tanzania has ratified the African Charter, regard must be had to the Charter when interpreting the Bill of Rights.

In *Abacha* v. *Fawehinmi*[104] the Nigerian Supreme Court clarified the status of the African Charter under Nigerian law. In that case, Fawehinmi, a human rights activist and lawyer in the country, had been arrested and detained in isolation for a week without being presented with an arrest warrant or given reasons for his arrest. Fawehinmi challenged the detention on the ground that it violated his fundamental rights under Articles 4, 5, 6 and 12 of the African Charter. The Supreme Court considered the effect of the African Charter under Nigerian law and held that the African Charter having been incorporated into the Nigerian

100 See generally M. Killander (ed.), *International Law and Domestic Human Rights Litigation in Africa* (Pretoria University Law Press, 2010).

101 [1993–94] 2 GLR 459 (SC); (2001 AHRLR 138 (GhSC 1993).

102 Ibid. paragraph 466 (Archer CJ).

103 *Director of Public Prosecutions* v. *Daudi Pete* [1993] TLR 22, 34–35.

104 *Abacha* v. *Fawehinmi* (2000) 6 NWLR (Pt. 660) 228.

domestic legal system is binding in the country. The court further held that if there is a conflict between the Charter and another domestic statute, its provisions would prevail over those other statutes because it is presumed that the legislature does not intend to breach an international obligation.

Another notable case from Nigeria is the Nigerian Federal High Court decision in *Gbemre* v. *Shell and Two Others*.[105] The *Gbemre* case was brought by Jonah Gbemre on behalf of himself and the Iwhereken Community in Delta State in the Niger Delta area of Nigeria against Shell Petroleum Development Company Nigeria Ltd, The Nigerian National Petroleum Corporation and the Attorney General of the Federation. The case was brought under the fundamental rights enforcement procedure in the Nigerian Constitution alleging violations of both constitutional provisions and the African Charter. The plaintiffs claimed that the oil exploration and production activities of Shell, which led to incessant gas flaring, had violated their right to life and the dignity of the human person under sections 33(1) and 34(1) of the Constitution and Articles 4, 16 and 24 of the African Charter. The plaintiffs alleged that the continuous gas flaring by the company had led to poisoning and pollution of the environment that exposed the community to the risk of premature death, respiratory illnesses, asthma and cancer. They also alleged that the pollution had affected their crop production thereby adversely affecting their food security. They claimed that many of the natives had died and many more were suffering from various illnesses. The community was therefore left in a state of gross underdevelopment. The defendants opposed the case on several grounds including that the articles of the African Charter referred to did not create enforceable rights under the Nigerian fundamental rights enforcement procedure. However, they failed to follow up their arguments during the proceedings due to procedural issues. The trial judge therefore proceeded to judgment without any findings of fact, which left the judgment bereft of robust legal analysis.

In its judgment the Federal High Court held that the constitutionally protected rights include rights to a clean, poison-free, pollution-free environment and that the actions of Shell in continuing to flare gas in the course of their oil exploration and production activities in the Applicant's community violated the plaintiffs' right to life and/or their dignity of the human person under the Constitution and the African Charter. Even though there is no apparent justiciable right to a 'clean poison-free, pollution-free and healthy environment' under the Nigerian Constitution, the Court relied on a cumulative use of constitutional provisions with the provisions of the African Charter (especially Article 24) to recognise and apply a fundamental right to a 'clean poison-free, pollution-free and healthy environment'.[106] This is in line with the decision of

105 *Jonah Gbemre* v. *Shell Petroleum Development Corporation of Nigeria Ltd and Others* (Suit No: FHC/B/CS/53/05), Federal High Court, Benin Judicial Division, 14 November 2005.

106 G. Fortman, '"Adventurous" judgments: a comparative exploration into human rights as a moral-political force in judicial law development' (2006) 2 (2) *Utrecht Law Review* 22.

the African Commission in the *SERAC* case, though the Court did not refer to the case in its judgment.[107] The implication of this decision is that there is a possibility of resorting to the African Charter for rights that are not available under national law.

It is important to note that the AU law role in relation to Member States is limited. For example, the Commission has generally refrained from considering and enforcing Member State laws itself. It has emphasised that its competence is confined to the interpretation and enforcement of the AU Charter. According to the AU Commission in *Groupe de Travail sur les Dossiers Judiciaires Stratégiques* v. *Democratic Republic of Congo*,

> Regarding the national laws, the Commission notes that it is not competent to decide if the actions of the Respondent State are consistent with its national laws. The Commission is only competent to verify if the national laws and the Respondent State's actions are consistent with the African Charter.[108]

However, as discussed above, the jurisdiction of the African Court is wider and the evolving jurisprudence of the African Court may lead to a more interventionist role by the Court. Indeed, in *Onyachi and Njoka* v. *Tanzania*[109] the Court's competence to evaluate evidence presented to the court of a Member State and the appropriateness of the penalty imposed was challenged on the ground that it required the Court to sit as a 'Supreme Appellate Court'. The African Court held that it was competent to do so because it has the power to examine whether the proceedings at the Member State's court was in conformity with the fair trial provision in Article 7 of the African Charter. However, the Court acknowledged that it does not directly apply Member States' law or examine the constitutionality of domestic legislation.[110]

Conclusion

The quasi-judicial origin of the AU continental judicial system negatively affected the ability to enforce the emerging AU law. It is notable that, despite the quasi-judicial nature of the African Commission, its jurisprudence has been

107 The African Commission on Human Rights held in *SERAC v. Nigeria*, Communication No. 155/96, 2001, that the failure of the Nigerian government to prevent the escape of toxic waste from oil reserves violated the **right to health** (Article 16) and the **right to a clean environment** (Article 24) of the *African Charter on Human and Peoples' Rights*. The Nigerian government had argued that the rights are vague and incapable of legal enforcement.

108 *Groupe de Travail sur les Dossiers Judiciaires Stratégiques* v. *Democratic Republic of Congo*, ACHPR, Communication No. 259/2002 (2013), paragraph 57.

109 Application No. 003/2015.

110 Ibid. paragraphs 37–39. See also *Mohammed Abubakari* v. *The United Republic of Tanzania*, Application No. 007/2013.

instrumental in the design of the African Court. Nonetheless, the introduction of the continental Court represents a remarkable change to the enforcement process. In theory, the enforcement process of the evolving Court appears more robust than that of the African Commission. Notably, the granting of provisional measures that started with the African Commission's procedure has been written into the instruments of the African Court. Furthermore, the granting of compensation and reparation is another major area that is expanding in the Court process. The development is further enhanced by the impact that the AU legal order is having on Member States. Member States' judicial systems are increasingly resorting to the African Charter and its jurisprudence in the domestic sphere.

11 Conclusions

It is acknowledged that the AU legal order may not be perceived as having acquired the same level of *acquis communautaire* as the well-established European Union. However, as shown in this book, there is an emerging AU *acquis* that is gradually evolving. At the core of the development is the AU Constitutive Act and the norms and standards developing around it. Viewed optimistically, it is credible to make a case that the AU is delivering the Pan-Africanism idea of a fully integrated African continent even if at a very slow pace. The ability of the AU and its institutions to generate norms and standards at the continental level that have consequences for Member States and their citizenry underscores the potential of the emerging AU legal order. An important example is the development of the norm on unconstitutional change of government under the AU legal order as a direct response to military interventions. As it has been correctly pointed out, military coups not only undermine democratic and constitutional rule, they also entrench bad governance that leads to the violations of rights of citizens.[1] The norm evolved gradually from the time of the OAU and became one of the foundational principles of the AU Constitutive Act,[2] which is also backed by a sanction regime. Other instruments of the AU such as the Protocol establishing the AU Peace and Security Council[3] and the Malabo Protocol[4] incorporated the norm and expounded on it. It has been observed that the approach of the AU in articulating the norm of unconstitutional change of government as a threat to peace and security even goes further than the United Nations' approach to peace and security.[5] The recent military intervention in Zimbabwe that led to

1 S. A. Dersso, 'Defending constitutional rule as a peacemaking enterprise: the case of the AU's ban of unconstitutional changes of government' (2017) 24 (4) *International Peacekeeping* 639.

2 Article 4.

3 African Union, *Protocol Relating to the Establishment of the Peace and Security Council of the African Union*, 9 July 2002, available at: www.peaceau.org/uploads/psc-protocol-en.pdf, accessed 24 November 2017.

4 African Union, *Malabo Protocol on Amendments to the Protocol on the Statute of the African Court of Justice and Human Rights*, 27 June 2014, available at: https://au.int/en/treaties/protocol-amendments-protocol-statute-african-court-justice-and-human-rights, accessed 27 November 2017.

5 *Supra*, Dersso.

the removal of former President Robert Mugabe and the Zimbabwean military strategy of ensuring that the process of removal and replacement of the President was done by constitutional means as required by the AU shows how the norm is shaping Member States' behaviour.[6]

The emerging continental court system in Africa is also notable and significant. Though nascent, the African Court has a better prospect with respect to effectiveness and enforcement when compared with the quasi-judicial African Commission in the field of human rights. The decision to introduce a court system to complement and ultimately take over the judicial function of the African Commission is a notable movement towards supranationality. In addition, the Malabo Protocol, though controversial, has further expanded the role of the continental court system going forward.

On the integration front, there are notable developments in some areas such as human rights, nationality and citizenship and economic matters. However, there are major challenges that the AU legal order will need to grapple with as it develops on this front. An example of such is reconciling the prevailing idea of morality and culture with the emerging legal order. The case of the controversial issue of sexual orientation and how the AU and its institutions is responding was discussed in Chapter 9. Developing institutional capacity to support the emerging legal order is an on-going challenge that the AU and institutions will need to respond to going forward. Nonetheless, these challenges are bound to occur in the emergence of any new legal order and could be overcome if there is the political will among Member States of the AU to address them.

It is notable that African leaders are aware of the need for institutional reforms in order to advance the continental agenda. In its *Decision on the Institutional Reform of the African Union*,[7] the AU Assembly appointed President Paul Kagame of Rwanda to conduct a study on the institutional reform of the AU in order to respond effectively to the multifarious challenges facing the Union. This exercise built on findings and recommendations from two previous reports, the 2007 Adedeji report and the 2016 Mekelle report.[8] The key findings on the challenges facing the AU from the report include failure to implement AU decisions, limited relevance of AU and its institutions to citizens in Member States, fragmentation and overlapping of institutions, accountability issues, funding issues and limited expertise in the running of AU institutions. From the perspective of the AU legal order, the report recommended that the role of the AU courts should be better clarified in order to make them more effective. In addition, the

6 *Statement of the Chairperson of the Commission of the African Union on the Situation in Zimbabwe* (21/11/17), available at: https://au.int/en/pressreleases/20171121/statement-chairperson-commission-african-union-situation-zimbabwe, accessed 5 January 2018.

7 Assembly/AU/Dec.606(XXVII) (2017).

8 A. Adedeji, *Audit of the African Union*, available at: http://osf.org.za/wp-content/uploads/2015/08/Audit-of-the-African-Union-Report-of-the-High-Level-Panel.pdf, accessed 11 December 2017.

report also recommended that the AU should clarify the legislative powers of the Pan-African Parliament and also the mode of elections into the parliament. The Kagame report also recommended the speedy implementation of the AU continental passport as part of the strategy to make the AU and its institutions more relevant to citizens. This report underscores the commitment of the AU to facing and overcoming challenges that have significant impact on the emerging legal order going forward.

Appendix 1

Constitutive Act of the African Union

We, Heads of State and Government of the Member States of the Organization of African Unity (OAU):

The President of the People's Democratic Republic of Algeria
The President of the Republic of Angola
The President of the Republic of Benin
The President of the Republic of Botswana
The President of Burkina Faso
The President of the Republic of Burundi
The President of the Republic of Cameroon
The President of the Republic of Cape Verde
The President of the Central African Republic
The President of the Republic of Chad
The President of the Islamic Federal Republic of the Comoros
The President of the Republic of the Congo
The President of the Republic of Cote d'Ivoire
The President of the Democratic Republic of Congo
The President of the Republic of Djibouti
The President of the Arab Republic of Egypt
The President of the State of Eritrea
The Prime Minister of the Federal Democratic Republic of Ethiopia
The President of the Republic of Equatorial Guinea
The President of the Gabonese Republic
The President of the Republic of The Gambia
The President of the Republic of Ghana
The President of the Republic of Guinea
The President of the Republic of Guinea Bissau
The President of the Republic of Kenya
The Prime Minister of Lesotho
The President of the Republic of Liberia
The Leader of the 1st of September Revolution of the Great Socialist People's Libyan Arab Jamahiriya
The President of the Republic of Madagascar

The President of the Republic of Malawi
The President of the Republic of Mali
The President of the Islamic Republic of Mauritania
The Prime Minister of the Republic of Mauritius
The President of the Republic of Mozambique
The President of the Republic of Namibia
The President of the Republic of Niger
The President of the Federal Republic of Nigeria
The President of the Republic of Rwanda
The President of the Sahrawi Arab Democratic Republic
The President of the Republic of Sao Tome and Principe
The President of the Republic of Senegal
The President of the Republic of Seychelles
The President of the Republic of Sierra Leone
The President of the Republic of Somalia
The President of the Republic of South Africa
The President of the Republic of Sudan
The King of Swaziland
The President of the United Republic of Tanzania
The President of the Togolese Republic
The President of the Republic of Tunisia
The President of the Republic of Uganda
The President of the Republic of Zambia
The President of the Republic of Zimbabwe

INSPIRED by the noble ideals which guided the founding fathers of our Continental Organization and generations of Pan-Africanists in their determination to promote unity, solidarity, cohesion and cooperation among the peoples of Africa and African States;

CONSIDERING the principles and objectives stated in the Charter of the Organization of African Unity and the Treaty establishing the African Economic Community;

RECALLING the heroic struggles waged by our peoples and our countries for political independence, human dignity and economic emancipation;

CONSIDERING that since its inception, the Organization of African Unity has played a determining and invaluable role in the liberation of the continent, the affirmation of a common identity and the process of attainment of the unity of our Continent and has provided a unique framework for our collective action in Africa and in our relations with the rest of the world;

DETERMINED to take up the multifaceted challenges that confront our continent and peoples in the light of the social, economic and political changes taking place in the world;

CONVINCED of the need to accelerate the process of implementing the Treaty establishing the African Economic Community in order to promote the socio-economic development of Africa and to face more effectively the challenges posed by globalization;

GUIDED by our common vision of a united and strong Africa and by the need to build a partnership between governments and all segments of civil society, in particular women, youth and the private sector in order to strengthen solidarity and cohesion among our peoples;

CONSCIOUS of the fact that the scourge of conflicts in Africa constitutes a major impediment to the socio-economic development of the continent and of the need to promote peace, security and stability as a prerequisite for the implementation of our development and integration agenda;

DETERMINED to promote and protect human and peoples' rights, consolidate democratic institutions and culture, and to ensure good governance and the rule of law;

FURTHER DETERMINED to take all necessary measures to strengthen our common institutions and provide them with the necessary powers and resources to enable them to discharge their respective mandates effectively;

RECALLING the Declaration which we adopted at the Fourth Extraordinary Session of our Assembly in Sirte, the Great Socialist People's Libyan Arab Jamahiriya, on 9.9.99, in which we decided to establish an African Union, in conformity with the ultimate objectives of the Charter of our Continental Organization and the Treaty establishing the African Economic Community;

HAVE AGREED AS FOLLOWS:

Article 1

Definitions

In this Constitutive Act:

"Act" means the present Constitutive Act;

"AEC" means the African Economic Community;

"Assembly" means the Assembly of Heads of State and Government of the Union;

"Charter" means the Charter of the OAU;

"Committee" means a Specialized Technical Committee of the Union;

"Council" means the Economic, Social and Cultural Council of the Union;

"Court" means the Court of Justice of the Union;

"Executive Council" means the Executive Council of Ministers of the Union;

"Member State" means a Member State of the Union;

"OAU" means the Organization of African Unity;

"Parliament" means the Pan-African Parliament of the Union;

"Union" means the African Union established by the present Constitutive Act.

Article 2

Establishment

The African Union is hereby established in accordance with the provisions of this Act.

Article 3

Objectives

The objectives of the Union shall be to:

Achieve greater unity and solidarity between the African countries and the peoples of Africa;

Defend the sovereignty, territorial integrity and independence of its Member States;

Accelerate the political and socio-economic integration of the continent;

Promote and defend African common positions on issues of interest to the continent and its peoples;

Encourage international cooperation, taking due account of the Charter of the United Nations and the Universal Declaration of Human Rights;

Promote peace, security, and stability on the continent;

Promote democratic principles and institutions, popular participation and good governance;

Promote and protect human and peoples' rights in accordance with the African Charter on Human and Peoples' Rights and other relevant human rights instruments;

Establish the necessary conditions which enable the continent to play its rightful role in the global economy and in international negotiations;

Promote sustainable development at the economic, social and cultural levels as well as the integration of African economies;

Promote cooperation in all fields of human activity to raise the living standards of African peoples;

Coordinate and harmonize policies between existing and future Regional Economic Communities for the gradual attainment of the objectives of the Union;

Advance the development of the continent by promoting research in all fields, in particular in science and technology;

Work with relevant international partners in the eradication of preventable diseases and the promotion of good health on the continent.

Article 4

Principles

The Union shall function in accordance with the following principles:

Sovereign equality and interdependence among Member States of the Union;

Respect of borders existing on achievement of independence;

Participation of the African peoples in the activities of the Union;

Establishment of a common defence policy for the African Continent;

Peaceful resolution of conflicts among Member States of the Union through such appropriate means as may be decided upon by the Assembly;

Prohibition of the use of force or threat to use force among Member States of the Union;

Non-interference by any Member State in the internal affairs of another;

The right of the Union to intervene in a Member State pursuant to a decision of the Assembly in respect of grave circumstances, namely war crimes, genocide and crimes against humanity;

Peaceful co-existence of Member States and their right to live in peace and security;

The right of Member States to request intervention from the Union in order to restore peace and security;

Promotion of self-reliance within the framework of the Union;

Promotion of gender equality;

Respect for democratic principles, human rights, the rule of law and good governance;

Promotion of social justice to ensure balanced economic development;

Respect for the sanctity of human life, condemnation and rejection of impunity and political assassination, acts of terrorism and subversive activities;

Condemnation and rejection of unconstitutional changes of governments.

Article 5

Organs of the Union

1 The organs of the Union shall be:

The Assembly of the Union;
The Executive Council;
The Pan-African Parliament;
The Court of Justice;
The Commission;
The Permanent Representatives Committee;
The Specialized Technical Committees;
The Economic, Social and Cultural Council;
The Financial Institutions.

2 Other organs that the Assembly may decide to establish.

Article 6

The Assembly

1 The Assembly shall be composed of Heads of States and Government or their duly accredited representatives.
2 The Assembly shall be the supreme organ of the Union.
3 The Assembly shall meet at least once a year in ordinary session. At the request of any Member State and on approval by a two-thirds majority of the Member States, the Assembly shall meet in extraordinary session.
4 The Office of the Chairman of the Assembly shall be held for a period of one year by a Head of State or Government elected after consultations among the Member States.

Article 7

Decisions of the Assembly

1 The Assembly shall take its decisions by consensus or, failing which, by a two-thirds majority of the Member States of the Union. However, procedural matters, including the question of whether a matter is one of procedure or not, shall be decided by a simple majority.
2 Two-thirds of the total membership of the Union shall form a quorum at any meeting of the Assembly.

Article 8

Rules of Procedure of the Assembly

The Assembly shall adopt its own Rules of Procedure.

Article 9

Powers and Functions of the Assembly

1 The functions of the Assembly shall be to:

Determine the common policies of the Union;

Receive, consider and take decisions on reports and recommendations from the other organs of the Union;

Consider requests for Membership of the Union;

Establish any organ of the Union;

Monitor the implementation of policies and decisions of the Union as well as ensure compliance by all Member States;

Adopt the budget of the Union;

Give directives to the Executive Council on the management of conflicts, war and other emergency situations and the restoration of peace;

Appoint and terminate the appointment of the judges of the Court of Justice;

Appoint the Chairman of the Commission and his or her deputy or deputies and Commissioners of the Commission and determine their functions and terms of office.

2 The Assembly may delegate any of its powers and functions to any organ of the Union.

Article 10

The Executive Council

1 The Executive Council shall be composed of the Ministers of Foreign Affairs or such other Ministers or Authorities as are designated by the Governments of Member States.
2 Council shall meet at least twice a year in ordinary session. It shall also meet in an extra-ordinary session at the request of any Member State and upon approval by two-thirds of all Member States.

Article 11

Decisions of the Executive Council

1 The Executive Council shall take its decisions by consensus or, failing which, by a two-thirds majority of the Member States. However, procedural matters, including the question of whether a matter is one of procedure or not, shall be decided by a simple majority.
2 Two-thirds of the total membership of the Union shall form a quorum at any meeting of the Executive Council.

Article 12

Rules of Procedure of the Executive Council

The Executive Council shall adopt its own Rules of Procedure.

Article 13

Functions of the Executive Council

1 The Executive Council shall co-ordinate and take decisions on policies in areas of common interest to the Member States, including the following:

Foreign trade;

Energy, industry and mineral resources;

Food, agricultural and animal resources, livestock production and forestry;

Water resources and irrigation;

Environmental protection, humanitarian action and disaster response and relief;

Transport and communications;

Insurance;

Education, culture, health and human resources development;

Science and technology;

Nationality, residency and immigration matters;

Social security, including the formulation of mother and child care policies, as well as policies relating to the disabled and the handicapped;

Establishment of a system of African awards, medals and prizes.

2 The Executive Council shall be responsible to the Assembly. It shall consider issues referred to it and monitor the implementation of policies formulated by the Assembly.

3 The Executive Council may delegate any of its powers and functions mentioned in paragraph 1 of this Article to the Specialized Technical Committees established under Article 14 of this Act.

Article 14

The Specialized Technical Committees

Establishment and Composition

1 There is hereby established the following Specialized Technical Committees, which shall be responsible to the Executive Council:

The Committee on Rural Economy and Agricultural Matters;

The Committee on Monetary and Financial Affairs;

The Committee on Trade, Customs and Immigration Matters;

The Committee on Industry, Science and Technology, Energy, Natural Resources and Environment;

The Committee on Transport, Communications and Tourism;

The Committee on Health, Labour and Social Affairs; and

The Committee on Education, Culture and Human Resources.

2 The Assembly shall, whenever it deems appropriate, restructure the existing Committees or establish other Committees.

3 The Specialized Technical Committees shall be composed of Ministers or senior officials responsible for sectors falling within their respective areas of competence.

Article 15

Functions of the Specialized Technical Committees

Each Committee shall within its field of competence:

Prepare projects and programmes of the Union and submit in to the Executive Council;

Ensure the supervision, follow-up and the evaluation of the implementation of decisions taken by the organs of the Union;

Ensure the coordination and harmonization of projects and programmes of the Union;

Submit to the Executive Council either on its own initiative or at the request of the Executive Council, reports and recommendations on the implementation of the provision of this Act; and

Carry out any other functions assigned to it for the purpose of ensuring the implementation of the provisions of this Act.

Article 16

Meetings

1 Subject to any directives given by the Executive Council, each Committee shall meet as often as necessary and shall prepare its rules of procedure and submit them to the Executive Council for approval.

Article 17

The Pan-African Parliament

1 In order to ensure the full participation of African peoples in the development and economic integration of the continent, a Pan-African Parliament shall be established.
2 The composition, powers, functions and organization of the Pan-African Parliament shall be defined in a protocol relating thereto.

Article 18

The Court of Justice

1 A Court of Justice of the Union shall be established;
2 The statute, composition and functions of the Court of Justice shall be defined in a protocol relating thereto.

Article 19

The Financial Institutions

The Union shall have the following financial institutions, whose rules and regulations shall be defined in protocols relating thereto:

The African Central Bank;
The African Monetary Fund;
The African Investment Bank.

Article 20

The Commission

1 There shall be established a Commission of the Union, which shall be the Secretariat of the Union.
2 The Commission shall be composed of the Chairman, his or her deputy or deputies and the Commissioners. They shall be assisted by the necessary staff for the smooth functioning of the Commission.
3 The structure, functions and regulations of the Commission shall be determined by the Assembly.

Article 21

The Permanent Representatives Committee

1 There shall be established a Permanent Representatives Committee. It shall be composed of Permanent Representatives to the Union and other Plenipotentiaries of Member States.
2 The Permanent Representatives Committee shall be charged with the responsibility of preparing the work of the Executive Council and acting on the Executive Council's instructions. It may set up such sub-committees or working groups as it may deem necessary.

Article 22

The Economic, Social and Cultural Council

1 The Economic, Social and Cultural Council shall be an advisory organ composed of different social and professional groups of the Member States of the Union.
2 The functions, powers, composition and organization of the Economic, Social and Cultural Council shall be determined by the Assembly.

Article 23

Imposition of Sanctions

1 The Assembly shall determine the appropriate sanctions to be imposed on any Member State that defaults in the payment of its contributions to the budget of the Union in the following manner: denial of the right to speak at meetings, to vote, to present candidates for any position or post within the Union or to benefit from any activity or commitments therefrom.

2 Furthermore, any Member State that fails to comply with the decisions and policies of the Union may be subjected to other sanctions, such as the denial of transport and communications links with other Member States, and other measures of a political and economic nature to be determined by the Assembly.

Article 24

The Headquarters of the Union

1 The Headquarters of the Union shall be in Addis Ababa in the Federal Democratic Republic of Ethiopia.
2 There may be established such other offices of the Union as the Assembly may, on the recommendation of the Executive Council, determine.

Article 25

Working Languages

The working languages of the Union and all its institutions shall be, if possible, African languages, Arabic, English, French and Portuguese.

Article 26

Interpretation

The Court shall be seized with matters of interpretation arising from the application or implementation of this Act. Pending its establishment, such matters shall be submitted to the Assembly of the Union, which shall decide by a two-thirds majority.

Article 27

Signature, Ratification and Accession

1 This Act shall be open to signature, ratification and accession by the Member States of the OAU in accordance with their respective constitutional procedures.
2 The instruments of ratification shall be deposited with the Secretary-General of the OAU.
3 Any Member State of the OAU acceding to this Act after its entry into force shall deposit the instrument of accession with the Chairman of the Commission.

Article 28

Entry into Force

This Act shall enter into force thirty (30) days after the deposit of the instruments of ratification by two-thirds of the Member States of the OAU.

Article 29

Admission to Membership

1 Any African State may, at any time after the entry into force of this Act, notify the Chairman of the Commission of its intention to accede to this Act and to be admitted as a member of the Union.
2 The Chairman of the Commission shall, upon receipt of such notification, transmit copies thereof to all Member States. Admission shall be decided by a simple majority of the Member States. The decision of each Member State shall be transmitted to the Chairman of the Commission who shall, upon receipt of the required number of votes, communicate the decision to the State concerned.

Article 30

Suspension

Governments which shall come to power through unconstitutional means shall not be allowed to participate in the activities of the Union.

Article 31

Cessation of Membership

1 Any State which desires to renounce its membership shall forward a written notification to the Chairman of the Commission, who shall inform Member States thereof. At the end of one year from the date of such notification, if not withdrawn, the Act shall cease to apply with respect to the renouncing State, which shall thereby cease to belong to the Union.
2 During the period of one year referred to in paragraph 1 of this Article, any Member State wishing to withdraw from the Union shall comply with the provisions of this Act and shall be bound to discharge its obligations under this Act up to the date of its withdrawal.

Article 32

Amendment and Revision

1 Any Member State may submit proposals for the amendment or revision of this Act.

2 Proposals for amendment or revision shall be submitted to the Chairman of the Commission who shall transmit same to Member States within thirty (30) days of receipt thereof.
3 The Assembly, upon the advice of the Executive Council, shall examine these proposals within a period of one year following notification of Member States, in accordance with the provisions of paragraph 2 of this Article.
4 Amendments or revisions shall be adopted by the Assembly by consensus or, failing which, by a two-thirds majority and submitted for ratification by all Member States in accordance with their respective constitutional procedures. They shall enter into force thirty (30) days after the deposit of the instruments of ratification with the Chairman of the Commission by a two-thirds majority of the Member States.

Article 33

Transitional Arrangements and Final Provisions

1 This Act shall replace the Charter of the Organization of African Unity. However, the Charter shall remain operative for a transitional period of one year or such further period as may be determined by the Assembly, following the entry into force of the Act, for the purpose of enabling the OAU/AEC to undertake the necessary measures regarding the devolution of its assets and liabilities to the Union and all matters relating thereto.
2 The provisions of this Act shall take precedence over and supersede any inconsistent or contrary provisions of the Treaty establishing the African Economic Community.
3 Upon the entry into force of this Act, all necessary measures shall be undertaken to implement its provisions and to ensure the establishment of the organs provided for under the Act in accordance with any directives or decisions which may be adopted in this regard by the Parties thereto within the transitional period stipulated above.
4 Pending the establishment of the Commission, the OAU General Secretariat shall be the interim Secretariat of the Union.
5 This Act, drawn up in four (4) original texts in the Arabic, English, French and Portuguese languages, all four (4) being equally authentic, shall be deposited with the Secretary-General of the OAU and, after its entry into force, with the Chairman of the Commission who shall transmit a certified true copy of the Act to the Government of each signatory State. The Secretary-General of the OAU and the Chairman of the Commission shall notify all signatory States of the dates of the deposit of the instruments of ratification or accession and shall upon entry into force of this Act register the same with the Secretariat of the United Nations.

IN WITNESS WHEREOF, WE have adopted this Act.

Done at Lomé, Togo, this 11th day of July, 2000.

Appendix 2

Protocol on Amendments to the Constitutive Act of the African Union

The Member States of the African Union States Parties to the Constitutive Act of the African Union

Have agreed to adopt amendments to the Constitutive Act as follows:

Article 1

Definitions

In this Protocol, the following expressions shall have the meanings assigned to them hereunder unless otherwise specified:

"Act" means the Constitutive Act

"Assembly" means the Assembly of Heads of State and Government of the African Union

"Chairperson" means chairperson of the Assembly

"Court" means the Court of Justice of the Union and Court of Justice has the same meaning

"Union" means the African Union

Article 2

Preamble

In the first paragraph of the Preamble to the Constitutive Act, the replacement of the words "founding fathers" with "founders".

Article 3

Objectives

In Article 3 of the Act (Objectives), the insertion of three new subparagraphs (i), (p) and (q) with consequential renumbering of subparagraphs:

The objectives of the Union shall be to:

....

i ensure the effective participation of women in decision-making, particularly in the political, economic and socio-cultural areas;

....

p develop and promote common policies on trade, defence and foreign relations to ensure the defence of the Continent and the strengthening of its negotiating positions;

q invite and encourage the full participation of the African Diaspora as an important part of our Continent, in the building of the African Union.

Article 4

Principles

In Article 4 of the Act (Principles), the expansion of subparagraph (h) and the insertion of two new subparagraphs (q) and (r):

....

h the right of the Union to intervene in a Member State pursuant to a decision of the Assembly in respect of grave circumstances, namely: war crimes, genocide and crimes against humanity as well as a serious threat to legitimate order to restore peace and stability to the Member State of the Union upon the recommendation of the Peace and Security Council;

....

q restraint by any Member State from entering into any treaty or alliance that is incompatible with the principles and objectives of the Union;

r prohibition of any Member State from allowing the use of its territory as a base for subversion against another Member State.

Article 5

Organs of the Union

In Article 5 of the Act (Organs of the Union), the insertion of a new subparagraph (f) with consequential renumbering of subsequent subparagraphs:

....

f The Peace and Security Council.

....

Article 6

The Assembly

In Article 6 of the Act (The Assembly) and where-ever else it occurs in the Act, the substitution of the word "Chairman" with "Chairperson"; the deletion of the second sentence of subparagraph 3 and the insertion of new paragraphs 4, 5, 6 and 7:

………

3 The Assembly shall meet at least once a year in ordinary session.

4 At the initiative of the Chairperson after due consultation with all Member States, or at the request of any Member State and upon approval by two-thirds majority of Member States, the Assembly shall meet in Extraordinary Session.

5 The Assembly shall elect its Chairperson from among the Heads of State or Government at the beginning of each ordinary session and on the basis of rotation for a period of one year renewable.

6 The Chairperson shall be assisted by a Bureau chosen by the Assembly on the basis of equitable geographical representation.

7 Where the Assembly meets at the Headquarters, an election of the Chairperson shall be held taking into account the principle of rotation.

Article 7

Functions of the Chairperson of the Assembly

The insertion in the Act of a new Article 7 (bis):

1 The Chairperson shall represent the Union during his/her tenure with a view to promoting the objectives and principles of the African Union as stipulated in Articles 3 and 4 of the Act. He/She shall also, with the collaboration of the Chairperson of the Commission, carry out the functions of the Assembly set out in Article 9(e) and (g) of the Act.

2 The Chairperson may convene the meeting of the other organs through their Chairpersons or Chief Executives and in accordance with their respective Rules of Procedure.

Article 8

The Executive Council

In Article 10 of the Act (The Executive Council), the insertion of a new paragraph 3:

……..

3 The Chairperson of the Executive Council shall be assisted by a Bureau chosen by the Executive Council on the basis of equitable geographical representation.

Article 9

Peace and Security Council

The insertion in the Act of a new Article 20 (bis):

1 There is hereby established a Peace and Security Council (PSC) of the Union, which shall be the standing decision-making organ for the prevention, management and resolution of conflicts.

2 The functions, powers, composition and organization of the PSC shall be determined by the Assembly and set out in a protocol relating thereto.

Article 10

The Permanent Representatives Committee

In Article 21 of the Act (The Permanent Representatives Committee) the insertion of a new paragraph 3:

....

3 The Chairperson of the Permanent Representatives Committee shall be assisted by a Bureau chosen on the basis of equitable geographical representation.

Article 11

Official Languages

In Article 25 of the Act (Working Languages), replace the title "Working Languages" by "Official Languages" and substitute the existing provision with:

1 The official languages of the Union and all its institutions shall be Arabic, English, French, Portuguese, Spanish, Kiswahili and any other African language.

2 The Executive Council shall determine the process and practical modalities for the use of official languages as working languages.

Article 12

Cessation of Membership

Article 31 of the Act (Cessation of Membership) is deleted.

Article 13

Entry into Force

This Protocol shall enter into force thirty days after the deposit of the instruments of ratification by a two-thirds majority of the Member States.

Adopted by the 1st Extraordinary Session of the Assembly of the Union in Addis Ababa, Ethiopia on 3 February 2003 and by the 2nd Ordinary Session of the Assembly of the Union in Maputo, Mozambique on 11 July 2003.

Index

For Product Safety Concerns and Information please contact our EU
representative GPSR@taylorandfrancis.com
Taylor & Francis Verlag GmbH, Kaufingerstraße 24, 80331 München, Germany

www.ingramcontent.com/pod-product-compliance
Ingram Content Group UK Ltd.
Pitfield, Milton Keynes, MK11 3LW, UK
UKHW021302190926
475701UK00009B/590

* 9 7 8 0 3 6 7 9 0 0 2 8 1 *